ESSAYS IN

Theology of Culture

ESSAYS IN
Theology of Culture

ROBERT W. JENSON

WILLIAM B. EERDMANS PUBLISHING COMPANY
GRAND RAPIDS, MICHIGAN

© 1995 Wm. B. Eerdmans Publishing Co.
255 Jefferson Ave. S.E., Grand Rapids, Michigan 49503

Printed in the United States of America

00 99 98 97 96 95   7 6 5 4 3 2 1

Library of Congress Cataloging-in-Publication Data

Jenson, Robert W.
Essays in theology of culture / Robert W. Jenson.
p.   cm.
ISBN 0-8028-0888-3 (pbk.)
1. Christianity and culture. I. Title.
BR115.C8J46 1995
261 — dc20   95-4970
CIP

To the memory of Joseph Sittler,
who launched a beginning theologian
on such reflections by suggesting me
as his replacement during illness, and
who remained my model in them.

Contents

Contents

Preface

IT MUST BE ADMITTED from the beginning: these are essays in *theology* of culture. That is, they are not religiously motivated criticism or experiments in religion-*and*-the arts or whatever; they are specifically and brazenly trinitarian and churchly. If the gospel is true, it must enable true knowledge about anything at all. Therefore theology, reflection about the gospel, must be a universal discourse — as it has been held to be in all times of its health. The following are theological essays that take for their subjects — usually on account of contingent assignment to the author — matters usually classified as "culture."

The essays here selected span a considerable period of time: the first was originally published in 1966, the last in 1994. Rereading them for this publication, I was struck equally by their variety of argument and topic, which occasionally rises to mutual contradiction, by an almost alarming persistence of certain material themes, and by the ease with which many could have been grouped — as Blanche Jenson and I decided not in fact to group them — under a few rubrics: the arts, language, politics, and liberal education.

I will allow readers to note the tonal and conceptual variety of these essays for themselves, except for one matter. Readers will feel in the earliest political essays a certain "sixties" abandon, followed by greater caution in latter pieces. Thus, for example, I would not now try to save the word "socialism," recognizing that the historical actuality to which that word applies is what it is, and should not even accidentally be encouraged. Whether this is the sign of wisdom or aging or both or neither, I will not speculate; and perhaps the change does not extend beyond emphasis and mood.

This may be the place to note that I have — as is, I think, demanded — very little edited previously published essays. Where an essay was published in a vehicle with a very specific constituency, I have sometimes stricken direct address to that constituency. I have fixed a few errors that arose in publication, and a few original linguistic infelicities so great as absolutely to prohibit comprehension. I have made no attempt to adapt earlier essays to the linguistic sensitivities and/or prejudices of more recent years.

Of the persistent themes, I will here note but one. I was myself surprised to see how early *nihilism* and its political manifestation as *fascism* appear as chief culture-diagnostic categories, and how regularly they are used in a variety of contexts. I should not have been surprised, remembering that I carried Nietzsche's works about as an undergraduate, alarming and boring folk by citing from them. To this theme, let me say this much that is not explicitly said in the essays: I much doubt that an *actually* nihilist society is possible, but the persistent *threat* of nihilism's advent is possible and actual. From my first attempts to help undergraduates understand our situation to my currently renewed attempts to do the same, it has become steadily more clear to me that the threat of nihilism's advent has been the chief spiritual determinant of life in the West since the turn of the twentieth century, as it still remains. Nietzsche promised simultaneous degradation and glory, when the nihilist eschaton should come; the "last man" is plainly on the scene, but something seems to be delaying the "superman."

As to the rubrics under which the essays could be grouped, these reflect contingencies of my career. I have always been an afficianado of the arts; and during the time when I was a professor of philosophy at a liberal arts college, I was with some frequency asked to speak about them. I have less often been requested to reflect on the sciences, but have responded when I have been. The concern for language arises from the character of my philosophical education, which has been disproportionately in Anglo-Saxon "analytic" philosophy and in German-French "hermeneutic" philosophy.

The political writings began sometime after I was, as were so many, politicized by the civil rights and antiwar movements. Normal political concern was transformed into motivated practice by life during the sixties and seventies in Gettysburg, Pennsylvania, a staging point for moves on Washington, D.C., and a nest of liberal academics; for years the "demonstration kit" was a standard item in our wardrobes. The impulse to speak and write then emerged above all in invitations from two Washington think groups: the Political Affairs Seminar maintained among "inside-the-beltway" types by the pioneering pastor Leopold Bernhard, and the Institute for Neighborhood Studies, a branch of the Institute for Policy Studies.

Finally, for the first eleven years of my career I taught at a churchly liberal arts college, and now — after twenty years teaching theology to future clergy — I am again at such a college. During both periods I have been deeply involved in curriculur and ideological discussions; hence the considerable number of these essays devoted in one way or another to the "liberal arts" and the general question about Christian intellectualism. The dates of various essays show how these concerns continued during the time I was away from undergraduate teaching.

The selection of the essays actually presented and the rejection of others, as well as most of the work of preparing them for publication, was done by my constant coworker, Blanche Jenson. And I have most heartily to thank William Eerdmans for the astonishing freedom with which he agreed to the preparation and publication of the volume.

Language and Time

From a Symposium on "Communication in the Arts"

A CONCERN for communication in the arts is, it seems to me, a concern
to remember something simple and obvious and therefore easy to forget:
that the human activities we call arts belong to the larger class of those
we call language. We could, of course, lose ourselves here, trying to
define language. But I think we know quite well enough what language
is, and I will bow to the passion for definition only enough to remind
of something: that other activities are language besides those done with
dictionary and grammar, that language is all those things we do to
come to understanding with each other in a world.

If you say "Good morning" to me, you break open my self-enclosure
and make me hearken to you, to an other-than-me. We take up the task
of coming together in our lives, of coming to an understanding, however
trivial. Nor do you enter my life alone: "Good morning" is more than
some rather unpleasant sounds only because of a multitude of conventions that you and I share with everyone who speaks English and that
form an impersonal apparatus between us. This apparatus functions by
making reference to all sorts of things other than you or me or the
immediate contents of our experience. If you say "Good morning" and

I ask what "morning" means, you will begin to talk about the sun, the earth, light, darkness, and all sorts of things. Thus your life and mine become intertwined only by a shared environment, posited by language, *in* which we meet.

Finally, this environment is the special human kind we call a *world*. What I mean is this: the language in which you say to me "Good morning" comes to us both from the *past:* the conventions that make words of these sounds were already set before you spoke, otherwise you could not have spoken. Yet the utterance of these words is the breaking into my life of someone other than me, and that means of something new and different from me. I am challenged to see what I was not seeing, to take up new tasks and expectations: utterance opens the *future*. A "world" is a communal and *historical* environment.

I think it indisputable that a great variety of human activities do these same things that "Good morning" does, that all of them are appropriately called language, and that those we call arts are among them. So much for preliminaries.

If now we ask what distinguishes the arts from other language activities, it seems to me that we need only point up a distinction implicit in what we have already said. What we are trying to do when we speak has two poles. On the one hand, we are trying to say something about the world. "It is raining out" does this. So does "Good morning." So does a painting like Mr. Shahn's recent cover portrait of Senator Fulbright.

On the other hand, we are trying to make language itself work. We are trying to bring off this remarkable event of being together in our world. But if it is so that language puts us in history, and that therefore the world we have to talk about has the kind of meaning a story has, then every occasion on which we address each other is new and different, and to bring it off will mean creating new language. This is the other pole of what we are trying to do when we address each other. We are creating the new language needed for that moment.

For example, as I now speak of "the future" or "language," it is notorious that I do not and cannot mean quite what other people have — and you will understand me only when you grasp what this particular "he" "means by it." It may not be obvious that this is so with such an utterance as "It is raining out," but it is. Whenever we address each other, we create new language. And that is to say, we work on the creation of the common world in which we can come together.

[2]

My proposal is this: within the whole range of language activities, the arts are those where the attempt to make language itself work, to find the perpetually needed new language for perpetually new situations, predominates — just as the natural sciences are those where the attempt to say something about the world as it is predominates. In the arts, the creation of language has become a goal for its own sake. In the arts, we talk about the common meaningful world only in order to add to it.

Unattainable limits lie in both directions. The attempt of positivism to create completely unambiguous languages for the sciences, with all meaning located in purely descriptive protocol sentences, represents the drive to attain the one limit. Here the goal is to banish from communication anything that could becloud what we want to say about the world. The kind of abstraction in the arts where there is no original image from which to abstract represents the drive to attain the other limit. Here the goal is to create new meaning entirely without reference to the world that is already there. Music lives always close to this limit.

These limits are unattainable, and therefore no art can be completely without reference to the world as it already is, just as no scientific hypothesis is wholly unambiguous. Both sciences and arts, abstract painting and pure music included, remain language. But we press toward both limits and must do so. A concern for communication in the arts means awareness of this pressure and caution about the drive, inherent in the arts, to cease talking about the world, to cease doing one of the things that language does. It is thus a concern for the *image* in the visual arts: for *song,* that is, music with texts, in music; and for syntactic and semantic *sense* in literature. It is a concern for the descriptive, "literary," iconographic element in the arts — for the element that tempts to paraphrase.

This concern for communication in the arts may also be stated in terms of time. Language, we say, is a gift of the past that challenges us to the future. All utterances both describe how things already are, that is, describe the past, and seek to add to the world, that is, to evoke the future. The sciences intensify language's description of the past; the arts intensify its evocation of the future. A concern for communication in the arts is a concern that the arts remain language, that is, that in stretching forward to the future, they do not lose hold of the past, do not cease to talk about the world that already is.

Why should the church have such a concern? The church is, in general, concerned for the unity of description and creation in language because the church is the gathering to perform a certain language act, to make and hear a certain address: the church is those who tell and hear the gospel. And the gospel is the story of a man of the past, Jesus of Nazareth, told as the story of the destiny of the hearers. "In what happened with Jesus," the gospel says, "you may learn what will happen as the final fulfillment of your life." The church is concerned with the unity of past and future in language, with the doing of both description and creation, because it exists to tell the story of a past event as the story of the final future of human life.

The church is concerned for the arts in particular because it discovers them springing up in its own interior life, in its worship. The church in its worshiping is drawn to the arts because pure description of what happened with Jesus and bald doctrinal statement that he is the coming Lord would not be the gospel at all.

The gospel tells about Jesus as the future, and in so doing impresses him on the hearers as a future for which they may live, calls up and evokes the coming Lord as the Lord of their present. Therefore, the gospel can never be only statements about Jesus; the gospel depends on the creative, future-evoking power of language. Of course, our ordinary language — whether of words, gestures, purely didactic pictures, or whatever — is itself more than descriptive, and will, therefore, often suffice for the telling of the gospel. But the church seeks to intensify the future-pointing power of its talk about Jesus; as a result, the church finds itself singing, rhyming, depicting, dancing, and playing his story.

The church is concerned for communication in these arts that live within it because it is not mere "futurity" as such that it seeks to evoke. The future it seeks to live and enact has a specific content: the church calls up as future the story of a particular man of the past, Jesus of Nazareth. And it calls him up as the future of the actual men who hear, with all they have made of themselves and speaking to all that is factually true of them.

The church has its own explanation of the desire for conceptual emptiness, for the suppression of reference to the actual world, in purely decorative visual and audible forms. The church has long experience of the attempt, endemic to religion, to flee from the world as it is and experience directly the fulfillment of life right now, to escape the present and live only in the future. The church's judgment on this attempt has always been the same as when Paul encountered it in the church at Corinth: we are not yet at the end; the world we have to be faithful in is this present world.

All attempts to pretend we are already at the end are a pretence, which can be sustained only by seeking forms of experience without conceptual content (for the only real content our life can have is what we experience in this present world). When religious forces appear in the church that must find expression in music without words and pure religious beauty, the church suspects that just such an attempt is in progress.

When purely decorative visual arts, textless music, and abstract dance claim an independent place as language in the church, they represent in the church the gnostic enthusiasm that claims to be already liberated from the facts, from the conditions of this world, and to directly possess the fulfillment. The phenomenon is not new; in the primitive church it appeared as speaking in tongues. Speaking in tongues was exactly language that almost ceased to be language by detaching itself from inherited rules and so from the need or ability to say anything about the given world. Speaking in tongues was an attempt to be the language of the angels, an experience of something like language that was life in the future fulfillment alone. Arts without literary content are the sophisticated church's form of tongue-speaking.

This is not a blanket condemnation. Paul saw value in tongues. He said that the one who already believed might very well so press toward the final consummation of his fellowship with the Lord as to acquire from time to time something like language that was freed from language's inherited conventions, that made no more provision for talk about this world. Yet whatever such eschatological language might mean in the experience of the believer, one thing it could not do: it could not be that sharing of a common inherited world by which the church could accomplish its task of speaking and hearing about the man Jesus and our lives now as those who follow him.

So also the hearing of a Mozart sonata may be a decisive and necessary event in the history of my personal life of faith, the moment perhaps of the first birth of a true longing for fulfillment. But when I and my fellow believer sit in a church and listen together to that sonata, each of us lives his own life. The common world of history in which we and Jesus of Nazareth are items, and in which we can come to believing understanding with each other about him, is exactly what we are here permitted for the moment to escape.

If there was to be tongue-speaking in common worship, said Paul, let it be interpreted, subsequently pinned to a specific set of statements in the common language. So also we can say: by all means let there be, when we gather to worship, an organ piece played that can lift each of us to an intuition of his private heaven. But let it then be interpreted: let it be a hymn prelude that is then given specific gospel content by the text of the hymn that follows. By all means let there be pure abstract or expressionistic decoration in our churches. But let it be interpreted: let it lead the eye to a crucifix, to a last supper, to a healing miracle — and above all to the space where the gospel story is to be told and acted out. Let it be part of the style of one whole depiction, which has the story of Jesus as its iconographic content.

In the life of the church, the relation of decorative art to art that is also didactic corresponds to that between private devotions and public liturgy: the first may well be "the burden of a sigh," the second must be communication. And in the life of faith, it is the public communication that is primary — no sighing, please, until we have worked this out about that fellow Jesus.

The concern of the church for communication in the arts is a concern also for the culture of man, in or out of the church. The mark of our epoch is the crisis of language, signaled by "But what do you mean?" as our typical question. One way of describing the crisis is that past and future disconnect in our language. The religious or metaphysical words that once both called us to live for a future and were used as names of present realities — "God," "soul," and the like — have ceased to illumine and instead have become puzzles. Therewith we come to experience our hopes and purposes as lacking all basis in reality, and our knowledge of reality as purposeless. We hear some of our talk as unreal and the rest as futile. Either way, we do not achieve understanding with each other.

Within the arts, this crisis appears as disharmony between the artist's seeing or hearing of the world as it is and his drive to *add* to the world of meaning. The artist has the task of reconciling what is and what shall and must be; the artifact is to be at once a reflection of reality and a step forward to new reality. So long as the language by which the artist's society realizes its community is religious or metaphysical, the faith of the artist's society, that what is and what ought to be are already one in God or the absolute, sustains the artist in his task of welding them together in experience. When this is no longer so, then the artist must unite the past and the future, the real and the ideal, by the unassisted force of his own act of creation, then he must contain their conflict in his own soul and without consolation from his fellows.

Such a calling is at the extreme limit of human possibility, and therefore our art is in permanent crisis. If the artist loses his grip on the past, then so long as the forms he casts up are new, they count as art. Even conscious direction of the shaping of these forms now seems unnecessary, for no communication is intended. So why not simply turn several radios on and off at random, calling whatever sounds result music? If, on the other hand, the artist loses his longing for the future, then why not make a statue that is simply a direct cast from the model? Better yet, why not just strip the girl herself and put her on a pedestal? What is the matter with things just as we find them?

Either way, the artist's activity is no longer language. Such art has nothing in common with even the most radical abstractionism or expressionism. It no longer merely presses the boundary of language, as art indeed must; it has leaped the boundary. Such art is, I suggest, the enacted suicide of language, the speech of those who have lost all faith in language and speak only to proclaim that loss of faith.

In this crisis, which may very well be permanent for whatever time is left our civilization, the church could make a healing contribution if it would. For the church is a community of persons who have reason to know that man does have a future, a future that does cohere with the past in the life of the man Jesus, who has come and will come again. The church is therefore a community of those who are able to have confidence in language no matter what, who even when the religious and metaphysical words die are able simply to keep talking.

If the community of believers and the community of the arts were to intersect, there would be that many more in the community of the arts who were able peacefully to defy our endemic doubt of the possibility of language, who were able to take with a grain of salt all the theories and programs by which art through some device is now still to be made possible for six more months, and calmly get on with the business. There are such men with and without faith. As in any community of work, the existence of one man who is able to get on with the job makes it possible for others to do the same.

The church should contribute many more. The church, were it a part of the community of the arts, should be a voice in that community, saying, in the most savingly superficial sort of way, "It isn't as impossible as you think. Here is your pen and paper. Sit down and write it." It should be a voice raised to debunk the mock heroics of suicidal artistic ideologies, a voice to free a few young artists in each generation from the sterility they impose. It should be a childlike voice ceaselessly betraying the emperor's new tailors, and so making jobs for honest craftsmen.

I have spoken of the church's active concern for the arts in the subjunctive mood, for the intersection of the church with the community of the arts is at present slight. As a result, the church is no kind of voice, helpful or otherwise, in the community of the arts. Before the church will be able to play the role in our culture to which God assigns it, it will have to overcome its own kind of fear of communication — which is another story.

But the church has every reason to seek to begin to play its cultural role, for as a community that exists by and for a message and worships a God who is a Word, the concern of the church is the concern for communication, in the arts or elsewhere. The care of language is the one thing on which the church is utterly dependent and to which it must be utterly dedicated. Nor is there any reason to fear the assignment, for past and future are indeed one as the love that is the deed of Jesus' life: we can and do communicate, also in the arts.

[1967]

God, Space, and Architecture

CHURCH ARCHITECTURE, to put it tritely, is the definition of spaces that are to be used for gatherings to worship God. Our question is, What sort of spatial definition does this activity require?

This question obviously presupposes the motto "Form follows function," but in the broad sense in which it is a priori true and serves mostly to raise further questions about the spatiality of the "function" in question. In the present case, considerations such as what sort of liturgy must be provided for or how many must be able to participate can be taken care of quite quickly and leave most of the important decisions unsettled: Shall the lines of the building be parallel, convergent, radial? What should be the shape of the floor plan? Should the design be harmonious and restful, or dissonant and nervous? Should the surfaces be richly decorated or bare?

To deal with these problems we must take up the question really posed by "Form follows function" and ask, Why does worshipping God need a space? In what sense is the relation of worshipers to God a spatial relation? And to deal with *this* question we must deal with some apparently remote reflections, which can here be asserted only in thesis fashion. They will, however, lead straight back to architecture.

Published in *Response* VIII (1967): 157-162. Copyright Liturgical Conference, 8750 Georgia Ave., Silver Springs, MD 20910. All rights reserved. Used with permission.

God enters our lives with the question posed by time — better, by the temporality, indeed the mortality, of human life. Because I have a future, because I not only am what I am but am going to be what I will be, I am always asked what will become of me — asked by family, profession, chance meetings, and myself. And because the only certain future is death, which is my cessation, I cannot dispose once and for all of my future, and so cannot bring its question to silence. That is to say, I cannot answer it myself — which is the entry of God into my life.

The question of the spatiality of our relation to God is, therefore, the question of how we move in space as we try to deal with the question posed by time. But what is space to time? Space is precisely the present as against the past and the future. Space is precisely that in which things are present, are now to me. Space is that in which *presence* occurs. The things in space are those that are now there for me, that neither no longer are nor not yet are.

One possible way of facing the challenge of the future to what I already am, of facing the threat of the future, is to use that which is now, which is presently at hand, to secure myself against the threat of the future. I can use space, the accessibility of things that are now, to defend myself against time, the uncertainty of what may come. This is the classical course of the man who built his barns and stored his goods, who used structures and what they could contain of things present to his hand, in order to be able to say to himself, "Soul, you have ample goods laid up for many years; take your ease, be merry." I can do this because things presently at hand in space are assured: there the thing is, and I can be certain at least of that. Thus if I define reality as presence, if I live by the maxim that what is real is what is here and now, what is in space, I can dismiss the threat of the future as unreal fantasy. I can assure myself against the doubtful and questioning future by what is assured, by what is in my barns or in my telescope.

There is, of course, a notorious hitch to this, pointed out by the parable. We cannot escape that we have a future. What we do, therefore, is to seek to broaden the present at the expense of the future, to expand the space of time that is assured and accessible and in our control. This is what the man with his barns was about. It is what all technology is about. But then we discover that within this broadened present the threat of time reappears: moth and rust corrupt the contents of our barns; the present things we rely on decay and become obsolescent, and so do we.

Thus the final solution is to posit an unassailably present being, a being who already is all that it will be and therefore has no future to threaten us, a changeless and therefore a pure and perfect presence. This is the solution of religion — and the God of religion is therefore the Absolute Presence. His mode of life is the *nunc simul,* the all-already-now-at-once of eternity. For him the future is already now, there is no not-yet, and in him therefore we have a present being, something now there, who is our perfect guarantee against all threats from the future.

To be sure, in order to be changeless, God must not be conditioned by the relations that exist between things in space. Everything in space changes — this discovery leads us to posit God in the first place. The God of religion is therefore not conceived as a thing in space. But he is experienced as the one in whom we find what we vainly seek in things in space, as the fulfillment of spatiality. He is the posit of the existential meaning of space. Our relation to him is therefore experienced analogously to spatial relations: we experience his presence, his being now for us, as nearness, and his transcendence, the unassailability of his presence, as distance.

Finally to the point: spaces that are defined for the worship of *this* God can provide spatially for the relation of the worshipers to the object of their worship. The transcendence of God can be provided for by establishing a distance, the nearness of God in worship by arranging this distance as one that is in some way overcome in the action of worship. Distance and its overcoming combine when the structure also establishes a direction to the place where God is.

Distance between the worshipers and God is most directly provided by building two separated locations, one the location of the worshipers, the other the location of the Presence — with worship including some sort of back-and-forth between these locations to experience God's nearness. The Gothic pattern of nave and choir comes immediately to mind. But the principle was well established long before Gothic times, and despite Protestant trumpetings about tearing down rood screens and so on, the principle is followed still in almost all church building, Protestant or Catholic — only of course in vulgarized form: Catholics have built holy theaters for viewing the sacred act, with the stage up front as the location for the Presence and an auditorium for the worshipers; Protestants have built holy lecture halls for hearing the sacred discourse, with the lecture-desk as the holy place up there and with sound rather than sight as the bridge between the two locations; and Lutherans and some others have made a clumsy combination of the two.

This arrangement automatically also establishes a direction to God — forward to the altar or pulpit. This direction can then be architecturally emphasized in the most various ways: by colonnades, strong lines that converge in perspective, and so on. The simplest way is to shape the building as one or another polygon and put the furniture and props of worship in one angle or against one side, so that when people worship, one focus of the building necessarily becomes the focus of their attention. The very crudest is to make the building rectangular and jam altar, pulpit, and font, as well as whatever decoration there is, all against one short side. This is the most popular method with modern church architecture, in which Protestants stubbornly persist even now when Rome is abandoning it.

The distance to God is architecturally definable also by one or another vastness of the structure, so that the defined space reaches out beyond that occupied by the worshipers. This vastness can be quite diffuse, as in Worms Cathedral or St. Paul's. Or it can be combined with direction, as in the great Gothic churches, where the vastness reaches upward and forward.

In Gothic churches the structure itself draws us through God's distance to his presence. Gothic architecture synthesizes all the means we have discussed for providing spatiality for the God of religion; it is the perfect religious architecture, and our hankering for it in religious moments is a sound, if reprehensible, intuition.

It will, I trust, have been divined that my intent is polemic against this apprehension of God and against the architecture that provides spaces designed for worshiping God as so apprehended. Every great age of the church makes its peculiar discovery about the gospel: the discovery of our age is that the God about whom the gospel speaks is not simply the same as the God of religion — indeed, that he is his antithesis. This discovery is omnipresent in the theology of all confessions and schools. It is therefore all the more remarkable that it has had so little effect on the appurtenances of our faith, including our architecture. I suggest that a main cause of the universally admitted emptiness of our worship is that we persist in building and using structures in which it is impossible to worship any other God than the God of religion, in whom the gospel no longer permits us to believe.

The gospel calls forth a way of living that is the opposite of religion. For faith it is precisely the threat of the future, the possibility of the new and different that separates me from what I already have and am, that gives me my true self. This is the life given by the word of forgiveness, which tells me I may forget the past and its determination of the present and live for the future. The gospel makes of the present the moment of decision, an act of commitment of the past to the future. Things presently at hand become opportunities for decision. And so space becomes the arena of meeting such opportunities.

In the pattern of life evoked by the gospel, God, far from being our posit to defend ourselves from the challenge of the future, is the challenger, the speaker of the word that detaches us from the status quo and lets us live for what is coming. The God of religion is the absolute and changeless Presence. In direct antithesis, the God of the gospel is the Coming one.

The present reality of this God, his being *now* for us, is therefore not a quasi-spatial nearness but rather the *event* of this word that opens the future being spoken. The God of the gospel does not now exist, analogously to things in space; he happens. Worship of this God is not a relation to a Presence out or up or in there; it is a relation to the future. The overcoming of the separation from God that occurs in prayer and praise is not an appeal to a distant one but to a coming one. And his present is not a presence, but the occurrence of the word of the gospel being spoken between us, the occurrence of our telling each other the story of Jesus as the story of our joint destiny, and of our acting that story out as we do so (the sacraments).

It is plain that we cannot provide spatially for the relation of worshipers to this God by distance and direction. For this God's separation from us, his transcendence, is temporal and not spatial. And his present is exactly what we do, so that his space is not a different space from the one we occupy as we worship him.

The space provided for the worship of this God, for his present, must be a space for this action, for the telling and acting out of the gospel. It must, that is, be wholly a stage. And there must be no auditorium, for here there are no spectators, here the telling and acting out is done not for the worshipers but between the worshipers; here the place of God is not a different place from that of the worshipers.

As with any good stage, the arrangement of the furniture to be used for the action should be completely flexible. For reasons that we will see in a moment, the best everyday arrangement will probably be central, with the table in the center, but it should be possible to clear this away at a moment's notice. It is not possible to decree in advance a changeless staging for any drama; and once it is recognized that the entire church building is a stage, with no auditorium, all basis for a permanent interior distinction of locations is gone.

The definition of the space to be used for worship should turn all lines back on the volume of space used by the worshipers, rather than away from it. It should direct us not to a holy location but precisely to each other. The whole idea of a common focus for all present is exactly what we must overcome in our church architecture. For God's present is exactly the moment of our action; his space, therefore, is the space that action takes up. A space for worship is the capsule of a moment.

The otherness of the God of the gospel is the otherness of the future. Thus it cannot be comprehended by a space, whether by distance within that space or by a direction of that space. Rather, the otherness of the God of the gospel means that the moment of decision and action for which a defined space provides a capsule has its meaning only in what will come of it, only in another moment future to it: that is, the otherness of the God of the gospel means that the space used to worship him, the space of the moment of decision and action, is not complete in itself and must not appear to be. Its forms should, therefore, be broken, restless, even nervous. The Renaissance ideal of harmony, of the creation of a space that allows us to rest content in the given moment, is here what must be overcome. We should not find a church soothing. The forms of church buildings should be ready to fall, or to take wing. They should have the dynamics of the temporary.

It is clear that these last considerations suggest that spaces defined for worship should be small. What about large congregations? Quite possibly this question will be answered by the disappearance of large congregations, as the full consequences of the end of Christendom work themselves out. Surely the erection of great buildings designed to stand a thousand years is now a most dubious undertaking. But if large churches are to be built, then perhaps the temporality of the moment of worship may be established by making them so diffusely large that any one gathering within them will seem an encampment, from and to which to wander.

The life of faith, the life of such tellings and enactings of the story of Christ, is itself a story: I proceed from one such enactment to another, and this succession has a plot established by the distinction of baptism, preaching, and Eucharist. Thus the relation between the parts of the life of worship is temporal and not spatial. Therefore, instead of defining one space for all parts of the life of worship, and then distinguishing and relating them spatially by putting the altar here, the pulpit there, the font in a third location, there should be several rooms for various purposes, so that as we worship we go from one to another. How far this could be carried out would vary with circumstances, but surely the original custom of separate baptistries should be reestablished.

Finally, the space for worship is the space for the enacting of a particular story, the story of Jesus as the story in which the worshipers may find their destiny. On this stage it is always the same play that is performed. But the structure as such cannot establish this; only what, for want of a better term, we call the decoration can provide the scenery that defines the space as one set up for enactment of this particular drama. As we live in a church building, the story of Jesus of Nazareth should surround us, in sculpture, fresco, stained glass, mosaic, and other forms. The passion for bareness of much modern church architecture was a necessary purge of cheap and irrelevant decoration, but it is inherently inappropriate to the purpose, for a bare church is too un-determined as to which God is to be worshiped. Nor should such didactic decoration be limited to a few areas, for this would again establish a holy focus. Rather, the eye and even the body should be led to make journeys of exploration through a church building, discovering here a crucifix, there a healing miracle.

These reflections may be accused of utopianism, with good reason. Yet it is surely realism to recognize that in contemporary architecture we have not yet found even partly satisfactory forms for spaces for worship. We have continued to build for a religious Christianity that has long since gone hollow. The want of theological reflection on what sort of space God in fact takes is the main cause of this failure.

Eschatological Politics
and Political Eschatology

❦   ❦

I

Politics is eschatological; eschatology ought to be political.

THE MAXIM will already seem a truism, so rapidly has the theological mood that affirms secularization coalesced with the theological program of setting the meaning of theological statements by pointing to a final future. The maxim is already in danger of being handled as an empty tautology: politics is eschatology; eschatology is politics. I associated myself with the maxim before it was a fad, and will stick to it — but only because I think it can be nonvacuously developed. One way of avoiding vacuity would be to remind ourselves that eschatology is not only politics: that there can and must be cosmological and aesthetic eschatologies as well. But that will not be our task here.

Published in *dialog* 8 (Autumn 1969): 272-278. Reprinted by permission.

II

To the first half of the maxim, it is no objection that politics have been practiced in societies that never heard the biblical proclamation of hope. For if that proclamation is indeed *true,* there could be no society whose religion wholly lacked an eschatological component. And it is a fact that those societies that have most nearly suppressed their own eschatological disquiet have also suppressed politics below ideological consciousness. Politics is eschatological because it deals with hopes, if only to manipulate live hopes in the service of past hopes safely dead. Politics is a society's hoping as an activity and a process.

But need hope itself be eschatological? Not, anyway, in the sense that one might want to hope for penultimate futures, for example, peace or righteousness, but not be able to do this without also buying a final future, that is, God. This would be just a new version of the "God in the gaps": here are *a, b, c, d . . . n* to hope for in life, and *b* and *d* you can't hope for unless you also believe in God. Merely relocating the gaps to be filled under the category "hopes" will not rehabilitate this preternatural God, supposing he was ever habilitated. We will encounter on our way no future possibilities that we can take up only by appealing to God.

But that life is a way on which we encounter possibilities is itself an interpretation; making this interpretation and believing in God are the same. There are no God-linked hopes. But hoping itself is confession of God. How one hopes is confession of which God one confesses.

Nor do we thereby set up hope itself as one among other human potentialities and as the gap that only God can fill: it is not that one might wish to hope and not be able to because one did not believe in God. For hope is reflexively omnivorous: to wish to hope is, in fact, to hope, and so also to believe in God. One can refrain from hoping only by interpreting the world altogether otherwise than as possibility — in which case neither the question of particular hopes nor the question of God arises. Thus there is no question of "having" to hope in God in order to hope politically — or otherwise. If one does not hope, one sees no objects of hope; and this is not a privation, for it could be a privation only within the interpretation of the world as occasion of hope. We will encounter nothing on our way with which we need God to deal; but we need God to be on a way. If we have no God, and so are not on a way, we do not lack something; we simply live otherwise. Whether this mode of existence is, in fact, possible is another question.

III

Of course, it is not that simple. Here is the complication: Is God himself a particular object of hope? Do we have something particular to hope for at the End, and so from God alone? If God is not a special object of hope, as our discussion so far might suggest he is not, then talk of God is syntactical metalinguistic description, in the material mode, of our talk of other objects of hope, and probably now best dispensed with. If he is, then there seems to be a particular hope that, tautologously, is God linked; and however we set up the relation between this hope and our other hopes, we seem back with God-in-the-hope-gaps.

Indeed, do not our hopes on the way and a hope at the End inevitably cancel each other? If we hope for pie in the sky, can we ever really look for potatoes on earth? And vice versa? Is not a particular eschatological hope the necessary enemy of political hopes? Thus we regularly see people led by hope in God to commit themselves to political hopes, like the Christians who gave themselves to the Mississippi project and other civil-rights enterprises, only to discover that in proportion as these hopes occupy their lives, their need of the being they had called God diminishes. It is sad but true that specific gospel proclamation is usually nearly absent from the communication of exactly those congregations most involved in community action and the like, so that a visit to the worship of these with-it congregations is often dreary and stale. Vice versa the political inaction and stupidity of those congregations who talk most of God's final reward in Christ is notorious.

I think the difficulty is solvable, or rather solved, by the gospel. I think also that seeing how the difficulty is solved will show that — and more important, how — politics is eschatological. We will examine the possible schemes.

We can eliminate one scheme immediately: that there are earthly hopes and a heavenly hope, and that they simply succeed each other. For the eschatological hope must be hope for all other hopes, or it is not eschatological. This refutation is emptily tautological, but just so appropriate to a vapid suggestion.

Another undialectical proposal, but a serious one, would make the eschatological hope the limit of an infinite series of reinterpretations of political hopes. Just so, the Old Testament is the result of a thousand years of repetition of this event: that a failed — or achieved — temporal hope was recognized in its ambiguity and partiality, and taken up into a new and whole hope, which again was antiquated and transcended in its time. The "land" was first Canaan, then Jerusalem, then a land raised above the mountains and inhabited by men with the law written in their hearts. So now it would be our task to find the interpretations of the "land" or of "righteousness" that could be born of the antiquation of older interpretations — as those, to continue the series, in postexilic Israel, the Constantinian church, or the social gospel — and of the peculiar needs and possibilities of our times as we can see them.

Such hopes would be eschatological because we would know that the fulfillment of our hope for, for example, social justice as we understand it, would occur precisely in that it was overtaken by a new interpretation thereof. That we thus knew about the process of interpretation and reinterpretation would be our difference from Israel. An end to the series of reinterpretations would not necessarily be expected, for even without it we would have, as the content of our politics in any one epoch of the history of reinterpretation, concrete hopes we could not surpass.

This is the way that eschatological politics are done today. I wish partly to affirm this way, and will return to it later. But this scheme poses a problem: death is given only ontic and not ontological significance. And this will not finally do, for the future is, after all, not only the time for hope. It is also the time of death, which will interpret all hopes so: "It might have been." Israel knew this, and spoke her knowledge without illusion. But she never did anything theological about it. She never gave Jahwe anything to do with death, or death anything to do with Jahwe: she never gave death ontological status. Her choice was right, for in advance of death the only mediation of hope and death is compromise, such as all other ancient cultures made — the alternative would be to be past death, like the New Testament Lord is claimed to be. But thus death remained in Israel a "remarkable theological vacuum,"[1] and the future only ambiguously occupied by hope. This is why Israel was never able to

1. Gerhard von Rad, *Theologie des alten Testaments* (Munich: Christian Kaiser, 1957-65), II, pp. 371-72.

carry the desacralizing of her world through to the end;[2] she needed an open retreat into cultic repetition of a healing past origin. It is why Israel was essentially liable to exchange her faith for a religion, one of "law." We have to take the step Israel did not, and confront death and hope in the question with which Israel ended: "Can these bones live?"

One way of taking that step, and preserving hope in the face of death, would be to eternalize hope, to fall back on the manna of religion hoarded by Israel and make faith altogether into a normal religion. We might envision our hopes always already realized in a timeless ground of being where there could be no death and no threat of the future because there is no not-yet, because there already is all that it will be. Precisely the failure of our temporal hopes would be the entry to this timeless Being — and death would be the gateway to heaven.

Eternalizing hope has been the standard move of the Christian religion. "Dialectical" theology transcendentalized instead, and made a variant that is the inevitable last stage of the Christian reception of religion and its timeless Being. Specific political or other hopes serve in dialectical theology only to open hoping itself as a mode of existence. What is to be hoped for is not this or that, but the grace of being able to hope. What is promised by God is not this or that, but the grace of receiving life as promise. Such hope is immune to death and everything else, for it has no content to be frustrated. Indeed, this sort of hope arises exactly when the knowledge of death removes the content of our hopes. It arises in the crisis of the past in the present moment of futurity, in a judgment upon all concrete contents of the present from a future which itself can never become past because it has no content.

Eternalizing or transcendentalizing our hopes is a perfectly feasible way of rhyming them with death. Together they are the way mankind has universally chosen, and seems likely to choose now. But they are also the depoliticizing of our hopes. For politics takes time.

So: political hopes in evasion of death, or ontological recognition of death by depoliticizing hope. What we need is a way to transcend the alternative, and Paul proposed one. He proposed *love* as the solution to this antinomy of hope. Love is a concrete content of hope: one can very well say he has loved and give evidence for the assertion. Therefore one can hope to achieve love and be able to describe what one hopes for.

2. Von Rad, p. 366.

Yet if we hope for love, we hope in precisely such a way that shipwrecked hope will but beget new hope, we hope in a way that cannot be frustrated even by death. For when I love, I await my life from whatever the loved one does, without wishing to bind in advance what that may be. I expect to learn what is good from what the other in fact does. Love is thus at once concrete and transcendent; it is a concrete final hope that does not cancel penultimate hopes, and a transcendent hope that does not lack temporal reality.

But this is too abstract. There is no such thing as "love," only particular loves. Dropping, therefore, the generalities: Jesus of Nazareth gave himself up to our hopes and interpreted his destiny for himself and us on the shipwreck of those hopes in death. That is to say, he loved us. It is also claimed that he rose again. That is to say, he succeeded at love. If I give myself up for the other, and therefore cease myself to exist, I frustrate the gift. Only if I give myself up for the other, and just in this death am the future of the other, do I succeed at love. Only death and resurrection could be successful love. The word of the New Testament promises Jesus' successful love as what we may finally hope for, as the last interpretation of Israel's promises. The dialectics of this promise — and only those of this promise — give us an object of hope that is also the transcendent possibility of hope, a hope that is neither timeless nor transcendental yet transcendent to every present.

Called to hope for this final object of hope, we can hope in death without either abandoning or detemporalizing our hopes. We can work hopefully for the "land" or for "righteousness" as we understand them, knowing that if we break on our hopes, the land and righteousness will rise up again. For love, the futurity of death, is hope rising again.

Our dying hopes will first rise, we may hope, in ever-new interpretations of what we hoped for — as out of the dying hope of integration of America's blacks into white culture there is rising the hope for a new American culture jointly created by independently powerful partial cultures. Thus we return to the standard position of eschatological politics — but with this difference: the new interpretation in which broken hope will live again is not something we must bring forth, nor is it demanded by that great abstraction, "history." Rather if we hope for love as the End, we may expect that a new grasp of the "land" or "righteousness" will be called out of every new catastrophe by the word about Jesus that promises that love. This word can be spoken again after every catastrophe, for it has its own content, independent of other contents of hope and therefore able always to survive them. Yet when it is spoken it is the possibility of all hopes. It is not a word adventitious to our penultimate hopes, since it is a narrative and what is narrated is the crucifixion of Jesus, the death of our hopes, now narrated as future.

Or translating back to the terms of the question with which we began, the final future whose possibility is God is indeed a particular hope. Jesus' love is the final hope. Therefore, God, as the reality of this possibility, is an object of hope. Yet this hope is not for pie in the sky, it is hope for the resurrection of our potato-hopes.

IV

Yet this cannot be the whole story. For if the Christian promise really has a particular independent content, it must also promise a particular time of its fulfillment. Religion's heaven can survive as no place, but faith's new heaven and earth must be sometime. Otherwise, as we have seen, we must either ignore death or eternalize or transcendentalize our hopes. To understand the Christian hope, we must speak of the final future as a time of its own. Refusal to do this was the fault of dialectical theology — its only fault, but one that drove it to otherworldliness despite its own primary intention.

So we come to the other side of the maxim: eschatology is and ought to be political. We have to describe a last object of hope; and if the object is to be the resurrection of our politics, it must itself be describable in political terms. The Christian promise must be interpretable as describing a last society for which we may hope.

What may we await? We may await a *revolution done by Jesus' un-defeatable availability to his fellows, and a consequent new society organized by that life.* Perhaps this hope is preposterous; those who find it so will have to consider for themselves whether or how they will sustain other hopes. Our present task is merely to try to understand it. To that end, we discuss four aspects of the above proposition and enter one disclaimer.

First aspect. This hope is hope for a free future action of Jesus, a man once made past by death. It is, therefore, hope in his resurrection. The chief difference between a dead man and a live one is that the live man can still surprise us. Every dead man is in a certain sense alive, if his achievement shaped the tradition that mediates my present possibilities. I can very well await a future shaped by Socrates, Napoleon, or Malcolm X. Indeed, I must. But despite "living on" so, these worthies are dead, for they cannot *surprise* us, their life in the tradition is a given, a deposit. If I am surprised by Socrates, it is because of my previous ignorance of the tradition, or because someone else has surprised me in connection with the tradition. This sort of aliveness and determination of the future will not do for Jesus, for the future we await from him is successful love, and freedom to surprise is of the essence of love. We await, therefore, that "this same Jesus" will surprise us again out of love.

But what can it mean to say that "this same" anybody will do thus-and-so when the anybody is one who has died? The question is about the criterion for the use of "same person." Here I will merely state and use that which to me seems appropriate to faith's grasp of reality, without arguing for or defending it — since I have done that elsewhere.[3] In a case where our first criteria of personal identity — in terms of appearance, known location in time and space, and so on — came in conflict with each other, we should mean by personal identity *dramatic continuity* and judge it by *dramatic appropriateness*.

We regularly make such judgments, as when we say that scene three did or did not fit the rest, or that such-and-such a deed "had to be" done by Jones, being just what we "should have expected" from him. So the content of the gospel message, "He is risen," is this: We may await unpredictable events recognizable when they occur to be dramatically appropriate as the conclusion of Jesus' life of self-giving, and recognizable as the dramatically appropriate conclusion of our stories as well. In political terms: We may await a revolution dramatically recognizable as the conclusion of his life. This stipulation is sufficient in itself, but it does raise metaphysical issues we cannot treat here.

Second aspect. In any period of the Gospel's history of interpretation, the hope for Jesus' love concretizes itself by drawing to itself the dreams of the time. Whether these dreams have themselves been influenced by the gospel hope or are purely "natural" makes no difference here. Such a vision of the last future can and will be mythologically or ideologically elaborated to whatever extent is appropriate to its particular character.

3. Robert Jenson, *The Knowledge of Things Hoped For* (New York: Oxford University Press, 1969), pp. 150-153.

Politically, such a vision of the last future has a utopian function, like a platonic idea but on a temporal horizon: it is an unachievable but endlessly approachable limit of political endeavor. There is no politician so pragmatic that he wholly lacks a utopia, even if it be merely the utopia of his own unchallenged rule. And that the man with noble goals is "hardheadedly" aware that those goals will never be wholly realized, and that to partially realize them endless compromise will be required, means only that he knows his utopia is one.

Believing utopias differ from others in this: It belongs to their content that the believer knows his dream will be broken — he knows about death and gives it ontological significance, but does not therefore despair. For part of what he hopes is just that the death of his dream will be the occasion of Jesus' story calling forth yet a better dream. He does not know what the gospel's new interpretation of the future will be; for that statement of faith's hope that is independent of all utopias, that we "await the conclusion of Jesus' love," is not itself utopian and does not therefore enable predictions of what new utopias it will call to its future interpretation.

So also, our formulation of faith's hope in terms of revolution and a new society is itself already utopian, though minimally so. It draws on the fad-words of the age, and will be transcended. This does not mean it is an as-if sort of thing. If the Christian promises are fulfilled, we will see that just this prediction has been fulfilled — but many other versions of our hope as well.

Third aspect. The most obvious thing about "revolution" is that there has never been one — not as the word is used ideologically. Nor will there be — until the gospel's promise is fulfilled. There have been and perhaps will be governmental and social upsets in plenty, while whole civilizations rise and fall, but none of these upsets has been nor will be what a Marx or a Fanon means by "revolution." Revolution is an intrinsically eschatological concept.

When SDS types or Paris student revolutionaries are interviewed about their goals they invariably frustrate their liberal interviewers by insisting the present "system" must be overthrown, but having no intelligible proposals about what should replace it — and by not even being bothered by their lack of proposals. Just thereby they show themselves true revolutionaries. For political description of the revolutionary goal would have to be operational, it would have to specify how to bring it about. And this would mean indicating structures of the existing system to be used as levers on other structures, that is, to remain themselves intact. At this point we would be back with reform — even if by coercive methods — which is what the liberal interviewers want, but is exactly what the rebels are fed up with.

It has always been so: consider the vacuity of Marx's description of the Communist society against the rich operational detail of his analyses of capitalist society. What revolutionaries do have, instead of operational proposals, is utopias — but utopias themselves do not need to be brought to pass, and revolutionaries want to bring something to pass.

Thus consistent revolutionaries, such as Mao, have been driven to make revolution its own goal, to proclaim "continuous revolution" — in not at all accidental correspondence to dialectical theology's hope for hoping. Of course, revolt for the sake of revolt is — unless it is nihilistic or merely adolescently suicidal — as nonsensical as hope for the sake of hope. Maoism, like the early Barth, is a titanic and decisively instructive dead end.

The only one who could make a revolution would be one who lived freedom from the established structures to its fulfilled end, without giving up on the historical human reality mediated in those structures. That is, only he could make a revolution who had freely abandoned his life, who had freely died and who had died of his total acceptance of his fellows in all their hate and alienation. There will only be a revolution if it is made by a loving one who has died. Those of us who say Jesus of Nazareth is risen say there is such a man, and await the revolution from him.

Therefore, also, we can invest revolutionary passion in utopias known to be utopias, without despair or fanaticism; he will make the revolution and not we. Just so, therefore, we are free from ourselves to attack each new status quo with abandon, in the name of that future that is the meaning of all presents.

Fourth aspect. The hope for a new society is not — except in the rhetoric of a Lyndon Johnson or Richard Nixon — merely the hope for a society different from, and by some scale of value, better than, this one. It is hope for the overcoming of something inherently "old" in all past and present societies and in all future societies operationally extrapolable from past or present societies. Our societies are qualitatively old because they live by the past: their continuity is the same as their persistence, their stability as their stasis, their existence as the preservation of some status quo. This is why revolutionaries invariably become conservative as soon as they get power; there is nothing else for those responsible for a pre-eschatological society's existence to do except conserve it. There are, after all, only two ways of having life: losing it in order to find it, or hanging on. A society that did the first would indeed be something new.

So the flower children who set out to be a society of love, of mutual self-surrender, indeed conceived the only possible new society. Their only problem was that pre-eschatological societies cannot love, as their elders tried legalistically and therefore vainly to warn them. Therefore, they were driven, like many other serious monks before them, to primitivism, to the attempt to be as little a society as possible: to nudity, sexual nihilism, vagabondage, antirational use of drugs, and the abandonment of language.

That our existence is social means that each of us is himself only in his place in an identifiable entity not coextensive with himself but rather including other selves in their places. I am myself and yet free from myself, that is, am personal, only in that I am something for you; and this something is a function assigned neither by you only nor by me only. So we have the perennially observed dialectic of social existence: it at once is the possibility and reality of free life for another and threatens that freedom by making us mere functions.

The problem is the problem of the center, of what joins you and me to be a unit other than either of us, within which each of us has a function for the other. If we are centered merely by a system or ideal, our society will be qualitatively old, and will reduce us to functions, for systems and ideals cannot love. Therefore, societies have regularly sought a person, a being who can love as the center: the King, the Führer, the *theios aner* of a state cult. But those who love and therefore die, and do not rise again, fail at love — so that all societies so centered are at last distorted by the frenzied attempts of their centering persons to be immortal.

A "new" society could only be a society centered on one who has loved his fellows unto death and risen from it. This is the gospel's political eschatology: we may await a society ruled by one who gives himself to each of us just as each is defined by his past, and in which the function of each of us for the others is defined by the particular sort of acceptance that his particular past imposes on this ruler. I will be for you a particular possibility of love, of free self-giving, a possibility defined in its particularity by the unique past that defines "I." The effective social goal of this society will, therefore, be God, the Transcendence of the futurity of love.

Finally that disclaimer. There is a problem that I mention here only to indicate I have not forgotten it: the participation in the end-society of those who shall have died. This participation must be affirmed, but the wrench that an eschatology with content gives to our notions of time and personal identity means that this participation, like all the rest of theology, must be rethought. There is, however, no space for that rethinking here: it will involve an entire new metaphysics. Anyone who suspects me of using this excuse to postpone a hard task is correct.

On Becoming Man; Some Aspects

THIS PIECE will have two main parts. The first will be a condensed statement of some dogmatic considerations, and will begin with two highly arguable but here unargued axioms.

Axiom I: man comes to exist in and out of the world of animals and plants and galaxies precisely when he realizes that he does not yet exist; men are those of God's creatures who have their own true selves not as possessions but as challenges. My humanity is not a set of characteristics that I may be counted on to exemplify: like being vertebrate or brown haired or sapient. My humanity is rather something that happens, and happens exactly as the event of choice and action in which I become something that I was not before. This axiom is a set of platitudes of contemporary philosophical and theological anthropology — but platitudes the consequences of which we have hardly exhausted.

Axiom II: that I am not yet myself and must become it, is after all something I cannot very well say to myself. Where would I get the location from which to say it? If I am to discover this peculiar sort of fact, if I am to discover that my selfhood is an opportunity and not a given, somebody else will have to tell me. The challenge to find what I am by becoming other than I am can only come from someone other

Published in the *Bulletin of Lutheran Theological Seminary* 50 (1970): 4-13. Reprinted by permission.

than me, by some person who is new and strange to me and communicates that strangeness. My humanity is our mutual work. This second axiom is a slightly less platitudinous set of anthropological propositions; and its consequences have — despite Buberizing on all hands — hardly been looked at at all.

Being man, therefore, is an enterprise rather than a condition. It is, moreover, an inescapably joint enterprise. I am man only in that I become it; and this enterprise requires more than one in the same way as marrying or playing football requires more than one.

Moreover, the enterprise of being human is also a fearsome enterprise — again like marrying or playing football. For who, after all, is to speak this word that can call me to my true self? You are — and that is what is fearsome. I am dependent on you. I am dependent on your sensitivity to perceive when I need your word; on your judgment to find the right one; on your compassion to risk speaking it. That is, I am dependent for my humanity on yours. And that is a risky bet.

There is not only risk here, there is mystery. For if I am dependent upon your humanity for mine, on whom are you dependent for yours? On me. No matter how many members we bring into this circle, it remains a circle. How does it ever begin to turn? The common enterprise seems to hang in time by its own bootstraps. It is obviously impossible that it should ever have begun, and yet it happens.

It is, I suggest, at the point of this mystery that we speak of "God" — who is therefore a hiding and a hidden God, for he is the mystery of our existence. He is the mystery that we do somehow live as response to a word that has not yet been spoken.

The fearsomeness of the human enterprise is not merely the fearsomeness of relatively high risk; it is the fearsomeness of mystery. We are called to live for a future that is not merely not in our own hands but is in unknown hands. We must live by each other, not merely knowing that we are mutually relatively untrustworthy, but with the endlessly reciprocal waiting of each for the other to speak that keeps even our relative trustworthiness from getting started.

Our lives, we have said, are response to an address we have not yet heard, and this is what is meant by the hiddenness of God. The situation is one to which we do not stand up. There is no saying we might not have stood up to it, but we do not. The way we break is that we deal with the futurity and hiddenness of our humanity by defending ourselves against them and that we use our communication with each other, the mutuality of our existence, to close ourselves to each other.

We wait endlessly for the word of love: each of us from the other, for none of us dares speak it first. If I promise myself to you before you promise yourself to me, I give my life up in that promise. I die. And only your answering promise, of which I cannot be sure, would be my resurrection. And so I wait, and so do you; and the word of love is not spoken, to which our humanity would be the response.

We may ask, of course, which comes first: our collapse before the mystery of our existence, or its fearsomeness. Do we fail before the mystery of our existence because it is so fearsome? Or is it so fearsome because we have failed before it? But to that question we will get no answer, for this is merely a form of the ancient theological conundrum whether God's predestination or man's sin came first. We will get an answer to that question when both God's predestination and our sin have been fulfilled and not before.

If I now come to speak of Jesus, it is not because he is "the answer" in the sense of ending these dialectics. The dialectics of our enterprise of humanity continue also in faith, only under changed signs. Moreover, the whole preceding analysis has been Christian from the very beginning: a view of man suggested by the Christian message.

But just so I do come to speak of Jesus; for if the recollection that the church preserves of him is true, then the word of love to which our humanity is the response, and for which we vainly wait, has once been spoken. Jesus of Nazareth interpreted his own existence wholly by his promise to his fellows. Which is to say he loved and so died. And without our response he heard the response of love: in that death he was called to live, though we gave him no answering word of love.

If he lives, then for us also. Then for us also he is not merely an item of the past; then we too may wait to hear from him that word of love. The word by which we might live, to which our humanity is the response, is still yet to be spoken, and we do not anticipate it; but we have a guaranteed promise that it will be spoken. The future remains the unknown future; but it is in known hands. And whoever spoke to Jesus that word of love that called him again to life — the word that he awaited from us and did not hear — that is God.

Being man remains an enterprise rather than a condition. But if he is risen, then the enterprise is the *specific* enterprise of finding a role in his self-giving, and it is an enterprise entered on with *promise.* Being man remains a fearsome enterprise; but if he is risen then the fearsomeness is that of all true human love. It is still true that we must call each other to our humanity, and that we withhold the call from each other; but if he is risen, then he will be one of us and will not wait upon our response. Therefore even when we defend ourselves against our future, it remains ours; and when we reject the word of love, the very rejection certifies the particular word of love he will speak, which is a word to those who reject it.

In the rest of this piece I want to examine these dialectics of becoming human both more secularly and more closely. And I propose to do this under two somewhat arbitrarily chosen headings. They are chosen from the western vocabulary for aspects of humanization; for better or worse the West is where we are. The headings are "reason" and "organization."

The concept of reason is fundamentally an *ethical* concept. Rationality or reasonableness is an ideal we hold up before ourselves and struggle to achieve. As with any ethical concept, what is really hidden in the notion of reason is a set of commands. I suggest that these commands are simply the expression, with respect to our knowing, of the two sides of the enterprise of becoming human: its task-character and its mutuality.

The first command is, be prepared to change your mind. To be reasonable is to subject oneself to this command and be trying to fulfill it. Or perhaps the command is better formulated: test your opinions. The ideal of reason is basically a prohibition. I am prohibited from holding my opinions to be true simply because they are my opinions. I am prohibited from holding my opinions to be true simply because I have always entertained them or even because my whole culture has entertained them. Putting the same command slightly differently, the ideal of reason prohibits me from holding my opinions to be true merely because it would be advantageous for me for them to be true. To be reasonable is to be ready to submit all beliefs to whatever is in each case the appropriate test: to the test of experiment and observation, or to the test of argument, or perhaps simply to the test of discussion. The command of reason, therefore, is simply the command to be open to the future in the matter of beliefs. It is the expression of the task-character of human existence, applied now to the cognitive side of human existence.

The policy that I should be ready to submit my opinions to a test seems, of course, to be obvious. Yet the sway of this demand is exceedingly rare in human society. The standard ethos of mankind has rather been to take precisely the fact that an opinion is held as a sanction of its truth. Normally, mankind has submitted its opinions only to the test of antiquity. This is the *mythic* pattern of human existence. Myth equates the deep truth about the world with description of an originating event before time and of a consequent primal state; and it appropriately finds its own sanction as truth in continuity of opinion back to that beginning. Most of mankind, including many high cultures, are still captive to mythic existence. It is a part of man's breakout from mythic existence and from traditional culture that he breaks through to the willingness to test his beliefs, that he breaks through to acknowledgment of the task-character of his knowledge.

The particular breakout by which we yet live was accomplished in Greece. But Greece's cognitive freedom hardly survived the moment of its birth, except where it was picked up by Christian faith. The great time that we remember when we speak of the supposed gloriously rational and clear-minded Greeks was in fact an extraordinarily short time in the history of Greece; Greek culture itself returned rapidly to mythic dreaming. Christian faith, of course, has the very best reason to pick up this commitment to testing beliefs. For Christian faith awaits a last judgment. That is, faith subjects the whole human enterprise, knowledge included, to a test, and to a test that we will never get safely behind us. The adventure and test-character of knowledge is something that Christians have the best possible reasons to affirm and practice.

We are, of course, endlessly ingenious in evading the cognitive adventure. But once we have acknowledged the ethos of rationality, once we have submitted ourselves to the command to test our opinions, we have to cover our evasions by making them look like reason. We have to "rationalize" them. Of those of our opinions that we are unwilling to test, and that we hold because they belong to the substance of our security in the status quo, we are likely to say they are known by some superior variety of rationality. Thus in the Western metaphysical tradition it has been usual to say that some truths about the world are known by direct participation in the mind of God. Conveniently, we let God do the testing of these opinions; we simply take them over, and say that as a consequence of being known by direct participation in his mind they are so blindingly clear that for us to test them would be absurd. If drugs take over God's role in this evasion, little is changed.

The most sophisticated defenses against the command to test are those produced by apparent radical obedience to it. One such evasion in particular is very popular just now. Every cognitive attempt, if submitted to the command to test, represents a wager we might lose. I throw my belief on the table, risking whatever part of my life I have committed to that belief. But there is a way of playing on the open-mindedness and endlessness of the adventure, by which I excuse myself from putting any money on the wager, by which I excuse myself from letting anything ride on the opinions I submit to the test.

The modern Nietzschean intelligence endlessly sees new sides to every question. Give this intelligence a problem and it can generate new facets of the problem through all eternity. This is a good thing. But the Nietzschean intelligence is liable, like every other, to its particular perversion: the *uncommitted* intelligence that empties the wager, that evades the possibility of losing anything of myself by making no bets on any option. So, for example, we reflect that there may be a God, or that there may not be a God; and decide that anyway we will wait and see. In the meantime we try to live so as to come out on top in any event. This appears to be radical openness to the future; but in reality, since the connection of commitment is cut between my life and the future tests to which I submit my beliefs, this ethos is radically reactionary: it allows everything in my life to stay exactly as it was.

The one who has heard of Jesus has heard reason both to submit all beliefs to the test and to bet his life on those beliefs. For he is called to live life as a wager; and he has heard the hope that precisely by losing his life he might find it.

The second command that constitutes the ideal of reason is that we submit our beliefs to *public* tests. I am commanded that the tests to which I point in justifying my opinions must be tests that you could also, at least in principle, perform. This command is merely a direct transcription of the other side of man's nature as the gospel sees it: that human existence is a joint enterprise requires that our knowing also be a joint enterprise — that is to say, that I be able to let you in on the reasons for my beliefs, and in such a way that you can judge those reasons.

We come here to the Western empiricist tradition. The point of that tradition is not some arbitrary restriction on what sorts of experience I may have. My experience is what it is, and that is the end of the matter. The point of the empiricist tradition is rather a restriction on how I use my experience to back up my claims to knowledge. Private experience is forbidden at this point. Private experience is any aspect or part of experience that, were I to advance it as justification of a knowledge-claim, is such as to prevent my also telling you how to check this use of it by me. The empiricist tradition rejects use of private experiences as clues to truth because truth is a joint enterprise.

The point of the empiricist tradition is not a restriction on what experiences I can have. The point is an analysis of the conditions under which experience can be critically shared. Quite evidently you and I can share experiences only by their mutual reference to our common public world, only by our experience's reference to that world that is neither inside me nor inside you but precisely between us. One may call it the "material" world, or the "sensuous" world, or whatever he likes.

We do not know in advance how many ways there may be of sharing the public world. But if I claim access to a putative reality and cannot tell you how to get the same access, my experience is disqualified as an experience relevant to truth. If I say I am experiencing something, you should in general take my word for it; but if I identify my experience by saying I am experiencing "pain" or am experiencing "God," then to make that identification I use a word out of our joint public language. That a language is public means that you are able to check the statements I make using it: they are statements you too are able to decide to make or not to make.

If humanity is a joint enterprise, then only with this emergence from privacy does our experience become human, does it become knowledge of the truth. My experience in itself is what it is what it is what it is . . . , as an animal's experience is what it is what it is what it is. . . . The privacy and irrefutability of my experience I have as an animal — and there is nothing wrong with that. I am an animal, and if I were not, neither would I be anything else. But I am also a man, and I am a man in that I emerge from privacy. I obey the command of humanity when I refrain from claims about human truth that are backed only by my private, that is, prehuman, experience. The command to be human enforces, therefore, a sort of asceticism, and much is undoubtedly lost by it. But no one ever said that the creation of man would be without loss.

Therefore the demand for reason cannot in itself conflict with the promise of the gospel. Indeed, I suggest it is but an expression of it. Why then do we often speak of faith versus reason? Because it can happen that God in fact withdraws from the public realm, or at least that God as a particular culture has understood him withdraws from the public realm of that culture. Then our communication with each other about God, our rational knowledge of him, will indeed become broken and difficult. And then we may be glad that rational human knowledge of God is not all there is to contact with God, that God is our God also as He is God of stones and sticks.

Just here, however, it seems to me that religious people face a terrible temptation in the attempt to save religion from these difficulties of public communication. We do indeed now experience such difficulties every day: we go into the marketplace and speak of God, and no one knows what we are talking about. Then we face the temptation to save religion by withdrawing it altogether from the demand of reason into the safe realm of private experience. Religion, we will say, is a matter of "intuition" or of "sincerity." We will comfort ourselves that it does not matter what one believes, that is, it does not matter what his public expression is, just so he is sincere inwardly about it. It is important to understand clearly that by this retreat we do not overcome the difficulties that the demand for reason does indeed, in the circumstance of God's silence, make for religion. By these means we simply capitulate altogether.

Believers in Christ, in any case, should not need this escape. Perhaps religion can be saved by this retreat, but Christian faith cannot. If we have heard the gospel, then we have heard reason to persist in speaking our God in the public arena. For then we have heard of a revelation under a man name Pontius Pilate, and of a God who will verify himself by judging the quick and the dead, that is, the entire public history of man. We are therefore called to say our piece about God in the open arena of all nations or not say it at all. And we are promised that the gates of hell will not at last prevail against this attempt. The effort of faith will always be to hold our ultimate concerns in the human realm of communication and to fight all weariness that would drop them back to the level of private prehuman experience. And this effort is one that has promise.

The second aspect of humanization here to be noted is organization.

It has two roots. First, the mutuality of human existence means that each of us is himself only as part of a larger whole he makes with others — only as an organ of a community. That I am an organ of a community is not a limitation of my humanity, it is its possibility. Second, if this community is to be open to the future, if it is not to dissolve under the impact of every change that comes along, then some of these organs must be continuing organs, and not merely ad hoc arrangements for particular occasions. That is to say, the community must be organized. The need of organization is therefore rooted in the mutuality and futurity of man. It is one of the requisites of human existence, and perfecting our organization is one of the ways we become human.

But we all know too well how we regularly turn this organization against our chances for humanity. It is exactly organization that gives opportunity to receive the shock of the future creatively. But instead of taking those opportunities, we can and do spend our time tending the organization itself, so as to wall ourselves up behind it in the status quo. That we may be antiestablishment types does not guarantee us against this at all — currently the Movement spends more time on its own nonorganization than on anything else.

Perhaps here is the main problem that now disturbs us about American life: the way in which status quo answers are built into the very structure of the decision-making machinery. On every issue, the organs of our society go through an elaborate dance, approach the very verge of change, and then produce the answer one knew all along would emerge: keep on with things as they are. Thus there have been years of agitation in the matter of the Vietnamese War, agitation that brought down a president — and the end result of it was that we recently heard Mr. Nixon give the same speech, in some places nearly verbatim, that Mr. Johnson used to give regularly.

Organization is nothing but the structure of our mutuality, and yet it turns incorrigibly against that mutuality. As has been repeatedly pointed out, the more highly organized a society, the more does our relation to each other occur through secondary roles: in such roles, it is not Robert Jenson but Professor so-and-so that needs your attention, it is not John Jacobowski but the bus conductor who confronts your morning. Harvey Cox is undoubtedly right in saying that the dominance of secondary roles in megalopolis is an opportunity of greater freedom, but this is true only for a very few. New York City is indeed for people like us an opportunity of greater freedom than Gettysburg provides. But most people who live in New York City experience the dominance of secondary roles in their human contacts as alienating and dehumanizing. The very organization by which we live with each other prevents us from getting at each other.

Technology exacerbates this character of organization. We will consider just one example: data processing. A "bureau" is merely a primitive data-processing mechanism, so that the replacement of a bureau by a computer is only a modest technological advance. But the consequences are great. Computers operate with binary arithmetic. So far as arithmetic is concerned, this creates no problems. But when we store such things as census responses or credit ratings in memory banks, the binary logic of computers dictates that the simplest way to do it is in the form of yes-or-no questions and responses. Out of the stored information, new questions will then be generated to ask us — and the difficulty is that the options posed will emerge from previous yes-or-no answers. Just thereby, the range of our future is narrowed.

We can fight this. Questions can be put with three options, or ten or twenty, and then translated from arithmetic on these bases into binary arithmetic for storage. But there is a point at which we will tire of the effort; and in fact programmers do not do much of it and cannot be expected to. The narrowing of our human options as a result of frail humans using computers is already a very real phenomenon — as any of you will know who have ever tried to get a mistake rectified in a computerized business office.

It should be no surprise, therefore, that history is dotted with rebellions against organization, or that we have such a deep rebellion against it now. But how would we go about being *un*organized? One tack now much in vogue is to make all mutuality momentary, so that it shall need little organization. We do not marry; we have meetings that are "beautiful" precisely because they do not impose on the future bondage to past commitments. But by this means what we do is transform life into a mere series of status quos, and in fact abandon freedom altogether. Another tack is to simplify communities radically, to the point where they need very little organization. Monks have tried to do this all through history; and communes try to do it now. A dozen or so communes scattered around Gettysburg would undoubtedly be a very good thing — as salt; but they are no solution to the problem, for to the extent to which this endeavor of simplifying society succeeds, we return to tribal society — which is the most static and rigidly structured of all.

As I have argued elsewhere, the problem is the problem of the center, of what holds us together to be a community. If it is only the organization itself, or some ideology, that holds the community together, then that organization will indeed try to enslave us. For only personal address, only your real personal challenge to me and mine to you, can set free. Societies have therefore regularly sought to put persons at their centers: royal families, divinized heroes, or dictators. But these attempts also have regularly proved destructive. For only that king or hero whose word to me was a word of love could center our society as a society of freedom — and where are we to find such a person? Unless, of course, Jesus of Nazareth should really be as we have remembered him, and really be alive and coming to us. In that case we may indeed await a society with a personal center, a society bound together by one who speaks to all other members of the society the word of love.

Meanwhile, what we have to do is anticipate the end-society, but anticipate it not gnostically but historically. I suggest this means a sort of unresolvable union of anarchism with devotion to the organization. We are at once cheerfully to refuse to be repressed by the organization and to remain devoted to the society so organized and even to the improvement of its organization. As protest marchers, we should carry the black flag in one hand and the Stars and Stripes in the other. We should build bigger and better data processors, and occasionally slip them a folded card.

Perhaps I can sum up all I have been trying to say about becoming man under one final heading, also taken from the vocabulary of Western humanism: "creativity." Creativity is not a particular faculty of man, so as perhaps to conflict with other faculties, as reason or will. Man's creativity is rather his entire thrust through time, accomplished as rationality and as organization and as an indefinite number of other aspects. Man looks back at himself as he lies back there, as he is already a product; and picks this past reality up and uses it as the block of stone out of which he carves himself anew.

We may dare this adventure, and every day invent ourselves afresh, because we are not the only creators. What we do with our creativity is merely to pile up raw material for love (in love openness to the future and mutuality definitively meet). The story I will at my end have written will be delivered over to Christ and to you, as a unique and particular set of possibilities for your love — and vice versa. We can, that is, dare the adventure of creativity because there is one who will not wait for the rest of us to be absolutely free and absolutely mutual — to be human.

Violence as a Mode of Language

❀   ❀

IT IS MY ASSIGNMENT to attempt the beginning — and I guarantee that is all it will be — of a systematic theology of violence. This will be done very much under the inspiration of Martin Luther and in the attempt to use the resources of the Lutheran theological tradition.

The first thing we should have clear about violence, if we want to understand it theologically, is that violence belongs to the reality of what Lutherans have called *word*. It is an aspect of communication. Violent behavior is something we do in order to speak with each other, in order to get things across to each other. When I go to work on the woodpile in the basement with a hatchet, no one demands that I be restrained and calls out for law and order; and though it might sometimes be said that I attacked the job "violently," this would be exactly on those occasions when I was trying by my behavior to tell my wife how ill-used I was in being asked to chop the wood in the first place. Violence is not just energetic and destructive physical behavior. It is energetic and destructive physical behavior that belongs to the reality of the word, of communication. In the Lutheran tradition, therefore, the doctrine of "law and gospel" is the locus within which we may seek to understand the phenomenon of violence.

Published in the *Bulletin of Lutheran Theological Seminary* 51 (1971): 33-42. Reprinted by permission.

More particularly, violence is a phenomenon of the way in which our bodies participate in our communication with each other. It is a phenomenon of the body's role in the flow of address and response, of call and answer, that is human life, a phenomenon of the way in which we use our bodies to say things. If you punch me in the nose, you say something to me. But if you have done it by accident, and there was no message you wanted to get across, I may become angry at your clumsiness, but I will not accuse you of violence.

Therefore, a necessary step is a cursory analysis of some aspects of the event of communication and of the role of the body in this event. I want to conduct the analysis in terms of the arrows of time — past, present, future — as the universal interpretative horizon of human life.

The word is the opening to us of the future. The word is the reality now between us of what neither of us is yet. Every address of one man to another poses to the hearer the possibility of becoming something other than he is. It poses to the one addressed the possibility of a self that he is not yet. And this is true from "It's raining out," at one extreme, to "Your sins are forgiven," at the other. "It's raining out" poses the possibility to me that I should run and fetch my umbrella; "Your sins are forgiven" transforms the entire way in which I have my future stretching before me.

Perhaps we can understand it so: by our words to each other, by our mutual address and response, we create a shared life, a life that is neither just my life, or your life, but our life. In that shared life, what comes from you is to me a new possibility, a new future, just in those ways in which you are in fact different from me. And what comes from me to you is a possibility of newness and difference for you, again just in those ways in which I am in fact different from you. And the shared reality that we create by these words, the reality in which we now come to live together, is something new to both of us. The word is the opening of the future.

But now we have to ask what our words are *about,* and *to whom* are they addressed. And we have to say that our words are of course about the world, and our life in the world, as it already is; for nothing else exists for our words to be *about.* Our words to each other are necessarily about the world as it already is, including you and me as we already are. Moreover, it is you and I as we already are, as we talk at each other, who are also the only possible addressees of our words. Thus we come to the *body.*

My body is me as I stand here (I use the objective case on purpose).

My body is me as an object in the world, like tables, trees, or whatever. My body is me as an item of the present scene, as an item of the way things just are. My body is me as I now and already am, shaped and molded by what has been done by me and happened to me in the past.

Thus — very schematically, and leaving all sorts of holes — in the event of communication the word and the body represent the two arrows of time: the word is the call that opens to me the possibility of things not being as they are; the body is me as you see me, warts and all.

An achieved communication, a word that comes off, is the opening of the future of new and strange possibilities to and for Jones and Jenson as they stand there. Whether it be the preaching of the gospel or "Hello," a successful event of the word is an occasion on and in which a transforming vision of the future opens up, as the realistically entertainable future of the ones who are already there to be addressed, defined by all that has happened to them and to their world. Therefore for Christians "*the* word" is the word of forgiveness, which opens a future that is ours no matter what the past may have been.

A successful event of communication is an exchange in which what we already are and what we may yet become come to *rhyme* with each other in our words. A word that works is one that opens the future to the past, to ourselves as we already stand there, and just so is an event in which the past *moves* into the future that the word poses.

But now — we as we already are, we as our own pasts, are in the word-situation present to each other as our bodies. If then it belongs to a successful word that we as we already are move into the future, one merely repeats this in other terms by saying that it belongs to the word that our bodies move, that we *do* something with ourselves as we stand or sit there as items in the world. In the situation of the word, the movement of our past, the freeing up of our past, is represented by the movement of our bodies.

As we live and grow in our ever-renewed address and response to each other, part of this is that our bodies move with each other. An intrinsic part of language is gesture, the way in which our bodies, representing our past given selves, respond to and turn toward the new possibilities that our words open to us. The motion of our bodies is that aspect of the event of the word in which the word establishes, or fails to establish, that the future to which the word challenges us is the future of and for the persons we already are.

Undoubtedly, the supreme example of the way in which our bodies participate intrinsically in successful community, in the word, is the act of love. Here we say something to each other with our bodies. *What* we say, whether we say "Damn you" or "Bless you," is determined by the words that go with and come before and follow after; but only the body can get those words across. Only with what we do to and for each other with our bodies can "I love you" really be said. For the content of the words is love, that is, affirmation by each of us of the other as the other really is. The content of these words is affirmation of the one body by the other.

Or why has the church always said we should absolve by putting hands on the head of the person being absolved? That sounds like a rather silly procedure, as if some kind of fluid flowed from one to the other — so now in Protestant churches we do not do it that way. Instead we confess everyone once just before the service and absolve them in a mass. And nobody feels forgiven: that this absolution is directed to *me* was the point of the hands of the priest on the penitent. Or why at a football game do we not sit down to cheer? Because you *cannot* cheer sitting down: the motion of the body is part of the act.

Liturgy, with its sitting, standing, parading, gesturing, and so forth, is the most comprehensive example of the way in which the body belongs to our communication with each other. Those who have been so misguided as to try to make the liturgy more personal and intense by eliminating the standings, sittings, paradings, crossings, and kneelings achieved, of course, the opposite result. It is exactly in these motionless liturgies, where we just sit for an hour and fifteen minutes, that it becomes impossible to experience rhetoric about "God" as in any real way true about us.

And now I want to take this word "liturgy" in an expanded sense, and pair it with "violence," as words for what I suggest are the two basic possible modes of the body's role in communication. On the one hand, when in the words that flow between us the rhyme of past and future comes off, when you call me to something to which I am able to respond as my future, then the movement of our bodies that therein occurs I want to call "liturgy." Liturgy is the free, celebrating turning of ourselves toward a future that opens, toward a promise that is made.

On the other hand, when the rhyme does not come off, when I am unable to apprehend the future that you pose to me as mine, and yet

[43]

you or some third party insists that it *must* be mine, the movement of our bodies that then occurs is what we call "violence." Violence happens when I want to say something to you that really cannot be said to you, that you are not in a position to hear, and when yet I insist that you are going to hear it. When my words do not move you, and yet I determine that you are going to move, then we have violence.

When the future posed in your word to me is not a possible future of the one I am, of the body that is here, this may be to your credit: if, for example, you open the possibility of my sacrificing myself for our society, and I refuse because I already have great possessions, the fact that your word opens no future that I can appropriate honors you and disgraces me. On the other hand, it honors *me* if you whisper defamatory words and I reject the whispered invitation. Or it may be that your words open a future that is not mine for morally neutral reasons, as the experimentation that must be done in the next years in order to determine the heredity mechanisms is not a future upon which I have the ability to enter.

Most significantly, perhaps the future to which your words call me is not my future because it is nobody's. Perhaps it is a fantasy that spooks in your words, like the "free elections" in Vietnam for which so many have died to no purpose, that is to say, to no future. Perhaps, worse yet, your words open no future that I can appropriate because the whole point of your utterance is to bind me to the past, as is the purpose of most political propaganda. Consider only the many generations in which the political representatives of corporate greed have kept their power by evocations of a "free enterprise" that unfortunately no longer exists, if it ever did.

What is communicated by violence is the alienation of what is to be from what is, the contradiction of the future that is posed and the present reality. If your words pose to me a future that I simply cannot accept, or vice versa, and if we then persist in our mutual address, whether because we really must or for less honorable reasons, the bodily reality of this negative communication, the gestures that accompany it, is what we mean by violence. Instead of free liturgical celebration of the future that has opened to us in the words between us, as with a kiss, we perform bound and binding action to compel the commanded future to come to pass, as with a twisted arm. Instead of our bodies together liturgically turning toward and into what is promised to us and joyfully accepted by us, the one body operates on the other to make the commanded future come to pass.

It is no accident that I have begun to speak of "command," "compel," and the like, that is, in the terminology of what the Lutheran tradition calls "the law." "Law" is the word of any future that is not receivable by the one to whom it is addressed as a joyful promise, that is in contradiction to what the hearer is and wants, that must therefore present the future to him in words like "must" and "shall." "Law" in the Lutheran tradition is utterance that opens a future that those to whom it opens cannot celebrate liturgically, cannot, as the ones they are, receive joyfully.

Therefore Luther bluntly called the power in the law the "sword" — that is to say, *violence.* The agents of the law are always agents of violence. There is no law without coercion, for the law says what must be whether we affirm it or not. Therefore also Luther did not view violence as altogether avoidable. For when the word-situation is already marked by alienation of what is from what is to be, that is, by violence, then we must call each other out of that situation: in this situation too there is a word that has to be uttered. But in this situation nothing can be said except violently. Therefore the call away from violence will be itself a violent call. That this situation will in fact recurrently be our case is part of what is meant by the fallenness of man.

Luther accordingly said that necessary and justified violence is that violence, and only that violence, which is the bodily aspect of the call to do what will terminate existing violence. The sanction of the law is violence to restrain violence — which is why Luther was so against taking the law into any more hands than it was in already. Finding necessary violence concentrated by history in relatively few hands, Luther was for leaving it there.

Therewith we have moved out of mere analysis into the many ethical problems posed by the fact of violence. Luther's solution is that everything depends upon what a given act of violence *says;* for one thing that it may say is "Let violence cease." I wish to accept this solution. But it seems to me that working this out is now far more complex than it was for Luther, because of a possibility he does not seem to have noticed. That possibility is the possibility of *a language of violence,* of a society that has so shaped its language that in it nothing can be said except violently.

A language of violence would be a language in which the alienation of the facts of the case from dreams for the future is built into the vocabulary and syntax of language itself. A language of violence would be a language which has no words by which it is possible honestly to face reality as it is and at the same time freely to project what might and must be. I suggest that this fearsome possibility is posed to us by the present situation in America.

If we want to understand the violence that increasingly characterizes our life, we must understand that insofar as we live with each other and talk to each other in the language of American politics, the language that we hear on TV in the thirty-second spots, the language of the local newspaper's comments on current affairs, the language of neighborhood discussions, most comprehensively, the language taught in the public schools, we are increasingly reduced to the position where we either say nothing or speak violently. We are reduced to this position because in the language that America is inventing for itself it is impossible to have any authentic relation to the actuality of American life and of the American role in the world.

So long, for example, as the phrase that is provided as a label for our economic system is "free enterprise," it is quite impossible to speak at all about the reality of our economic life; for in fact the system is not free, for "enterprise" or anything else, and in the sense of the phrase never was. Or so long as the pairing that our official language provides for our relationship to other nations of the world is that some nations are "developed" and some nations are "undeveloped," we will have no clue to what is really going on; for this pairing presupposes a continuum along which we have come quite far and on which other nations are also moving, only a bit further back. But this is just not the case at all: the so-called undeveloped nations are highly developed, but as the exploited parts of one worldwide monopoly-capitalist system of which we are the beneficiaries. The whole purpose of such language is to separate us from reality, thereby preventing any action upon that reality.

Anyone not yet convinced that the era of doublespeak is upon us, need only examine any random statement of Mr. Nixon or Mr. Laird on social justice, the state of the economy, weaponry, the Indochinese ward, the SST, or whatever, and then reflect that these collections of pseudopropositions are taken as perfectly intelligible and acceptable by the American public. Americans faithful to the language they learn in school and from our public life inhabit an entirely imaginary world. And that is just the purpose of this language: to prevent us from trying to change the real world, to prevent the future from intruding. In a society with such a language, anyone with something to say is in a position where he will be driven increasingly to violence in the attempt to say it.

So we come to our question: in such a general word-situation, what of the Christian community and of the word that the Christian community has to say in the world? It is the task of the Christian community to interpret every aspect of human life, and every aspect of the world in which we live that life, by the story of Jesus of Nazareth and by the promise that story makes. The story of Jesus of Nazareth is the gospel-promise only if it is a word about and to the actuality of the world. The gospel is a missionary message: a word addressed to the world, intending to interpret the reality of the world to itself. Therefore we cannot avoid politics, economics, movements of culture, and all the rest of that dangerous reality out there.

The conclusion is clear: given the language of the world we inhabit, which is a language of violence, the church too will be driven to speaking violently. Only by saying nothing to or about the real world, and that means only by refraining from the gospel, would we be able entirely to avoid involving ourselves in violence. That at certain times in history we should find ourselves in this situation, should, after all, be no surprise; for the one of whom we speak did say, "I come not to bring peace but a sword," and where the Christian message has gotten through it has repeatedly brought just that. On the other hand, believers are clearly commanded to nonviolence. This side of the matter seems to me so evident in Scripture and the whole tradition that I will excuse myself from arguing it here.

What then are we to do? As the last part of this essay, I wish to advance a tentative suggestion. I base the suggestion on the following considerations: the gospel brings, as Jesus said, "not peace but a sword," because of a way in which it is like the law. The gospel is like the law in that the future that the gospel poses to us is a future in absolute contradiction of every status quo, of everything that we are and of everything that our world is. Yet at the same time, the gospel is the message that the suffering of this contradiction is the very reality of God; and therefore the gospel, which speaks of a "kingdom of God" utterly against everything we think we want, is nevertheless a promise to which we can respond liturgically. The bodily reality of the gospel communication is the free liturgical anticipation of the way in which God — Glory Hallelujah! — will overthrow everything, of the way in which God will create the future — God be praised! — in utter contradiction of every standing order.

Thus my suggestion is that the body-aspect of this message, insofar as it is a missionary message, must be a peculiar sort of violent liturgy. We are called to preach in the language of the world; this is now a language of violence. We are called to speak to a society that understands only violence, and to speak of the utter overthrowing of all that is. But we are called to be nonviolent. I suggest that the body-side of such a word will be *violent* action in contradiction of injustice and hate, that is, transformed into liturgy by being done uselessly, as *play*.

I have an example here, an example I never thought I would find myself using, until I began preparing this essay: the destruction of draft records by the Berrigan brothers and their friends. I have no information about their theology or their motivations; I want to point only to the deed. Nine of them broke into a draft office, took the files out with apologies to the inconvenienced clerks, and set fire to them, meanwhile praying. I cannot help seeing a parallel to Luther, Melanchthon, and their students burning the papal bull, meanwhile praying. Was this action violent? Certainly, in a way; they went to jail for it. Was anybody *compelled* by it to anything? Was anybody's arm twisted? No. Then did it do any good? Did it help end the war? To that question Daniel Berrigan replied that it was "a square question." "Did it do any good?" is American pragmatism at its worst. What occurred was a *liturgical* celebration of the future that the gospel promises — done in the violent body-vocabulary that is the only vocabulary with which we Americans are provided.

I suggest we must become inventive of such liturgy. Not all of us are called upon to burn draft records — I have burned none and have no intention of beginning. But we must always be finding just such liturgical violence to be the body-reality of our mission. I suggest that the words for our preaching must be so outrageous in their contradiction of conventional perceptions that they are a kind of body-violence in themselves, that they are "a slap in the face." I suggest that the church's mission — whatever its interior reality may be — is to function as a band of watchmen in the world who violently resist the way things are, but without hurting anybody, and so *uselessly, pointlessly, playfully,* in honor of *God.* And finally I suggest that such action will of course release real violence, as it always has, so that the second step for believers is to determine so to act that when their nonviolence lets loose violence, *they* are the ones to suffer.

The Kingdom of America's God

I

AN AMERICAN CHRISTIAN who ponders the spiritual history of his nation finds two phenomena nearly beyond belief: (1) the size of the hopes for human fulfillment under God, by which this nation has been animated, and (2) the spiritual vacuity and hopelessness to which we have come, and amid which we now live. The matter of this essay is how the one came to the other, and what new possibilities there may now be.

I make no claim for a general explanation of our history. I will examine what seem to me fatal flaws in our hopes themselves, and ask what possibilities might lie beyond them. How much of history such ideational analysis explains, I do not know. I will limit myself to the more explicitly religious of our hopes, and to the religious mainstream.

I begin with a passage from *Our Country,* by Josiah Strong, executive of the Evangelical Alliance at the end of the last century, who summarized, already somewhat desperately, a century of mainline American evangelical movements:

The two great needs of mankind . . . are, first a pure, spiritual Christianity, and, second civil liberty. . . . It follows, that the Anglo-Saxon, as the great representative of these two ideas . . . , sustains peculiar relations to the world's future, as divinely commissioned to be, in a peculiar sense, his brother's keeper. . . . There can be no reasonable doubt that North America is to be the great home of the Anglo-Saxon, the principal seat of his power. . . . I believe it is fully in the hands of the Christians of the United States, during the next fifteen or twenty years, to hasten or retard the coming of Christ's kingdom . . . by hundreds, and perhaps thousands, of years. We occupy the Gibraltar of the ages.[1]

It is easy to show how the sort of vision represented by Strong was morally blinkered and practically disastrous. It is also easy to be amused by his naivete. But this vision of America's destiny and task, proclaimed from thousands of pulpits and in thousands of pieces of popular literature, was indisputably inspiriting.

It cannot be said that we are now inspirited by anything. We share no vision of a common mission; though, of course, an abstracted and contentless notion of American mission is still used to summon support for various bureaucratic ventures. It is not true that America has been a nation without historical consciousness, without vision of a destiny granted by its particular past; but it is rapidly becoming such a nation. Indeed, even what might be called the "natural" historical existence that occurs in families and schools seems to have ceased for many of our people. The post-Vietnam generation contains persons barely aware even of their personal pasts. With no hopes at all, not even able to grasp what a hope would be, they are human molecules moving at random in moral space, giving no more than pragmatic allegiance to any community whatever. In this they but mimic their parents, in whom nihilism was concealed only by the last tatters of the success ethic.

1. Josiah Strong, *Our Country* (New York: Baker and Taylor, 1891), pp. 208-227.

II

Strong's sort of vision was simultaneously Christian and political. Whatever we may criticize, that much at least was good.

The Christian community bears a promise through time: that Jesus the Nazarene is Lord of all, so that he must finally triumph. Believers call this promise the "gospel" — a "cheering message" — because, Jesus being who he is, it is good that he and his cause will triumph. If the message about Jesus is indeed to be cheering, it must be spoken to the dreams and terrors by which those who at a time and place hear it afright and comfort themselves. The promise of Jesus' triumph *interprets,* and interprets itself in terms of, the shorter-range promises that at a certain time and place preoccupy life. Thus arise the great eschatological visions of the Christian proclamation: the starving behold the "Great Banquet," the alienated see their citizenship in the "New Jerusalem," the ignorant seek the "Vision of God."

The great eschatological visions have throughout Christian history been visions of *communal* fulfillment. The Lord's triumph will not be his private justification; the life that will triumph was lived and given up "for" us. His triumph must be a communal event. Just so, the gospel-promise matches our penultimate hopes, for these too are communal: each person's hopes are invested in others, and depend for fruition on the approbation of multitudes.

Moreover, some of our penultimate communal hopes are inevitably not only communal but specifically *political.* They concern participation in or exclusion from the process of setting rules for common life, as against merely living under them. So also many of the gospel's eschatological visions are political: the "City" of God, the "Kingdom" of God, the "Rule" of the Saints. It is so in principle and is exemplified by history that the gospel must be promise to and about the polity, about the arena in which the community settles its future.

Since Christianity's visions arise as interpretation of penultimate hopes shared by believers and unbelievers, a secularizing interpretation is also possible by which eschatological hopes in turn come to be shared by believers and unbelievers, in forms marked by the gospel with absoluteness and radicality. Millions dream of the Great Banquet who do not expect Christ to be host.

Both processes of eschatological interpretation are extraordinarily visible in the spiritual history of America. I am not a historian; and my knowledge of America's history depends on others' work. But the *plot* of such a story and its discernibility depend on basic theological choices; perhaps a systematicians's habit of mind may help discern the plot.

III

We celebrate the American Revolution, the first great epoch of the story I wish to tell. The Revolution positively volunteers itself to theological analysis, for in that its makers came to call it, as we continue to call it, "revolution," they and we understand the event eschatologically. In the language born of the American and French struggles, a "revolution" is a turn of human events, having universal significance and universal force and dividing human events into an old sequence and a new. What is new is *liberty* — a public space for debate and decision, which citizens may enter to determine together the future of their community and not merely endure it,[2] to practice creation of the new as a continuing principle of common life. Such an event is the very pattern of what theology calls "eschatological"; and the hope of such liberty is the very kind that goes back and forth between theological and secularized interpretations.

The American Revolution was made by Puritan Whigs and deistic Whigs. Of the American population in 1776, 75 percent had at least a distant Puritan religious background;[3] most of the revolutionary leaders were deists, some of them leaders of the international Enlightenment. Puritanism first and most. . . .

Puritanism was the Calvinist Reformation in the Church of England, cast as a church party by beginning within a national church antecedently separated from Rome. When the Stuart monarchs made a Calvinist Reformation of the English church seem unlikely in England, thousands went to *New* England to carry on from there; and so much of colonial America was populated.

Certain traits of Calvinism were to be fateful for America. To begin, Calvinism (unlike early Lutheranism) maintained the patristic and

2. Cf. Hannah Arendt, *On Revolution* (New York: Viking Press, 1963), pp. 21-58.
3. Sidney Ahlstrom, *A Religious History of the American People* (New Haven: Yale University Press, 1972), p. 124.

medieval doctrine of God unchanged. Traditional Christian thought was formed as a synthesis of biblical proclamation with the religious and intellectual heritage of Western antiquity. The least stable part of this synthesis was its doctrine of God: in standard theology, two quite different statements of what it means that there is God stand superficially connected beside each other.[4] On the one hand, there is the metaphysical God, the final explanatoy Ground of reality as we find it, who is reached by argumentative and mystical penetration back through reality as we find it. On the other hand, there is the proclaimed God, the Power of the future to differ from reality as we find it, who is known by words about Israel and Christ, addressed to the historical and contingent hopes and fears of hearers.

Neither body of doctrine was, of course, unaffected by its juxtaposition with the other. When talk of the great Explanation is infiltrated by the gospel's assumption that God is above all *free,* the image is evoked of an utter and unfathomable Will as the final explanation of reality as we find it: the Ground of all things becomes a *distant* Ground. When the gospel's promises are made in the name of the metaphysical God, the promises also come to serve as explanations to establish a rationally perspicuous relation between God and believers: the inwardness of hearkening to words becomes the experience of penetration to an inner Ground of the soul analogous to the outer Ground of the world.

Thus the traditional doctrine of God shimmered with polarities: between the two starting identifications of God, inside each, and crossways. In the system of medieval Christianity all these were reconciled and made religiously fruitful by the existence of the church. The church was a rationalized institution — of miraculous grace. It was a public and political administration — that administered inner power. It was a main structure of the standing order — to make available eschatological transformation. It was the mediator between the distant exterior and public ground and the inner and private experience of Christ's presence. Remove this sort of church, leaving most else as it was, and you have classic Reformed theology.

In Reformed tradition the two identifications of God, and the two appropriate relations to God, stand unmediated against each other. They

4. Cf., most compendiously at present, Wolfhart Pannenberg, *Basic Questions in Theology,* trans. G. H. Kehm (Philadelphia: Fortress, 1971-72), vol. 2, pp. 119-183.

are very nearly two different religions, united only by fiat. The *Medulla Theologica* of William Ames,[5] "chief theological mentor of the New England puritans,"[6] can provide a typical and directly relevant example.

In Ames, the doctrine of God comprises the doctrines of his "essence" and his trinity. Ames's doctrine of God's essence is no whit different than if Israel and Christ never were. He begins with God's self-evident unity, aseity, and immutability. From these he deduces all God's attributes.[7] These attributes in turn tell both "what he is and who he is";[8] thus even to *identify* God no reference is made to the historical content of the gospel. God's power[9] and choice[10] are defined by his essence, and his creating[11] and governing[12] flow from his choice.

With God's governing, we come to the key concept of the theological movement to which Ames and the New Englanders adhered: the "covenantal" relation of God and man. God governs "rational creatures in a moral way."[13] This moral government consists in "teaching" and in carrying out "what is taught."[14] God's teaching is "making law and . . . establishing it."[15] And from "this special way of governing . . . arises a covenant . . . , a kind of transaction of God with the creature whereby God commands, promises, threatens, fulfills, and the creature binds itself in obedience. . . ."[16] The whole development is exclusively in terms of "law," and contains no word the deists would not be able to repeat.

On the other hand, the rest of the *Medulla* is animated by a profoundly christological and eschatological piety, and its talk of God is peculiarly biblical. In a medieval system, the doctrine of the Trinity would provide

---

5. William Ames, *Medulla Theologica,* 1623. Cited from the translation of J. D. Ensden (Boston, 1968).

6. Ahlstrom, op. cit. p. 131.

7. Ames, op. cit. I, iv.

8. Ames, I, iv, 31.

9. Ames, I vi.

10. Ames, I, vii.

11. Ames, I viii.

12. Ames, I, ix-x.

13. Ames, I, x, 1.

14. Ames, I, x, 4.

15. Ames, I, x, 5.

16. Ames, I, x, 9.

both the speculative clarification of this other talk of God and some unification with the metaphysical doctrine. This does not happen in the *Medulla* — which, of course, does have a section on the Trinity,[17] but shrunken, arbitrary, and unconnected to the main section on God.

In New England, this tendency seems to have reached its extreme; perhaps the total absence of the old church promoted the development. Perry Miller's great work on the seventeenth-century New England mind is a 461-page catalogue of unresolvable polarities: between miraculous and transforming inner experience and pragmatic rationalism, between God as utter mystery and God as all-too-reasonable haggler for souls, between God as pure distant Reason and God as inexplicably forgiving Presence, between the image of reality as a ladder for the soul's ascent and the image of reality as a world-mechanism.

A second feature of Reformed theology was its tendency to meliorate these tensions by giving the civil polity some part of the role that had been previously played by the church. In America this took a particular form.

Puritanism in England had adopted or created the idea of the *social contract,* to fight Stuart divine-right claims. We need not decide whether the concept of God's individual and ecclesiastical covenant with believers was suggested by the concept of social covenant or vice versa; whichever, Puritan thinkers quickly joined the two.

In general the covenant-theologians worked to mark out an area of God's rule within which he would rule no less omnipotently than by the necessities of natural process, but in a way appropriate to moral creatures, in an order of freely entered compacts and their obligations.[18] Since by ancient Christian doctrine, the state is a chief means and sphere of God's reasonable rule, it falls within this doctrine of covenant.

Indeed, God's covenant with men was taken simply to include men's social covenant with one another; the former was itself understood in legal terms and was the basis of all legally definable rights and duties. To "own" the covenant with God is simultaneously to make sociopolitical covenant with other men. In America the necessity of creating governments from scratch gave opportunity for actual practice of the

17. Ames, I, v.
18. See for this and the following, Perry Miller, *The New England Mind* (Cambridge: Harvard University Press, 1954), pp. 399-431.

idea that polity is created by contract of the citizens; suddenly all this theory was transformed into reality.[19] This had three consequences.

First, polity making in New England, and to a lesser extent in other colonies, was an attempt to create "holy commonwealths," polities based on covenant with God. This holiness was not abstract or moralistic. It was a role in history: the Puritans had seen England as the nation "elected" to complete the *Reformation;* now New England took up the task.[20] The covenant was thus a social and political covenant for the completion of the Protestant movement. This theme has never been abandoned in America's self-conception.

Second, in one half of their theory, Puritans anticipated much of eighteenth-century Enlightenment liberalism. So Governor John Winthrop: "No common weals can be founded but by free covenant." No sovereignty is rightly over men except "according to their will and Covenant." Or John Cotton: "all power that is on earth" must "be limited." Magistrates must possess only such authority as "will do them good, and the People good."[21]

Third, the task of founding commonwealths turned attention to the future, and the task of founding *holy* commonwealths turned attention to man's end of glorifying God, that is, together, to eschatology. When the Reformation is finished, what can follow but the millennium? As Jonathan Edwards would later say, "The two great works of the devil ... are ... his [Papistic] and Mohammedan kingdoms. . . . It is in the destruction of these that the glorious victory of Christ . . . will mainly consist."[22]

This brings us to the last of those characteristics of Puritan theology fateful for America. Like Lutheranism, but unlike some of the Reformation sects, Calvinism perpetuated the traditional eschatology, in which the polarity of the traditional doctrine of God is precisely mirrored. In traditional eschatology, the eschaton is on the one hand the *fulfillment* of temporal history, with its contingency and community, and on the other hand the individual's private escape therefrom. The importance of this will occupy us later.

19. Compare the "Mayflower" civil covenant and the Salem church covenant.
20. Ahlstrom, op. cit., pp. 93, 135.
21. Quoted from Miller, *New England Mind.*
22. Jonathan Edwards, *A History of the Work of Redemption, 1739/1774* (New York: American Tract Society, 1839?), p. 389.

The Revolution was made by Puritans and deists. What was deism? It is a fair description to say that it was the one great side of English Puritanism's inner polarity, gone off on its own: the distant Explanation-God, a rationally perspicuous relation to him, a humanity bound only by its own covenants in all that concerns it specifically as human, reality as world-mechanism, political reality as social contract. The Enlightenment was English export wherever it appeared — even and especially in France — and may be understood as the religion of Puritans who had lost their christological faith.

When deists appeared in America, the Puritans denounced their "infidelity" to Christ, but understood them marvelously well in everything else. Between the deists' assertion of God's existence, essence, and rule, and his own, Jonathan Edwards saw no difference; indeed he regarded the agreement as an argument for the truth of the gospel, since through so long a list of weighty matters the gospel teaches what even the christologically unbelieving must agree to.[23]

Our "founding fathers" were mostly from the deist side. The explicit vocabulary of the Revolution and Constitution came from them. They envisaged, and largely brought to pass, a state that was the very mirror of a particular God: the world-Ground half of Reformed deity, the Puritans' God minus all occasions of christological or mystical piety. Jefferson affirmed that "life, liberty, and the pursuit of happiness" are endowments of the Creator; simultaneously he regarded "religion" as politically irrelevant. He could do both at the same time because by "religion" he meant that inner christological piety that in Puritans he saw added to affirmation of the world-Ground, but that was clearly also subtractable therefrom.

As the deist God is an engineer, who follows the laws of Newtonian physics to construct his creation as a perfect machine, so when intelligent creatures participate in creation, as when the constitutional fathers sat down to make our polity, their task too is that of designing engineers, and their product a machine. The lengthy discussions in the *Federalist*[24] of, for example, the most suitable ratio of electors to representatives, the forms of government suited to territories of various sizes, or the precise mixture of "federal" and "national" responsibilities and

23. Edwards, *Work of Redemption*, p. 39.
24. *The Federalist*, 1852 ed.

powers vested in the new government resemble nothing more than the discussions of design engineers about a new model-series of automobiles.

God's great machine, besides being a marvel merely as clockwork, turns out God's blessings for us. So the constitutional fathers designed a machine to turn out political blessings: of justice and liberty, the latter defined as "self-government," as general access to the arena in which the community's future is decided.[25] Design of such a polity had heretofore proved impossible; but as Newtonian mechanics had revealed the laws of physical reality, enabling vastly improved technology in that sphere, so also "the science of politics . . . has received great improvement."[26] Precisely in that the deists' ideal state is a freedom and justice machine, if it is properly designed it produces liberty and justice independently of the goodness, that is, the dedication to these values, of those who at any time are its cogs and pulleys. Laws of political motion derived from analogy to the Newtonian laws of action and reaction pit interest against interest, faction against faction, power-center against power-center, to the good of all.[27] The construction of such a polity was the great goal of those who established America's institutions.

IV

The Puritans described earlier are those of the seventeenth century. To understand how Puritans and deists formed our eschatology, we must move to the eighteenth-century Puritan contemporaries of the deists. Two important things have happened in the meantime.

First, the creation of commonwealths holy as such proved hard. In a variety of ways, the project was openly or tacitly replaced by the project of a commonwealth *in* which holiness might flourish, a polity within which a holy people might be raised up. With respect to the state only, this cut the connection between the two sides of Puritan reality also for the Puritans; that severance once endured, Puritans could affirm the entire deistic proposal and ideology for the state, it being only one half of their own proposal reappearing in an autonomy they too had now

25. *The Federalist*, pp. 103, 174, 241.
26. *The Federalist*, p. 39.
27. *The Federalist*, pp. 39, 43-45, 238, 241.

been driven to acknowledge. Even the mechanisms from which the deistic founders would construct the constitutional machinery were familiar items of Puritans' parish and civic practice.

They not only could affirm revolutionary state building, they could greet it with holy enthusiasm. Both Puritans and deists made liberty the goal of their state building; and insofar as this meant liberation from something, the enemy was the same for both — every remnant of the tyranny of the "dark" times before the Reformation. So John Adams, half Puritan, half Enlightener, in his *Dissertation on the Canon and Feudal Law* of 1765:

"Thus was human nature chained fast for ages in . . . servitude to [the Pope] and his subordinate tyrants. . . ." These subordinates are the divine-right civil rulers, and between religious and civil "systems of tyranny" was "a wicked confederacy. . . ." "Thus as long as this confederacy lasted, and the people were held in ignorance, liberty, and with her, knowledge and virtue . . . seem to have deserted the earth, and one age of darkness succeeded another, til God in his benign providence raised up the champions who began . . . the Reformation. From the time of the Reformation to the first settlement of American knowledge gradually spread; and in proportion as that increased . . . , ecclesiastical and civil tyranny . . . seem to have lost their strength. . . ."

The task is now for America to complete the Reformation, by establishing balances of power in givernment to protect "Rights derived from the great Legislator of the universe," against "the whore of Babylon, the mystery of iniquity, [the] great and detestable system of . . . usurpation."[28]

The second development was a new kind of eschatology. Throughout the Western history of Christianity, the arrangement of two versions of hope, matching the two versions of God, has been a vexing problem. On the one hand, Christians have hoped for *fulfillment* of the biblical promises about such things as liberty and justice and the unity of earth and mankind; on the other hand, they have hoped for escape from all

28. Cited from E. L. Tuveson, *The Redeemer Nation* (Chicago: University of Chicago Press, 1968), pp. 20-25.

such temporal worries. Turn-of-the-century Puritans were attracted by a relatively new solution: that a period of fulfillment of the historical promises would precede the return of Christ, thus remaining continuous with history, to be followed by the return of Christ and the final transformation into eternity ("postmillennialism").

They liked this solution because by positing a sort of preliminary eschaton continuous with history, they could use the biblical eschatological images to interpret the experientially apocalyptic events they had to deal with. In particular, they unanimously interpreted the completion of the Reformation as that fall of Antichrist that in Revelation immediately introduces the millennium. Jonathan Edwards was the great American exponent of this view, followed by such disciples as Timothy Dwight, who laid it at the root of the revivals and crusades of American evangelicalism.[29]

But if American state building completes the Reformation, then it is the prelude to millennium. And if the millennium is causally continuous with preceding history, then American state building — this deist enterprise! — is the final active preparation for the millennium, and thus the American nation is nothing less than the to-be-prepared place for Christ's return. Moreover, this preparation is necessarily a universal mission: it is Christ's return to the world that is to be prepared.

So already but cautiously, Jonathan Edwards himself: "This new world is probably now discovered, that the new and most glorious state of God's church on earth might commence there; that God might in it begin a new world in a spiritual respect, when he creates the new heaven and new earth."[30] Timothy Dwight had no more such caution: "HAIL LAND OF LIGHT AND JOY! Thy power shall grow / Far as the seas, which round thy regions flow. / No more on earth shall Rage and Discord dwell, / But sink with 'envy to their native hell. / Then, then, an heavenly kingdom shall descend, / And light and Glory through the world extend."[31]

Edwards described the coming of millennium, and catalogued its marks, thus also stating the goals of American destiny:

29. See Edwards, *Work of Redemption,* pp. 419-428. Cf. C. C. Goen, "A New Departure in Eschatology," *Church History,* xxviii, 1, pp. 25-40.

30. Jonathan Edwards, *Thoughts on the Revival of Religion in New England,* in *The Works of Jonathan Edwards,* vol. 4, ed. C. C. Goen (New Haven: Yale University Press, 1972), p. 354.

31. Timothy Dwight, *America . . . ,* cited from Tuveson, op. cit., pp. 105-106.

The Spirit of God shall be gloriously poured out for the wonderful revival and propagation of religion. . . . Concerning this overthrow of Satan's visible kingdom . . . : 1) Heresies, infidelity, and superstitution . . . will then be abolished. . . . 2) The kingdom of antichrist shall be utterly overthrown. . . . 3) Satan's Mohammedan kingdom shall be utterly overthrown. . . . 4) . . . and then shall the house of Israel be saved. . . . 5) Then shall also Satan's heathenish kingdom be overthrown . . . , the heathen nations shall be enlightened with the glorious gospel. There will be a wonderful spirit of pity towards them, and zeal for their instruction and conversion . . . it will be a time of great light and knowledge. It shall be a time of great holiness. . . . It shall be a time wherein religion in every respect shall be uppermost in the world. It shall be had in great esteem and honor. The saints have hitherto for the most part been depressed, and wicked men have governed. But now they will reign. . . . In that day, such persons as are eminent for true piety and religion shall be chiefly promoted to places of trust and authority. Those will be times of great peace and love. There shall then be universal peace. . . . Then shall all the world be united in one amiable society. It will be a time of excellent order in the church. . . . That will be a time of the greatest temporal prosperity. Such a spiritual state as we have just described has a natural tendency to health and long life.[32]

Edwards's description is the very program of the great campaigns of revival and reform that from his day almost to ours form the history of American Christianity, and that there is no need to rehearse. They were all aimed at saving the nation for its mission of saving the world; and the deist state that guarantees liberty has been both guarantor of the possibility of the enterprise and often part of the blessed condition to be promoted. The ideology of New England's destiny continues in these campaigns, only now this purpose is understood as the people's, not the state's. The state is ruled by the distant Ground of the status quo — though creation of that state is itself part of America's equipment for eschatological destiny.

It is not quite correct to say, therefore, that American evangelical religion privatized Christianity. No religious movement in which anything of the Puritan impulse lingered could entirely abandon outward

32. Edwards, *Work of Redemption*, pp. 451-465, 474-481.

reality and the public arena. What evangelical religion did was to create a sort of second public arena, alongside the political arena, missing only the specifically political function of direct public decision making, having a liberty defined as liberty from the state and as socioreligious rather than political.

This second public reality of the nation has been in its way "political," in that the existence of a state dedicated to political liberty itself became a part of the millennial vision and also in that the second public sphere necessarily sustained an advocate's role over against the state. The religious movement that carried the civilizing of the West, abolition, prohibition, female enfranchisement, and the social gospel (the activists were in each generation the same persons), was eminently "political," but in a particular and odd way.

Thus the American religious settlement divided reality. It put politics proper under one God, the deists' God, the religiously distant Ground of things as they are. For the other God of active religion, it created a new kind of public space, embracing every aspect of public life except that no actual decisions about the community's future are made there — these are under the competence of the first God. This second public space was assigned to be the home of Christian faith's eschatological vision, and indeed of religious passion and the quest of transforming divine presence in general.

V

Throughout our history, these two spheres have been symbiotic. Our deist civil religion was by itself not adequate to its function, though so long as the symbiosis endured, this was not noticed. For great occasions it has always drawn from the reservoir of evangelical religious hope. A religion entirely without eschatology can sustain a society wholly dedicated to preservation of the status quo (as was ancient Egypt for most of its history); but a nation committed to such hopeful realities as liberty or the "pursuit" of happiness cannot function without some vision of common purpose. Therefore the greatest American state leaders have at every epoch or crisis legitimized national undertakings by invoking the millennial visions of evangelical religion.

On the other hand, evangelical reformism has depended on the state, for none of its projects, public by intention, could be accomplished without the state's cooperation. This also reflects the theology of the situation. Because God's Creatorhood had been invested in the polity's distant Ground, evangelical faith's God was something less than omnipotent, and for great deeds needed the help of his big brother.

The great symbiosis seems to have exhausted itself; and this, I suggest, is the more precise statement of our present spiritual vacuity. Our state is increasingly a machine in truth; and our Christian religion is increasingly driven back to truly private spheres, there to exhaust itself in dimly sensed futility.

Deprived of identification with evangelical religion's God, the deist state-God ceases to be an object of religious devotion, and so becomes incapable of grounding the polity from beyond the polity. When Mr. Madison's polity-machine is not judged from beyond itself, it becomes indeed a machine-polity, a great apparatus grinding along oblivious of all human quest for transcendence and community. As it ceases to be true that almost all Americans are, of course, also committed to the reformist millennial vision, we lose both memory and hope.

Were we ancient Egypt, this might not matter; but we are committed to such temporal values as "liberty." When communal vision of transcendent destiny fails, temporal values become demonic; then, for example, the "liberty" for which our state exists exhausts itself in the liberty of the state, and national security becomes the functioning political value. Since this turns rule over to police and army, who are servants of the state, such a state has no actual rulers; it is but a self-perpetuating mindless process, a self-sustaining institutionalized public disorder, the usual word for which is "fascism."

Deprived of identification with the state God, evangelical religion's God ceases to have power over outer reality. Religion becomes a "private affair." This dogma, often taken for American tradition, has in fact scarcely fifty years' standing among us. We no longer pray, "O Lord, succor the poor"; we pray instead, "O Lord, make us feel better toward the poor" — giving God as light tasks as possible. Unable either to guide or condemn what we do in the polity or the economy, our religion's only relation to these arenas is now that it bucks us up for what we would do in them anyway; just so, evangelical religion becomes in truth the comfort of the oppressors and opiate of the oppressed. In this setting, the Bible is, of course, a stumbling block. We could get rid of it by generally adopting authentically privatist Eastern religions, or religions invented specially for the purpose; and that is actually what many are doing.

After the fact, we may judge that the symbiosis *could* not have endured, in that it always constructed a life of alienated liberty. As the deists' half of the Reformed God was a distant utter Freedom, so the deists' polity is a sovereignty marked by distant and alienated freedom. Our state has been and almost remains indisputably the "freest" on earth; nowhere does it contain a home for tyranny. And yet when we try to grasp that freedom, it always seems to elude us, to be someone else's. Exactly those who grasp most persistently, and "go into politics," find themselves most captive to something-they-know-not-what and lust for inspiriting religious vision.

As the evangelicals' half of the Reformed God was a very near but not quite world-ruling inspiriter, so the evangelical crusades grasped a freedom that was all too much man's, and again elusive. The omnipotent God, the God who could be a God of grace, was busy with state matters. American Christians have asserted on this continent nothing less than the glorious liberty of the children of God. But the finally liberating entry of God was postmillennial, always dependent on the success of the next crusade. And so the enterprises of freedom turned one after the other into obligating burdens. If only the other half of God, theoretically concerned only with state matters, would help out. Also for our religion, freedom has always been just over there.

The way of our divided vision of God leads to nihilism, to a society of isolated moral atoms interacting by the amoral laws of a machine-polity — that we have come in fact so far on this way, and whether we travel to its end, depends of course on many other factors besides those discussed here. Yet I am hopeful. If God wills it, the self-defeat of alienated sovereignty can break down the divisions between God and God, and liberty and liberty. From the death of the old American settlement, God can create a better.

VI

On the one side, we may hope that the end of evangelical reformism as religion's assigned sphere will set the church free to be much more decisively and peculiarly Christian, more sectarian even, than it has lately been. Such a church might even be able to preach the gospel again: it might reclaim the omnipotence and universality of God, so long predicates of an inactive state-God, for its Christ. The church might become so specific as again to have a specific thing to say in and to the world, and so become again a messenger-community to the — in this instance, American — ecumene. It might become a messenger-community of God's future that is not bound to America, which if need be will come, both ultimately and penultimately, over America's dead body, and which can be hope also for America just when America can have little hope in itself.

On the other side, we must hope for a new civil religion and theology, meaning by "civil" religion not the average religion of the populace, but the religion that matches and so sustains the actual functioning institutions of a polity. We need new civil religion both because the old one is moribund and because our polity needs some new institutions. No doubt we still need the republican machinery for some purposes; but precisely for the important political questions of education and local distribution of resources and relations with specific faiths, we need institutions whereby the citizens can themselves enter a public arena of debate and consensus, there together to decide the future rules of community.

Some are at work on these now; their creation offers America's best alternative to fascism. Such a polity would invoke a God far more easily to be identified with the Bible's God than is the deists' God: a God who *is* Freedom for man, a God self-invested in what is not yet but will be, a God who affirms love among men, and therein affirms face-to-face argument and joint decision and self-government, a God who is the last Reconciliation of all our human meetings.

The two sides of so good a future fit each other. A penultimately saved America would invoke, in the midst of citizen debate, and for judgment and promise both, a God whom believers could recognize as theirs. To help sustain such judgment and promise to the polity would in turn be believers' political good work.

Is There an Ordering Principle?

MY ASSIGNED SUBJECT is the process by which the numerous social and human purposes that present themselves to the American polity may be ranked with respect to urgency, may be, as we now all say — and God will just have to forgive us — "prioritized." The question is urgent because, as the American government governs less and less, only those causes that have top national priority, or those that have such low priority that they slip through without notice, have much chance even to be discussed, to say nothing of being acted upon.

How does, how can, how should the ranking of social and other human priorities be done? You will hear a great number of experts on segments of this problem. And you have invited a theologian, as a presumed expert on being in general and nothing in particular, to introduce it.

The first point that it seems to me must be made is that if we consider the problem in the terms in which it usually poses itself to us, there is no problem. When we talk of "priorities" and "prioritizing," and indeed of "ranking," the model of polity with which this language leads us to work is of an enormous data processing device. The multitude of interests that individuals and groups present to the polity-device are

Lecture to the "Public Affairs Seminar" in Washington, D.C., 1978. Previously unpublished.

processed in two steps. They are first assigned a weighting according to how large the constituency is, how rich the constituency is, how loud the constituency is, how much blackmail the constituency can put on other constituencies, and so forth. Then the complex calculation of these weightings is carried out by the logic circuits, these being composed of a great many people. The weighting formulas and the logical assumptions are the program of the device.

This procedure is in itself entirely unproblematical. The process I have just described does in fact happen; and no moral reflection or argument is either involved in it or called for about it. It is possible, of course, for one interest that is presented to the polity to be a desire to change the program. But any data processing device that is sufficiently large and sophisticated can change its own program; and all polities are that sophisticated. My desire to have my interest differently weighted than it has heretofore been will simply be computed by the device itself, along with other peoples' similar desires. It may even be that we wish to change the structure of the device: we think that it is inefficient or that it can't handle a great enough load. But again, polities have long anticipated the third generation of computers; they have been designing their own improvements and indeed their own successors for millennia. Thus also our desires to change the device, our revolutionary impulses, are simply computed along with similar impulses.

The model of public reality that we have in mind when we discuss it in terms of priorities, the weightings of these priorities, and the rankings of those priorities, is thus of a public reality that is entirely self-contained and offers nothing to discuss. If I think that some cause of mine is coming out short from the polity, the thing for me to do is try to increase the weighting of my cause: by "organizing" perhaps, or by putting on a little pressure — but that is to say, by another sort of input into the device. If I think the program misconceived or the device outmoded, my course is the same: I should organize to improve the weighting of *this* "input," namely my concern that the device is outmoded or the program should be altered in some respect.

Both of these, of course, are what Americans are busily doing. Once you get your name on the standard mailing list of either side, you are conceived to be a patsy either for "liberal" causes or for "right-wing" causes: you get five letters a day entreating you to lend your weight to some input into the great American data processing device.

But members of the Public Affairs Seminar apparently want to *discuss* something; indeed, to conduct a moral, even a theological, discussion. Such a discussion can only be of whether this whole model is itself adequate as a description of political reality. Or better: what can be discussed morally and perhaps theologically is whether polities that can be described by such a model are themselves adequate to human reality.

I suggest that when we worry about how our system "prioritizes," our real worry is that prioritizing may in fact be all that our polity does. We think, I suggest, that it should do something more. We want to be able to say not only that our polity in fact ranks social needs in such and such order, but that it ought to rank them in just that order, that it is right when it does so. And when we think needs should be ranked differently than they in fact are ranked, we want this concern of ours not to be just another input with its own weighting and ranking; we want it somehow to transcend the device. We want our concern — let us say that the environment should have higher ranking than it does compared with the problems of inflation — not to be merely another input; we want it to be a moral judgment, expressed somehow from outside the great data processing device.

The problem of course is of the Archimedian point. Where do we stand to make such judgments?

What we want, if we think there is something to discuss here, is to posit a "common good," a common moral judgment by which inputs into the polity of need and want are weighted by a value that is entirely independent of how many people support them, of how firmly they support them, of what kind of cash and other resources they can support them with. We want to be able to say that even if one person — and that the poorest person in the South Bronx — is the only one on God's earth who says that this is what the United States should do on a particular point, he may be right. And we want to be able to say that if he is right, and if the United States does not obey him, the United States is to be judged for not doing it.

Obviously a concern that is backed only by the poorest person in the South Bronx will not be adopted. But we want to be able to say that there is something the matter because it is not — if indeed that person is right. We want, that is to say, the polity not to be a prioritizing device at all, not to be properly describable on the analogy of a computer.

We want the polity rather to be a moral agent, a decider and discoverer of right and wrong.

I take it that the assignment given me by your committee was to consider what conditions must be fulfilled if in fact we are to judge our priorities by the concept of a common good. It seems to me that there are two such conditions, one of them metaphysical and the other political.

First the metaphysical: if we are able to judge the concerns that are presented to the body politic not merely by their interest weighting, but by whether they are right or not, by a common good, then the good must be knowable. The good must be not only decreed, but also discovered; not merely chosen, but also found.

Such a supposition flies in the face of the development of philosophy and of practical daily life in the Western world since the eighteenth century. The whole development has been toward the supposition that all there is to be done about the good is to choose it: that one cannot as a matter of fact know what is good, that one cannot say, for example, "I know that it is wrong/right to allow abortion on demand prior to such and such a date" as a statement of fact like "I know that my papers are on this podium." The whole development of our culture has been toward a situation where I think of myself always as an advocate: this is how I want it to be, and this is how you want it to be, and so we must struggle. But if there is to be a common good, then the good must be known: not only decreed but discovered, not only willed but also apprehended.

For a common good must be intersubjective. It must be a good that you and I share; and it is what we know, not what we choose, that we share. If I tell you that the cat is on the mat, but do not give you any signs by which to recognize the cat or the mat when you find them, so that you have no way to discover whether you also think the cat is on the mat independently of listening to me, my claim to know that the cat is on the mat is just thereby disqualified as a claim to knowledge, because it fails in intersubjectivity. The claim to intersubjectivity and the claim to knowledge are the same thing. We are interested in the other way around: if the good is to be shared, if it is to be intersubjective, then it falls into the realm of what we can discover. I must be able to say that I know this is good, and trust that you will by investigation come to agree.

It may not be quite absurd to think of my decreeing my own good and of this becoming my good simply by my having decreed it, a la Jean Paul Sartre. So long as I think of myself as a sort of moral atom, the conception may work, just barely. But I cannot decree *our* good and make it be *the* good simply by my decreeing it. For what if you choose a contradictory good? Then neither choice is complete until one or the other has prevailed. And then what completes the choice is again the struggle of weightings, of relativity factors, of conditions, of the whole apparatus. If nothing can be said about the good other than that it is what we want to happen, then the permanent condition of every society is the struggle of each against all, and the only possible polity is machinery such as James Madison devised for ameliorating the struggle.

What sort of good can be known and not merely chosen? The good is what *ought* to be: that is to say, it is what may not be now and may never be, and is no less the good for all that. But how can we *know* something that may not be real and may never be real?

We can do it if and only if public human reality is teleological; that is to say, only if the human process is not a process at all but a drama, a story, only if the public human reality simply *has* a goal that will be achieved and that lives in the present as the principle that in fact makes the daily choices.

Such is the Bible's promised kingdom of God: the good that God is determined to achieve, that because he is God will be achieved, and that is being achieved in all that happens whether we perceive or want it or not. Or such is Aristotle's intuited perfection of each kind of being as the inner dynamic principle of that being's growth: in the acorn there is already the oak tree, and everything that happens to the acorn as it grows is determined by the oak tree that is its always internally present goal. Or such is Plato's dialectically approached eternally ideal society and ideal humanity: of which all that happens in time is the cyclical reflection. Or such is Marx's "scientifically" discovered necessary course of society: that leads by the mere natural laws of all societies to the classless society.

These posits are very different from each other, but they share one character. They posit that reality has a teleological quality, that, quite apart from our choices, or in or through our choices, or sometimes in spite of our choices, reality is going somewhere.

When there is an understanding of common good, or even a hope for it, this is always on the basis of some such teleological grasp of reality. For only if reality is in some way teleological can the good be known; and only if the good can be known can it be shared, can there be a common good. The grasp of common good, of that from which an ordering principle may indeed arise, occurs as and only as teleological vision: as a vision of destiny which we do not invent and to which we are called.

America has traditionally had such a vision. With the founders of this country, the vision was nothing less than that America was to be the landing pad for the return of Christ. Things were watered down a bit after that, but the genuinely political history of America has continued to be the history not just of a crusade, but of a sequence of them: America was to make the world safe for democracy; America was to bring the blessings of "purified" religion — in the language of the mid-nineteenth century — to the rest of the world; America was to make the world democratic. Always America was to be in one sense or another a city set on the hill.

It is exceedingly easy to debunk this sort of vision. Looking back on other people's visions of destiny, it is no great achievement to perceive their naivete and the damage it did. Earlier Americans were indeed naive, and did a lot of damage. But the first great enterprise of America under the leadership of their debunkers, of "pragmatic," "nonideological" liberals, was the war in Vietnam.

When America has not done merely evil — and of course we do evil, every nation does that — but also some good, it has been because the nation shared some vision of destiny, some teleological metaphor. When we have been historically creative, it is because we have shared some look into the future, a metaphor of freedom or goodness or purity or mutuality, that could draw us forward through time. Nor is there any dearth in American life of great causes to be adopted now. It is not as if the world were so enormously improved that there were no longer any need for vision. Only how is eschatological vision to be evoked?

Whenever teleological vision appears, it is essentially religious. In America, the great visions by which in succession the nation has been animated have invariably been interpretations of the biblical proclamation of the Kingdom of God.

The proclamation itself lives only in and through such interpretations. Simply to say that God will triumph somehow is neither here nor there. To say that God will triumph is a meaningful utterance only when it is addressed to the living hopes and fears of some community, that is to say, only when it interprets those hopes and fears and is itself interpreted by them. In the Bible, we find, for example, the great vision of the Messianic banquet. And that interpretation of the promise of God's triumph is good news indeed to people who are hungry or longing for fellowship. Or again, in medieval theology we find the interpretation of the Kingdom of God as the vision of God: when God triumphs we will all behold him face to face and will live and breathe only in that beholding. And again, if you have a people for whom the life of the mind and spirit has come to constitute the hopes and dreams by which they live from day to day, this is indeed the message of the gospel.

Such mutual interpretation of penultimate hopes and Christian ultimate hope has been the substance of America's actual political life. It was not the budget or defense that animated the citizenry so long as we had a citizenry, but suffrage or abolition or the extension of education; and in each case it was most explicitly the promise of God's Kingdom by which the past was renounced and the vision of a better future evoked. It is the cessation of this interpretation that is responsible for the stasis in our political life that we all so painfully apprehend.

It is true, of course, that Mr. Madison's machinery deliberately excluded such interpretation from the government itself. The American vision of common good has therefore had to live in a sort of second public space, a public space constituted by congregations of famous preachers, by lyceum and Chautauqua, by traveling evangelists and lecturers of all varieties.

During the Mexican-American war, the governor of Pennsylvania proclaimed a day of meditation and prayer. The town fathers of Gettysburg thought they should do something about that. So they invited the town's leading citizen, Samuel Simon Schmucker, founder both of the seminary and of the college, to address a meeting of the citizens. What he addressed them on was the illegality and iniquity of the Mexican-American war, in a town of war hawks, and the evils of slavery, in a town of Southern sympathizers. If I tried that in Gettysburg these days I would get run out — in fact, during the Vietnamese war, I very nearly did. But in Schmucker's day, the town fathers and community of Gettysburg were perfectly able to hear and discuss the radical opinions of their leading citizen.

It has been in this second kind of public space, outside the whole machinery of government, that the American dream of a common good has lived. And it is still perhaps in the synagogues and churches, and in such groups as this, that eschatological vision for our country will or will not be rekindled, to make possible apprehension of common good.

The metaphysical condition of a notion of common good is teleological vision. I said there was a second condition, a political condition, on which I have already been trespassing.

The political condition of a conception of common good is that the community, and not merely the individuals who make up the community, shall be a moral subject. The political condition is the existence of the community as a chooser and an actor. What that requires above all is events like that incident in Gettysburg during the Mexican-American War: the assembly of the citizens to argue what is good and what is bad.

I as an individual am not a moral subject merely because I have such and such wants and needs and express them. I have many wants and needs; and I express them by whatever channels are open, in the polity and elsewhere. The real income of professors of theology has declined every year since 1968. It is therefore my decided want and need that the rate of inflation slow drastically; and if that throws workers in Detroit out of work, that does not change my need at all. Moreover, if there are enough people like me, and we register our wants, that input will go into the great device and the prime rate will shift another quarter of a point. But I am not a moral subject simply because I have this want, or even because I express it, or even because I express it vigorously, or even because I express it by the holy ballot. I am a moral subject only if I *deliberate* whether it would be *good* that my needs be satisfied, given the cost of satisfying them.

So also the community is not a moral subject merely because a head count is taken from time to time to find out who wants what how badly. The community is a moral subject and can have a conception of the good only if the community can actually discuss, argue, and deliberate what is the good.

Therefore, if we are concerned about priorities, in the way I have suggested, then what we must work for is the creation of places where people can talk with each other about the good of their nation and their global community and their neighbors. Indeed, what I would hope would be that as your year in this seminar goes on, it would itself become such a community. If out of the discussions of this group, even the shakiest conception of common good were to emerge, that might be the most important political event of the year, because it certainly is not emerging anyplace else.

Finally, here we are; and I am doing the talking at the moment. So what do *I* propose as an eschatological vision for our time, as a mission upon which American might embark?

Eschatological vision always starts with the perception of damnation. Might it be that America, having taken the lead to structures of community with no place for assembly and no eschatological vision, having taken the lead to polities that are in fact data processing devices, could also take the lead beyond them? What if the vision of a society of face-to-face mutuality could itself be implanted somewhere in the political life of this republic? Then once again we would have a worthy teleological vision. If we had that, we would not need a ranking principle for priorities. Our priorities would simply string themselves out behind that vision, entirely by themselves.

What Academic Difference
Would the Gospel Make?

❦   ❦

I

CLEARLY, CHRISTIAN CLAIMS must make some difference to higher education, since the history of higher education since the mid-seventeenth century is almost entirely the history of attempts to escape them. No doubt the effort had to be made. The ancient marriage of the gospel with the mature products of Greek experience and reflection meant that the Christian claims appeared as a comprehensive metaphysics and worldview, within which all research and explanation was to be done. This framework proved unable to contain the critical and quantifying investigation that was born in the sixteenth century; and the specifically modern forms of knowledge broke out from it, drawing others after.

But two additional observations should be made, lest the naive conclusions usual among half-educated academics be drawn. First, the breaking of the Hellenic frame is itself an event *within* the history of Christian faith and theology. The gospel had to break the marriage with Greek wisdom also for its own sake. Moreover, much is now known

Published in *dialog* 18 (Winter 1979): 24-27. Reprinted by permission.

about the dependence of the new sciences on Christian impulse for the reorientation of vision that made them possible.

Second, insofar as modern knowledge has simply gone its own way, merely apart from the gospel, it has been anything but an unmixed blessing, on anybody's terms. Few, other than Rip van Winkles, would now argue — as I myself sometimes did many years ago — that secularization is simply a manifestly good thing and should be left alone.

In any case of the historical facts, conversation between the gospel and our sundry pursuits of worldly knowledge *must* be important to both sides — if, that is, the gospel is *true.* The gospel is the proclamation that the will and love named Jesus must win, for all persons and in all the hopes and fears of life. If the gospel is true, there can therefore be no human pursuit to which it is irrelevant, and so no department of a college or university that cannot with profit to its own enterprise confer with the gospel's messengers. The gospel occurs as an act of mutual interpretation between the claim that Jesus is risen and must therefore triumph and the passionate hopes of communities and individuals. The disciplines of knowledge are each in fact — if not in self-illusion — a specific complex of just such human passion.

It is indeed of "conversation" that we must speak. For the moment, a comprehensive framework of interpretation determined by the gospel is a goal and not a possession. And even that this is the goal is unlikely to be accepted by many of those whose contribution will be necessary to achieve it, for intrinsically irrelevant but psychologically powerful reasons. What we must hope for is a commitment to talk.

II

I can best make the case by examples, showing how such a conversation might go in a few areas. I will begin with a tough nut: the "hard" sciences, physics and its neighbors.

We often implicitly suppose that the habits of thought that make the modern scientific movement, and that we canonize as "scientific method," are a pristine, existentially neutral set of procedures, which were always there in some platonic storehouse of intellectual possibilities and which folk "discovered" in the sixteenth and seventeenth centuries. It suffices to describe this supposition to see its oddity. On the contrary, "scientific method" is the actualization of a particular complex of passionate human expectations. It is in fact a prime case of the sort of thing in the interpreting of which by the claim of Jesus' resurrection the gospel occurs.

Scientific passion has at least two components. One is dedication to what the seventeenth and eighteenth centuries called "critique," that is, the policy of being tenaciously from Missouri with respect to "appearances," to the world as it immediately presents itself. The classical case of critique is, of course, Copernicus: "It certainly looks like the sun goes around the earth. But does it really?" The other is fascination with the mathematical portions of language, that is, with language purified of the first and second persons.

Human dedication to the policy of critique is a declaration of independence, indeed of alienation, from the world of daily experience, from the world that all of us, including theoretical physicists and cosmologizing astronomers, first inhabit. It is a refusal to take given reality as final; it is the quest for a reality that hides itself. And the signal that this reality has been detected is the cessation of need for other language than mathematics, that is, of the need for the first and second persons. The signal is the cessation of personal involvement with the world.

What is hoped for here? What is the human content of this passion? Every such question is a demand for interpretation, which brings us to the possible conversation with which we are concerned. No doubt there are many possible interpretations. I will suggest two.

The scientific quest may be for a pure object-world, for a world from which we as cognizing subjects are alienated and therefore independent. That is, the scientific quest may be for *control* and *use.* Between a human passion and its interpretation there is no clear division; to the extent that the scientific quest has been so interpreted among us, to that extent we have in fact created a technocratic society, a society that understands itself as a vast factory situated in a world that is a heap of "raw materials," a society that confuses leadership with engineering and democracy with "inputs."

But the scientific quest for a detached world may equally well be interpreted as a quest for the free space in which community is possible, for a world that is not my world and not your world, in order that it may be our world. The passion for the world's otherness may make the world into — not a mine, but — a theater, a structured space within which the drama of human history can be played.

The scientific enterprise will not, of course, so understand itself except over against a human history that is in fact a drama, that has some plot. But such a plot is just what the gospel tells. More abstractly: the gospel promises the triumph of free mutuality through all the realms of being. If this promise is allowed any interpretive force, the world is thereby interpreted as the place for such community, and the scientific enterprise becomes a different enterprise than the one we are most used to. A scientific community that so understood itself — or even faced the possibility of so understanding itself — would have a different historical impact, undertake different projects, and even get some different results.

III

When the human knowledge whose object is humanity itself followed the initial sciences out of the Western synthesis to create the "social sciences," the wrench was especially profound. In that human being is ineradicably self-transcendent, our knowledge of ourselves is always knowledge of purpose, of what we are for. Therefore emergence from biblical tutelage meant, for the social sciences, renunciation of the biblical eschatology, that is, of the only available agreed statement of human purpose.

But practitioners of the social sciences continue to be asked how we should live, and will continue so to be asked as long as they are around. For it is to provide certified experts about human life that society maintains social scientists; and it is for the rewards of this status that persons enter the disciplines. As things usually stand, their advice must be reactionary.

Since the social sciences have renounced the only available wisdom about the purpose of life, they must find the warrants of their arguments elsewhere. The only other place to look is to the antecedent given circumstances of life, that is, to the past rather than to the future to which faith looks. Thus, for example, standard political science is able to speak of the good state only as an ideal of efficiency in satisfying ascertainable antecedently given needs of the human species, never as a possible creation to transcend all such needs, that is, to create freedom. In one form or another, "contract" theory, the notion that society is created to satisfy fixed felt necessities, and so succeeds to the extent that these are in fact satisfied, continues to be the framework of all ordinary social science.

If the social sciences are pursued merely apart from the eschatological vision from which they were once born, then when their practitioners are asked how we should live, they have only one recourse: they must find a replacement eschatology in the temporal pattern — that is, the method — of the disciplines themselves. But that pattern is one of constant argument to what must be on account of what has been and is. Behavioral science that generates ideals from its own method will therefore generate ideals of stability, of the satisfaction of unexaminable needs, of the balancing of undeliberated interests, even of mystic escape from time.

The laissez-faire university, in which students decide what is an educated man by voting with their feet for what already interests them, in which truth is supposed to be discovered by the competition of fixed ideas, is no accident. It is simply the university that has asked its own social scientists how to do things. Nor is it an accident that political science and economics departments are regularly so stodgily and ob-tusely mild-liberal or, if maverick, orthodox Marxist. Nor is it an accident that pop-psychological technique and bowdlerized Eastern religion cooperate so nicely.

There could be — and indeed is — a political science that began with the conviction that history and calling are real, that grasped political reality as the freedom that occurs in mutual ethical debate. There can be, that is, a political science that grasps politics as openness to God's future, and goes on to behavioral study of the institutional conditions of such openness. There could be — though I think there nowhere is — an economics that investigated the material conditions of such prophetic freedom. There could be — if the gospel were a partner of the discussion.

IV

A last case. Why do we read "literature" in school? At a few places, like St. John's College in Annapolis, they still have a straightforward reason: to be made wise by discussion with the deposit of our culture's humane wisdom. That was once, of course, the justification of all "liberal" education in the West; but except at a few odd places like St. John's it is not now believed — though it may occasionally appear in the fictional parts of college catalogues. The evidence suggests that no other justification is available. At any rate, in its absence, the actual reading of our literature has nearly ceased in the schools, from first grade through doctoral seminars in criticism.

It is at least arguable that the traditional justification for the study of literature can, at least in our time, be sustained only by conversation with Christian theology. This justification requires an anthropology in which the tradition of the past is constitutive for human beings, precisely for the sake of open future possibility. For a very long time, humanistic studies went on under the mere assumption of such an anthropology, by the mere memory of Christian humanism. Now that the memory has faded, our society simply does not see any sufficient reason to read Dostoevsky instead of Vonnegut, Shelley instead of Dylan. If the gospel is heard, there is such a reason. There may be reasons also if the gospel is not heard, but they do not seem to be historically available.

V

I come to a second and last main contention. I have been talking about "conversation" between various modern cognitive enterprises and the gospel. But what conversation both creates and depends upon is community. And indeed the modern cognitive enterprises are all essentially communal undertakings. They are even essentially democratic undertakings: when science works, the lowliest lab assistant can falsify the hypothesis of the greatest genius. Perhaps the heart of our problem is that the academic community itself is in dissolution.

The bond of the academic community is the conviction of the unity of truth. Through Western higher education's long history, the demand for "synthesis," "interdisciplinary studies," or just "a place to meet" has been one of academia's chief moral imperatives. In the version of the medieval scholastics, "unity" and "knowability" are both transcendentals, whose final application is to the whole of reality as such. Or stating the aspiration more crudely: if two bodies of assertion and reflection have nothing helpful to say to each other, at least one of them is merely thereby proven false.

I know no way to argue the doctrine that all truth hangs together. It seems to me so primitive an apprehension of our situation in reality that if it is not justified, nothing is. I will therefore assume it from now on. Aspiration toward the unity of truth can be enabled by a comprehensive theological or metaphysical system, by which all reflection and research are guided and within which all assertions are tested. Just this, of course, is what we lack. American education has by and large been guided by the weaker unifying posits of "liberalism," laid down for "truth" by John Locke. These are a perfect corollary of capitalism: let there be unrestricted competition of opinion, with each individual pushing his hypothesis; then an invisible hand will arrange the contribution of the winning ideas to the one truth.

Manifestly, liberalism of ideas is a halfway station: pluralism of fundamental opinion was a necessity in England after their civil war, and Locke salvaged what could be salvaged of the aspiration for truth's unity. But liberalism had to run out; and it can safely be said that it has. Its problems are the same as capitalism's. There is no reason whatever to suppose that competition does in fact function as a guiding hand to the greatest good of the greatest number. And even if it does, dedication to the unity of truth belongs only to that impersonal guiding hand, not to us. We are positively exhorted not to worry about it, to push our views by all means that do not damage the system itself.

The outcome is that fragmentation of the universities and colleges of which everyone has complained for a century at least. The ultimate outcome, indeed, is nihilism. For the aspiration to truth's unity remains; and to the extent to which I do not grasp my study and reflection within that unity, the value of my work is lost to me. If I then continue my work nevertheless, the vacuum of value will be filled with some other value than truth itself: vocational utility is in at the moment, which in colleges and universities is a sheerly nihilistic motivation.

In that the gospel comes to speak of God, it affirmatively interprets the aspiration for truth's unity: if there is God, all knowledge must finally be knowledge of him or his gifts. And while the gospel's promise of the unity of truth in God has often been made in the terms of a comprehensive metaphysics, it can get along without any such system.

For the unity of all knowledge and wisdom as the knowledge of *God* is in any case a unity in hope and not in possession, God being precisely the Power of the last future. It does not yet appear how all our competing and transitory efforts to know can be contributions to the revelation of the one God and his gifts; but the gospel promises that this is what God will yet make of them. And that is quite enough to be going on with.

I come back to "conversation." That our various and diverging cognitive enterprises are united *by conversation with one* claim about reality is the only form in which the aspiration for truth's unity can now be actual among us. That would be a counsel of despair, were inescapability its only reason. Believers, however, may suggest it for a more cheering reason: it perfectly matches the sort of unity that truth can anyway have in this particular conversational partner, which is unity in hope. That we *persist* in one common argument — made common by one constant partner — about the humane hearts of our disciplines *is* hope for the unity of all our disciplines. And hope is precisely the true present reality of that unity.

VI

There is, perhaps, great historic work for believing academicians and churchly institutions.

The Triunity of Truth

I

TEMPORARILY LEAVING OFF the "Tri-," my topic is "The Unity of Truth." I must confess that nothing absolutely compels anyone to be concerned with the unity of truth. But if colleges and universities are not concerned with the unity of truth, they will not be communally concerned with anything. For there is, after all, nothing for a school to be uniquely concerned with except truth. And if truth is not one, or if its oneness is not our concern, then a school has no one concern.

That truth probably is *not* one that has been the American academy's general assumption since shortly after the Civil War. Therefore our schools have also lived by the practical self-understanding that we cannot be communities. That does not need to mean we go out of business. But what then shall we be? In the United States there is really just one alternative: we can be "agencies," that is, operating units of the bureaucracy by which late capitalist societies hold together.

After all, a whole multitude of "services" reasonably can be assigned to bureaus possessed of the "capabilities" that schools have. A school can provide baby-sitting for the final segment of our extraordinarily

---

Address to the faculty of Augsburg College, Minneapolis, MN, 1979. Previously unpublished.

long infancies. A school can provide certification by which other bureaus can recognize their proper clients and/or their potential functionaries. A school is a good place to park eccentrics — folk hung up on the Hittites, or actual philosophers — for whom the society no longer has a use but whom for old times' sake it does not wish to put on other varieties of welfare. A school can be a laboratory for social experiment, or a consumer protection agency for the consumers of culture, or a boot camp for coopted revolutionaries. And so on. But if these functions were disassembled and each of them assigned to some other agency in the system, nothing would be lost. For these functions will not in themselves provide the life of a learned community. In the case of schools, that will be provided by the unity of truth and the cultivation of that unity, or it will not be provided at all.

For most of America's higher schools it is too late to worry about these matters. They have no communal existence, are smoothly integrated into the social mechanism, and only a few of those parked eccentrics complain. But it is just possible that some colleges, themselves eccentric, may yet be communities as well as bureaus — that is, that their denizens may yet see themselves as somehow engaged together in one defining task. And it is possible that the significantly churchly colleges may be among them. For such colleges, the unity of truth must be *the* imperative joint concern.

Indeed, it may be that the churchly colleges are the *only* ones sufficiently eccentric to have a chance still to live as communities around the unity of truth, the only ones for whom the unity of truth, and therewith their own communal selves, can be a concern. For the question of the unity of truth is inescapably a *theological* problem. And where theology is barred, so then is all reflection on truth's unity.

II

The phrase I have been using until now — "the unity of truth" — has been capitalized in my own mind, because it and "God" are alternative names for the same thing. The identity between the unity of truth and God obtains no matter how truth is interpreted. If truth is interpreted, as classically in Western history, as the correspondence of the mind to its objects, then truth will be one only if there is some one object known when any object is known. Such an object I think we will agree to call God. Or if truth is interpreted not as the appropriateness of the mind to its objects but as intrinsic to the mind, as the mind's contribution, then truth will be one only if there is one Great Mind in which we all participate. Or if truth is, as interpreted by the idealist tradition, the transcendence of the difference between the mind and its object, if truth is therefore in itself the unity of all things, then truth simply *is* God.

There is no way to assert the unity of truth, however one understands truth, except by statements that the American Civil Liberties Union will label sectarian. That is undoubtedly the chief barrier to effective education in our time and place, a barrier against which perhaps only the churchly schools — permitted to be a *little* sectarian — can make any progress.

One may ask, If the unity of truth and God are the same thing, then why drag the *word* "God" in, why not just talk about the unity of truth? Could not a secular university undertake a communal investigation of truth's unity and just not call it God? The answer, I fear, is negative; and that will bring me to a first material imperative.

However the unity of truth is interpreted, it is — as the philosophers used to say — transcendent. That is, the unity of truth, however interpreted, will elude our cognitive grasp; it will not stay still to be an ordinary matter of our research and discussion. If truth's unity — and now let me go through the same three possibilities I instanced before — is that there is one great Object known whenever we know anything, just so the one great Object is not in an ontological line with those other objects. We will not be able to study paramecia in one class and truth's unity in another. If truth's unity is the unity of the one great Mind in which we all participate, we can only indeed *participate;* none of us can think directly as that mind, none of us has it. Finally, if truth's unity is the unity of knower and knowing, then strictly speaking it cannot be known at all.

Since truth's unity is transcendent, "God" is the only accurate label for it. And more important than labels, in that truth's unity is transcendent, in that "God" is the only appropriate label for it, we will be grasped by the unity of truth only as we are grasped by God, and that is to say, in *prayer*.

III

If academics are concerned for their communal life, they will have to be concerned for the unity of truth, for that is the only communal life they have. If they are concerned for the unity of truth, they will have to do theology, for God and the unity of truth are the same, so that the *logos* of God and the *logos* of truth's unity are the same. And there is no doing theology outside the context in which the matter of theology is present to us, that is, worship. Any attempt to sit down in a committee or study or library and individually or communally stir up concern for the unity of truth could only end in utter boredom. It would be word games only, because the reality toward which this concern is directed does not make itself available that way.

The alliance of common prayer and common learning is the most ancient feature of Christian civilization — and indeed, of all high civilizations. The ancient alliance of common prayer and common learning is exemplified in the statutes, the polity, and even the architecture of nearly every college in this country in its founding period, as of the great European universities in their founding periods; and that alliance is not arbitrary or legalistic, it lies in the nature and logic of the case. For there is no way for the learned enterprise to be *one* except in the context of prayer.

The moment when we said that of course the "academic side" of things at churchly colleges, whether Harvard or a midwestern denominational school, could be just as well done with or without participation in the "religious side" — to put it as offensively as possible, the day we dropped required chapel and put nothing in its place — was the day we sold not our religious souls, but our *scholarly* and *pedagogic* souls. That was the day we condemned ourselves not to be communities of scholars and teachers but to be instead agencies of the state.

I cannot guess what could replace the previous religious life of the American colleges. The old style is surely gone for good. Reintroducing compulsory chapel seems a nonstarter. But if indeed there are to be colleges in this country that are communities of truth, unified by truth's unity, that will occur only when by some means or other the cultivation of truth's unity is rescued from being only a matter of words to each other, and placed in the context where it is also a matter of words to God who is that unity.

IV

I have come as far as I can without the "Tri-" part of my title. The foregoing considerations are true, I think, no matter which God we are talking about, no matter who or what we may say God is. But in an actual community gathered aroung the unity of truth — and that is to say, around some God or other — the question of God's identity, of which God we have in mind, will be decisive. For the answer to that question will be the same as the answer to the question *how* precisely truth is one and how that unity may be grasped and cultivated.

The foundational theological task, in this connection as in any, is the *identification* of God. The question of whether there is any God is profoundly uninteresting — nothing whatsoever follows from its answer. The religiously and intellectually interesting question is, Which candidate do you mean when you say "God"?

The function of the doctrine of Trinity is to identify which God we mean when in the Christian church we talk of God. And that carries directly into our present concern. The question about which God we mean is the same as the question, How, actually, is truth one? Thus the doctrine of the Trinity is the Christian church's answer to the question, How does truth hang together? And how may it be grasped as one?

V

There is also a historical diagnosis involved in turning at this point to the doctrine of Trinity. The unity of truth is mostly lost to us. To understand our situation we must ask how this happened. I suggest: the Western academy's grasp of truth's unity could fail and then did fail, because it was associated with an erroneous identification of God — erroneous, that is to say, if the Christian church is right in how it identifies God.

The defining characteristic of deity — under any identification — is eternity. A God is someone or some thing or some aspect of things that holds past and present and future together. Every human act is done in the confidence that I, as I now am, created by and carrying with me my own past, can choose and enact a future that will be new and surprising, that is, the future, and yet mine. Every human act is done in the supposition that the successive events of my life are not a mere succession, that they are not simply one damned thing after another, but that they somehow make a plot, that somehow they are a story with a beginning and an end, a complication and denouement and resolution. The fundamental religious word "eternity" denotes whatever facet of reality it is on which we rely for that coherence.

There are very many possible eternities. There is, for example, the Platonists' still center of the turning world, which because it is the center of the wheel, makes time into the wheel's rim, on which every point always returns where it began, and *so* holds beginning and end together. At the other extreme is the Christian eternity, in which God is not the still center of the turning wheel but the one who whips the wheel along. He is — to use Bultmann's language — the Power of the future to overturn all settled arrangements, all fixed presence, all apparent immobilities, and *so* to hold past and present and future together. In between there are indefinitely many ways in which humankind has supposed that it grasped eternity.

At the beginning of our civilization, in the great marriage of socratic and biblical interpretations of humanity and the world that defines our civilization, God's eternity was understood in a particular and, I suggest, erroneous way: eternity was interpreted as immunity to time. God, it was said, transcends time because time means nothing to him. God transcends time, and can hold past and present and future together, because he has no time. That is, he has no future; he already is everything he is going to be.

On this interpretation, God can be known, and in him the unity of truth known, only by a special kind of knowing, a knowing that abstracts from everything about reality that is determined by time. So we say, to take a standard case, "God is loving."

"What do you mean by that?"

"It means he is like my father."

"*Just* like your father?"

"No."

"What is the difference?"

"My father is subject to all the restrictions of life in time, and God is not."

This special knowing abstracts from the particularity of persons and events, from history. It abstracts from all hypotheses that can be confirmed or disconfirmed only by waiting on events, only by experiment and observation. It abstracts even from God's revelation of himself, in that this too is conceived as merely the temporal arrangement God makes to begin our journey to his true reality beyond time.

Thus the unity of truth was classically grasped in our civilization by a metaphysical natural theology that tried to penetrate through history and through the temporal flux of nature and even through the historical reality and practice of the religions, to a timeless structure of reality of which all these are but the reflections. When one grasped the timeless structure behind everything experienceable and observable, one just so grasped the unity of truth, for then all the separate truths of history and science and even of religion could be taken as so many illustrations, as so many reflections of the one timeless truth hidden behind them. So, for example, ballistics and grammar and the liturgy of the mass were brought together, in that the appropriateness of verbs to subjects, and of the one variable of a ballistic trajectory to the other, and the inherence of blessing in the bread, were all taken as so many reflections of a single timeless principle of being, the analogy of attributes to substances.

This metaphysics of timelessness has broken for our civilization. And with it broke our access to the unity of truth.

VI

Diagnosis of what broke the metaphysics of timelessness has been one of the great historical games of the twentieth century. For present purposes, it is enought to point out that the distinctively modern cognitive enterprises established themselves in the first place by a declaration of independence from the realm of timeless truth.

To speak of the historical disciplines, since the mid-eighteenth century the study of the past in Western civilization has been carried by a distinctively historicist consciousness, for which separations in time make a real difference. For the consciousness behind modern historical studies, Caesar's time is, just because it is Caesar's time, *not* my time. The space of time between Caesar and me is not a bridge but a barrier, a gulf, which has to be climbed over by research. Therefore also Caesar and I are not equidistant from the eternal God, and nor then are we contemporaneous before him.

Modern historical studies have been carried by a historicist conscious-ness for which precisely narrative — the stipulation of temporal sequences — is a vital form of truth. As soon as that consciousness was present, the historical disciplines could no longer submit to being unified with the other disciplines by abstracting from the temporality of their objects, by making Caesar and me both reflections of one timeless truth. Caesar is not I and I am not he, and just that is the historically important thing about us.

To speak of the sciences, since the seventeenth-century study even of repetitive processes in nature has found the truth of its own study precisely by rigorously restricting itself to the formulation of hypoth-eses, that is to say, to propositions left defenseless over against time, that can at any moment be falsified by experience. Of course the whole body of scientific hypotheses is not actually up for grabs at any one time; but the principle lies at the root of scientific self-understanding.

Thus the natural sciences could no longer submit to unification with the other disciplines by way of a metaphysics, a doctrine of God, whose basic principle was that time is meaningless for truth. For the old metaphysics of timelessness, any proposition whose truth we must wait to discover is just thereby qualified as an inconsiderable proposition. The modern sciences take the opposite view; for them what makes a proposition meaningful is exactly that we must wait for its verification.

Also theology joined the revolt. Sporadically since Luther and with near consensus since Hegel, Christian theology has seen more clearly than it had for millennia that in the case of Christianity the distinction between God himself and his revelation of himself in time is not a metaphysically ultimate distinction. Jesus of Nazareth is not in Chris-tian theology an image or illustration or paradigm of God; rather, as the Creed puts it, he *is* "very God." The Christian God is thus essentially identified with a historical phenomenon; if Jesus had not risen from the dead, the God of whom the Christians speak would thereby have been proven not to be.

However we are to conceive *this* God's eternity, we cannot rightly conceive as we have been taught to conceive it, as sheer timelessness, as mere immunity to time. The chief theological labors of nearly two centuries have been an attack on the way in which our civilization classically conceived the eternity of God, and so the unity of truth.

VI

For all the havoc the fall of this metaphysics has caused, Christians cannot mourn its good old days. We must judge that the old metaphysical union of the disciplines rested indeed upon a misidentification of God. The God whose eternity is his timelessness is not the God of the Christian gospel. Clarity in this judgment has been and is a distinguishing concern of twentieth-century theology.

Therefore the doctrine of God's Trinity is a preoccupation of contemporary theology, for the doctrine of the Trinity is the Christian church's identification of its God, and so also its attempt to say how its particular God is eternal if *not* by being timeless. Asked, "Which God do you mean?" Christians answer, "God is whoever raised Jesus from the dead." "Whatever did that, that's whom we mean by God." The doctrine of Trinity is simply an elaborate expansion of this proposition.

The Christian identification of God ties God's reality to a temporal phenomenon, Jesus, and to a temporal event, his death and resurrection. Thus this God's eternity cannot be mere immunity to time; this God does not stand outside time's past and present and future. Rather, this God unites past and present and future *from within* time. This God's eternity is itself a temporal event: the resurrection of Christ.

In the resurrection, one whom we *remember,* who is a past reality, is the living Lord who comes to us not from the past but from the future, whose judgment we await as the outcome of our lives. Just so, for Christian faith, past and future are joined together; and just so, for Christian faith, God is posited. All the strange formulas of the Trinity doctrine are simply elaborate refusals to fall away from that insight and go back to the more usual understanding of eternity as timelessness.

God appears in trinitarian discourse as the One who raised Jesus, as the *antecedent agent* of his own defining event, as God past, God the given, God the starting point, God the Father. But God also appears in this discourse as what *comes* of the resurrection: God is the Possibility that we may now live awaiting a determinate good outcome of time. He appears as the power of the End to bring all things well to an end, as the Power of the future, God the Spirit. And God appears as the love of Jesus, which, within time and from inside it, *joins* this beginning and this end; he appears as God present, God the Son.

All the complexities about "three persons and one substance" are simply elaborate attempts to resist the temptation to fall back from this vision and say that God after all is a fourth, *timeless* reality, of which the three are the temporal manifestations. No, the trinitarian formulas say, "These three are all there is to God." The Christian God is the last Past; he is the last Future; and he is the Unity of the two from *inside* time, not from outside it. Christian theology has had to learn to say: the reality of God is what happens between the man Jesus and the one he called Father and the rest of us. God's reality is a life, and therefore essentially includes and involves past and present and future; it does not abstract from them.

VII

So, finally, the unity of truth. How God is eternal is how he unites truth. How then is truth one, and how may we grasp its oneness? I have three points.

First. God's eternity is accomplished in and through time; therefore the unity of truth is accomplished in and through time. And that, then, is also how it is grasped. *Debate* between the disciplines — between, that is to say, those who claim in some way, shape, or fashion to possess truth — is the way the Unity — the Triunity I must now say — of truth can be perceived. The unity of truth is not just there somewhere, to be studied and applied; the Triunity of truth achieves itself in time, in discourse, in argument, in confrontation. As between the Father and the Son and the Spirit is achieved the reality of God, so the unity of truth is achieved in the confrontation between the historical disciplines and the natural sciences and theology. It is not *there,* waiting to be found; it *will* be. It waits to be argued out.

Second. Debate about what? About the last future and so about the course of time. The form in which the unity of truth is to be sought is as the unity of a narrative of universal history. What we have to debate with each other, if we are concerned with the unity of truth, is the coherent story of reality. As my past, present, and future hang together somehow, to make some kind of story — even a bad story — so the truth of our world and our reality occurs in that a universal story is hammered out, encompassing what we call history and what we used to call "natural history" and what theology used to call "saving history."

Since time continues, since the end of God's enterprise is not yet, truth is not simply one but rather is now *being* unified. That is why argument is the mode of our cognition of that unity. And what we have to argue about is the temporal process in which truth is being unified.

There is no point in a biologist calling in a theologian to reproduce his or her results with an unexpected genetic break. Vice versa, I will not ask biologist readers to analyze my presentation of trinitarian doctrine's history. But we *can* argue with each other about how, for example, that stretch of universal history told by the theory of organic evolution — the teaching of organic evolution is, after all, history telling — and the stretch of history told as the moral history of the human race might go together to make one history.

Third and last. That past and future do cohere in this way, that this is how God is eternal and therefore how the world hangs together, that this is how truth is one, is said in the first place by the resurrection of Jesus Christ. The impetus to the argument I have asked for and clarification of the concepts to be used in such an argument are therefore dependent not on faith in the resurrection of Christ, but on the presence in the argument of witness to the resurrection. And therefore the argument will not flourish unless theologians are invited in. The argument will not flourish unless theological argument and discourse is taken to be a normal part of the scholarly argument and discourse, not necessarily taken as the emperor of the discourse — if perhaps the queen — not necessarily even accepted as true, but hearkened to as present.

The only now possible living scholarly community will be constituted by *argument* about how to hammer out the *story* of reality, done with the presence of witness to the event in which reality makes a story, and in the context of *prayer.* That is itself the truth, however unlikely to be believed.

Faith and the Integrity of the Polity

❦   ❦

I

THE CHIEF political question is always, Where is sovereignty located, where in the community is the decision about the community's future taken? Sovereignty is not necessarily located where the most pomp and circumstance is found nor even where the most power is found. Sovereignty is located where the decision is made about what sort of community the community will be.

The chief religious question is, Which is God? The world is full of candidates for deity. At most one can be successful. The great question is not whether we pray. We will pray to someone or something. The question is, To whom?

My contention is that these two questions and all possible answers to them are paired, that for any given answer to the question, Which is God? there is a correlated answer to the question, Where is sovereignty located in the community? Or vice versa, if we know where in a community sovereignty is located, we have a least a good start at knowing which god they honor. There is perhaps no logical stringency in this pairing: we cannot simply deduce polity from theology or vice

Published in the *Center for the Study of Campus Ministry Yearbook* IV (1981): 32-39. Reprinted by permission.

versa. But to a community that locates sovereignty in a particular place, it will be natural to honor some candidates for deity rather than others — and vice versa. Let me try to convince you that this is so.

Politics is the whole process by which a community chooses what sort of community it will be in the future; politics is the process of communal moral choice. It is important to emphasize "moral" at this point. It is only when a community deliberates what it *ought* to be that politics are afoot. All the rest is housekeeping: it takes place in the *economy* even if it is done by the state.

To get this distinction across, let me use an illustration I have used too many times. Suppose that we have a polluted river, and that what is polluting the river is a series of factories built along it. The community of those who live by the river deliberates what can be one about the pollution and comes to a decision, choosing one of the devices sometimes used in such situations, a pollution tax. The amount of the tax depends upon the number of parts per million of such and such pollutants that a firm adds to the river. Every firm located along the river then has decisions to make. But these decisions will contain no moral component. The firms will put their computers to work, calculating how much, given the tax rates and their manufacturing processes, they should invest in antipollution equipment in order to get the best deal. There is nothing wicked about that; it is what the firms ought to do. But it is important to note that their decision making is morally entirely neutral. They do not ask — they *should* not ask — "What ought we do?" They ask instead, "Given the parameters of our manufacturing processes and the rates of this tax, what will be the best level of investment in antipollution equipment?"

A few years pass. The water in the river has improved considerably, but some in the community still worry about it. Others say, "Look at the improvement." Now the issue is whether to raise the tax. This is a moral question because again the community is balancing the future against the present and indeed the future against the future. Some of the firms along the river no doubt say, "If that tax goes up another penny, we are going to close the plant and do our manufacturing in Puerto Rico." So there are jobs at stake, and that is a moral value. Yet on the other hand, there is the question of the future viability and health of the community fifty years, a hundred years, two hundred years hence. *Now* the community has a political choice. The choices the companies made were not political. But the choice that the community has to make, whether or not to raise the rate, is a political choice.

Politics, then, is the whole process by which a community chooses what sort of community it ought to be in the future. But moral choice, whether done by communities or families or individuals, depends upon the posit of eternity. It depends, that is to say, upon the faith that, in some way or other, what I have been and what I will be cohere, that in some way or other the person that I now am, determined by all that has happened to me, and the future person about whose coming into existence I am now called to decide, in fact make one person, so that indeed I can decide about that person.

There is the existent lazy Robert Jenson. And there is the future vigorous Robert Jenson who will start jogging and be up early. Is that a possible future Jenson? Or is he a pipe dream, another entity altogether? Do the two Jensons cohere? If they do not cohere at all, my talk about that future Jenson is not moral discourse; it is fiction.

Notice the deep issue raised by this chatter about present and future Jensons. It is not at all clear abstractly that the several moments of a life are moments of any one entity, "a life." It can in certain states of contemplation become directly problematical; Jean Paul Sartre's fiction depends precisely upon persons to whom it becomes problematical that they, at any one instant, are the same entity as in any other. That my life coheres, that past and future are somehow held together, is not obvious. When I posit that they are, I posit *eternity*. For what we mean by the word "eternity" is whatever it is about reality upon which we rely for the coherence of past and future.

Moral choice, therefore, depends upon the posit of eternity, of some coherence of past and future. So then does *communal* moral choice. The possibility of politics depends upon the community's faith in some eternity or other, in some aspect or piece or level of reality in which past and future hang together. Moreover, if this dependence of moral choice upon the posit of some eternity becomes reflective, so that we do not merely depend upon the reality of eternity but seek eternity or invoke eternity or otherwise act specifically over against eternity, then we tend to speak of "God." To the extent, then, that the life of any community becomes reflective, so that it does not simply practice its moral decision but begins to wonder what it is doing when it does that, the moral processes of the community depend upon some posit of God.

There never was, and in my view never can be, a polity without its religion.

But there are many putative eternities and correspondingly many putative gods. There is, for example the kind of eternity of which Plato spoke, that is to say, the still point at the center of the wheel of time, a depth of reality in which time simply does not move, a great *nunc stans,* a standing present tense. At an opposite extreme of sophistication, the point about ancestors in animistic faith is that an ancestor is someone who has gotten so old that nothing surprises him or her any longer, so that in consultation with the ancestor the surprising things that time brings forth are unveiled as not surprising at all.

There are many putative eternities and correspondingly many putative gods. Similarly, there are many sorts of polity, differentiated by where sovereignty is located, that is to say, by who participates in the act of communal moral choice. Thus we speak, for example, of monarchy, meaning that there is some one person who makes the choices and whose ability to make the choices is legitimate, that is to say, is consented to by the community. Or we speak of democracy, meaning that all the people are somehow or other the subject of choice.

Given the way in which moral choice, whether exercised by individuals or by a community, and therefore politics, which is the moral choosing of a community, depend upon the posit of God, I think it then reasonable to claim that these two sets, the set of possible eternities and the set of possible politics, match one to one. Let me try to convince you further of this by analyzing one case: Periclean Athens in the few decades of its glory.

Sovereignty in Athens, for those few decades, was located in the assembly of all those in the population who had time to think. In Athens the free man — and here one has to say "man" because they were all, in fact, male — as over against the slave, is free from "necessity," that is to say, from the imposition of tasks by time, from the occupancy of his energy, his time, and his intelligence by what he does not choose, by tasks that daily life brings with it willy-nilly. He has one or more slaves and a wife taking care of the tasks that time imposes upon life; he need not constantly concern himself with what he has to do now because now it is time to do it. He is liberated from concern with what *must* be now, for concern with what *ought* to be and ought at any time and place to be; what he is free from is precisely the way in which time dictates.

The free man is free to concern himself with what ought timelessly to be. Such a free man may be trusted to choose the good for himself and his wife, children, and slaves because he has the time, that is, the freedom, to seek what ought to be. And the joint deliberation of such free men can be trusted to decide what is right and good for the community, for the joint life. Thus there arises Athenian democracy, the system of governance by the assembly of thinking men.

This sort of location of sovereignty, the government of the assembly of thinkers, pairs precisely with the general character of Greek religion and with the precise religion of Athens in those decades. The remembered and effective history of the Greeks began with a catastrophe, a national experience of death and meaningless power. A centuries-long flood of barbarians from the north, the so-called Dorians, destroyed the great and flourishing religious monarchies of the Achaeans. When Greek civilization revived centuries later, it was descendants of those conquered Achaeans who revived culture and created the Homeric religion. Such were Homer and the philosopher-scientists of Asia Minor's refugee settlements; such also were the Athenians. Greek religion, therefore, was tragic from its root. Its founding memory was the exact opposite of Israel's. Israel's founding memory was of utter despair and subsequent glorious liberation; Greece's founding memory was of glory and subsequent destruction. As Sophocles' *Oedipus Rex* ends, "We must call no man blessed until we have seen his last day without disaster."

This origin imposed three characters on Greek religion that are important to our story. First, its driving question was, Can it be that all things pass away? Can this indeed be the whole story, that glory, if we just wait, will be undone? Greek religion was the lived-out determination that time, who devours all his children, not be supreme. The one gift sought from the gods was stability. And the defining character of the gods was their immortality. The only difference between the Olympians and the rest of us is that they are immortal, immune to destruction: disaster never will come to them. If the God of the Old Testament is eternal in that he makes promises and keeps them, in that through time he remains faithful, deity among the Greeks is timelessness; what happens in time simply makes no difference to God.

Second, Greek religion thus took its decisive shape in an extraordinary act of human self-defense against mysterious fate, irrational power, overwhelming accident, transcendent intrusion — against, that is to say, everything that the rest of humanity has called God. Our chief witness to this is Homer, who provided the Bible of classical Greece. Homer and his audience insisted that human history have a comprehensible pattern. If gods were to appear in history, their behavior too had to be comprehensible, predictable, and sensible. And if they acted stupidly, as Zeus or Hera regularly did in the stories, that too had to be comprehensible, had to be traceable to something like jealousy or wrath that one could understand and predict. They would tolerate no "Lord God Almighty" who chooses Israel because he chooses it and to all questions says, "Because I choose." The Ionians rescued themselves from chaos by enlightenment, by the posit of an entire reality, including the gods, that made rational sense.

Finally, Homer's successors as religious thinkers were the philosophers of Ionia, the Greek coast of Asia Minor. With them the reduction of all the characteristics of God to one, immortality, and the inclusion of the gods within one comprehensible scheme of events led to the notion of "the divine." There is no such notion anywhere in the Bible. "The divine" is godliness merely as such, a godliness that then manifests itself in and through the gods of everyday religion. "The unbounded has no beginning. It seems rather to be the beginning of all other realities and to envelop and control them. This is the divine. So thought Anaximander and most of the natural philosophers" (Aristotle). For many educated persons of the classical period, this abstraction, which they sometimes for purposes of worship called Zeus, was the true religious object. What people worshiped was immortality, immunity to the rush of time, simply as such.

In sixth- and fifth-century Greece, this experience of divine timelessness, which is the content of all Greek religion, was carried by a trio of religious movements. Dionysian religion, the religion of the mysteries, cultivated the experience of ecstasy, of the immediate felt union of the self with the divine. Here the escape from time was achieved by penetration back into the self, to a level of the self where time does not operate, where I am myself timeless, that is, where I am myself one with the divine. This religion of the transcendent inner self eventually created the doctrine of the immortality of the soul. Like all mysticism, Dionysian religion was subject to a pendulum-swing between abstract individualism and collectivism. On the one hand, if God is my inner self, what do I need you for?

On the other hand, if I am one with abstract divinity as such, then I am absorbed into a featureless collectivity. But for a brief historical moment in Athens, Dionysian mysticism was rescued from this pendulum swing by being established as part of the public cult.

A second movement, the Delphic cult of Apollo, represented the timelessness of universal law. The rustic polities of the old city-states had collapsed, and as the Greeks struggled through three centuries to remake their institutions, they turned to the Delphic oracle for wisdom to build their new cities on the rock of godly laws. Priestly counsel customarily is an authoritarian voice for the status quo. But for just a few moments in Athens, priestly counsel, the voice of eternal law, was paired with the Dionysian religion; they were two branches of the same publicly supported faith. Indeed, Delphi itself married law and ecstasy: the temple was Apollo's, but it was Artemis, the goddess of ecstasy, speaking through an inspired prophetess, who gave the advice.

Meanwhile, Homer's theology was the civil religion of the state, in Rousseau's very sense: it was the ideology by which the state exercised control. The official cults of the city-states were always on the verge of turning into Nixonian civil religion, and eventually in fact they did. But for a short time in Athens, fusion into one community experience of this civil religion with the vital cults of ecstasy and of eternal law, of Dionysus and of Apollo, kept the official religion of the Olympian gods a living religion.

In Athens there was, then, for just a few decades a fusion of individual mystic experience, communal search for right law guaranteed by God, and state cult. The synthesis lasted only for a moment, but it created the political ideals of our civilization. And this joinder of the freedom of the individual with the community's search for the right, held together because they were both part of a publicly practiced religion, is the exact match to the polity where sovereignty is exercised by the assembly of individuals who are entrusted to have insight in themselves into eternal good and right.

II

In America there have been two pairings of polity and God. The one pairing is of the deist god, the eternal universe-maker, with a polity in which sovereignty is not located with persons but rather in the machinery. That is the whole point about Madison's constitution: nobody is sovereign in it. The President has a piece of sovereignty, the Congress has a piece of sovereignty, the Supreme Court has a piece of sovereignty. But it is the machinery that bangs these up against each other by which the decisions are made. Such a polity, in which nobody is sovereign but the machinery, is obviously a perfect match for the religion of a God who created a perfect world machine and then let it run.

The other pairing is between the covenant-making God of Calvinism and a polity that locates sovereignty in assembly as in Athens, but not in the assembly of insightful persons but in the assembly of righteous persons. The assembly of righteous persons, those who, as the Calvinists said, "own the covenant," who accept their place in the covenants that God makes with humans and take up their duties in it, rules. The righteous are trusted and trustworthy in their own and in their familial lives to make right decisions — and trusted and trustworthy to come together and make right decisions for the community.

Both of these pairings of a location for sovereignty with a specific God were present and practiced in the United States nearly from the beginning. The sovereignty of righteous persons was here first, of course; but the Enlightenment rapidly brought the other over. After the Revolution, it was decided to adjust the two by dividing the territory. The public sphere within which you will expect to find sovereignty was divided between the state, which worships the deist god (the reason that the state does not seem to worship is merely that the deist god does not take much worshiping), and a second public sphere of the great public activisms that have made so much of the history of the United States, where sovereignty rested in assemblies of right-thinking citizens, those willing to show up for the school board meetings, to attend athenaeum, to march around with signs in a righteous cause. This assembly of righteous persons worships a God who makes covenants, who agrees with us that it is a good thing that such and such be done and promises to provide at least the chance of success.

Through our history the two have lived in a sort of symbiosis. The symbiosis was necessary because whenever there was a challenge to national consensus, whenever the nation's standard moral posits were challenged — as by the questions of slavery or suffrage or by the Mexican and Vietnamese wars — it has developed that the constitutional balancing machinery is of no use. On no occasion has Mr. Madison's apparatus in fact surmounted a moral challenge. Always the state has had suddenly to appeal to the moral and eschatological passion alive over in that other polity. The deist god does not care about blacks or Mexicans or Vietnamese, for he does not *care* about anyone. The machinery of the universe grinds along and grinds up a few people as it goes; and that is just the way it is, also for the great watchmaker God. If religion is to support efforts to change how the world goes, a quite different God must be invoked.

The symbiosis is not stable. For the exclusion of lively, morally impassioned religion from the official polity of the state has progressively driven religion into strictly private realms. The movement from the evangelical religion of, say, the social gospel movement to the evangelical religion of Billy Graham may serve to display the phenomenon. But as the second public sphere diminishes, the deist god is left more and more on his own. And as he is left on his own, he proves to be the profoundly reactionary god of a profoundly reactionary polity.

The deist god is perfectly matched by Mr. Madison's republican machinery built on Newtonian principles: each of us is a mass in motion with an "inertia" of personal "interests"; we bang against each other, and the engineered structure is there to make the impacts productive. But what of me can be present in that machinery, can be "represented," is indeed my inertial self, my interests, never my moral personhood. What can be represented is always and only what I already want. No doubt I am able morally to justify what I want; but what cannot be represented is my moral creativity, my ability to create new wants in response to new possibilities opened by the future. And therefore when established norms are challenged in our communal life, when moral creativity is needed, the Madisonian machinery can produce no decisions at all; it is, I claim, a profoundly reactionary machinery in its design. It has not always functioned so, but only because for moral purposes it has been parasitic on the other public America.

III

Whether a fresh start of the American dream is possible is up to Providence. If there is to be a new beginning, it must be, I think, an increment of direct democracy, the kind of democracy that does not merely reckon with my wants but admits me as a moral person to be present at decisions and contribute my moral creativity. And if such a direct democracy is to be possible, it must be paired with a new birth of *civil religion,* for which I think the Christian church and the synagogue must take responsibility.

We cannot continue any longer simply to execrate bad civil religion without saying what we think would be better. Moral discourse that dares to be creative can be sustained only by *promise,* by religion that at once opens the future, makes it plausible that things can be different, and makes it tolerable to step into that open future, by saying that knowable good is waiting there. That is to say, moral discourse that dares moral creativity can be sustained only by religion that is a religion of promise.

For when we are not called to choose what is to be done on the basis of existing moral standards but to choose new standards — as we were, for example, over against slavery — then we turn dizzily in the sphere of freedom: we do not know anymore what is the right; we are to discover what is the right. Humans cannot stand to enter that sphere if it is empty, if a la Sartre the only thing that will fill it is our own determination. Only faith that the future is indeed open, that there is indeed space for moral creativity, and that the step we are called to take into openness is not a step into the abyss can sustain communal moral discourse at moments of moral challenge.

The hope, if there is one, is for a chicken-and-egg process. Which comes first I have no idea; it does not matter. There must be a renewed proclamation of churches and synagogues that speaks a word of hope to the concerns and problems of the polity and lets whatever civil religion that produces be valid. And there must be struggle, provoked by crisis, for direct democracy. Each will feed the other.

The Doctrine of Justification
and the Practice of Counseling

THE RELATION between the doctrine of justification and the extended one-to-one pastoral care that we now call counseling, but that has always gone on in the church under some name, is complex; several talks could be given on it. But I think that concretely, given our historical situation, the fundamental function of the doctrine of justification over against counseling has to be the critical, warning function. At least in my part of the church, counseling is the clergy's favorite activity. Enormous amounts of "pastoral counseling" are done, very little of which, I fear, is pastoral. Most of it is not different from that going on in secular agencies. The danger, of course, is in the anthropology.

Our society's and the church's enthusiasm for "helping" is still dominated by the image of the human person as fundamentally a patient in search of health. At the seminary where I teach, for example, our students must spend the summer after the first year in a supervised program of exposure to the troubles and needs and realities of the world, it being assumed with some justice that many have had little encounter with them previously. Despite all efforts, it is impossible to persuade

Published in the *Center for the Study of Campus Ministry Yearbook* IV (1981): 40-46. Reprinted by permission.

either the seminary or the church that there are places in the world other than hospitals where supervised exposure to the realities of the world could take place. Some of us have argued the students could spend the three months in a factory or with the police or in all sorts of places. But it has to be a hospital, because the dominating image of what ails humankind is that we are "sick."

From California there now do come waves of counseling ideology and practice that are too laid back to think of anyone as sick. Here the vision is of infinitely continued self-fulfillment, on the path of which different persons are merely at different points. But the basic value is the same also for this wing. The basic value is wholeness, accession to the self of all those characteristics appropriate to it, and — what is then really analytic — their harmony with each other.

I want to make two points. First, this is not a new anthropology. On the contrary, it is an only slightly bowdlerized version of the standard Western anthropology inherited from Socrates. And second, it was precisely as an attack upon this anthropology that the doctrine of justification was first formulated.

The anthropological question, What sort of a thing am I? is not asked everywhere and always. Humankind seems able to survive and even to flourish and create great civilizations without worrying in this fashion. For our purposes, the one who initiated such questioning was Socrates, who could not decide whether the human being was a god or a mechanical contrivance or "a worse monster than Typhon." I must, despite inevitable caricature, quickly sketch the religious and intellectual tradition within which Socrates asked his question, narrowly from the viewpoint of the question.

The Greeks' dominating concern was to find a rock to which we may cling against the flow of time. To be real was somehow to hold out, if only for a moment, against time, to be not simply swept along. This passion produced the conception of reality as "substance," a conception most adequately analyzed by Aristotle. Let me quickly sketch his analysis.

Said Aristotle: if we take any possible possessor of characteristics, any X that can be green or absentminded or heavy or gaseous or whatever, any possible be-er (which is the only translation that really fits the Greek word *ousia*), clearly there is nothing to this be-er, to this X, apart from what it is, that is to say, apart from greenness or heaviness or gaseousness, apart from those characteristics that it possesses. But given those characteristics, given that this X is in fact, let us say, green and heavy and lazy, then it *is*. Then it has the reality precisely of a possessor of these characteristics; it is no blank X but a book or a general or a god or whatever. Moreover, with any possible such be-er, we can divide the characteristics in which its reality is lodged into those that it possesses temporally and those that it possesses timelessly.

So I, Robert Jenson, am both brown haired and vertebrate. I was myself before I had brown hair or hair of any color, and I could lose my hair without ceasing to be myself. On the other hand were I to cease to be vertebrate, I would simply cease to be. Thus, to the relationship between being Jenson and being vertebrate, between this particular thing that I am and vertebrateness, time is an irrelevance. Whenever there is Jenson, there is also vertebrateness; taken strictly in itself, the relationship between being Jenson and being vertebrate is timeless. Time can only abolish the one by abolishing the other; it cannot change the relationship. Therefore, a be-er that had *only* characteristics of this sort would itself be timeless, would be endlessly persistent, since it would possess its reality by possessing its characteristics timelessly.

On the other hand, an X, a be-er that only possessed such characteristics as brown hair, would have no reality at all. For its grasp on its own being would be limited to characteristics that could vanish at any moment, and one or another of them would be bound to vanish right at the start.

The be-er that possesses all of its characteristics timelessly and so, because its reality is its possession of those characteristics, is itself timeless, is God. And to be real at all is to approximate in some degree God's self-possession. To be is to have some characteristics that are not the gift of time, some characteristics to my possession of which time is an irrelevancy and by which therefore time may be for a time overcome. Such be-ing, whether God or an X that is a little bit like God, is "substance."

So to Socrates' question, the first comforting answer that can be given is "I am some sort of substance." I can know this because if I were not some sort of substance, I would not last long enough to answer the question. Indeed, what Socrates really meant when he asked, "What sort of substance am I?" was "How long will I persist?" I have some grasp with which to resist time — how good a grasp? How long will I persist, and by virtue of what about me?

In Socrates' worry about himself, therefore, not only is it posited from the beginning that he is some kind of substance, but two exclusive possibilities are posited. Some substances — or at least one substance — endure forever, others endure only for a time. In Socrates' worry about himself these two basic ontological kinds were posited and in fact constituted his problem. For Socrates was a mystery to himself because he experienced himself in a way that fit neither category very well.

He could not fully understand himself as a temporal being; for all that made the dynamism of his life — true justice, authentic community, genuine beauty — seemed to him not to be temporal. Yet neither could he see himself as a very likely god. So Socrates' solution, which in part followed suggestions from mythology, was that human beings are put together of two realities, one of each sort: the body temporal and the soul timeless. It may be that Socrates himself never propounded the doctrine quite that bluntly, but Plato did and thereby created the anthropology that still shapes Western humanity's understanding of itself. Those who now deny it have not yet replaced it; they deny only one half and say, "We are only body," or "We are only soul," and just so affirm thoroughly Greek propositions.

Standard therapy and standard psychagogy still presuppose the Socratic anthropology in the guiding images of wholeness and health. The person is seen as the possessor of "potentialities," that is, attributes in the form subject to time. These potentialities are to be "realized"; and this self-realization is understood precisely in Socrates' sense as the straining of the person from temporality to permanence, to approximation of himself or herself to the ideal form of humanity, that is to say, to the form in which all the potentialities are actual, in which time can do no more damage.

For the most part, it is still supposed that the therapist or psychagogue has some defined concept of what ideal humanity is. Generally speaking, even when counselors do not admit it, they know what they want to make of their patients. That is, it is still generally supposed that there is a direction and a limit to our journey, to the ecstatic ascent of self-realization, just as Socrates found the goal and limit in the gods. Also when it is now sometimes supposed that there are no gods, in consequence of which each person undertakes the journey of self-realization in his or her private direction, there being no one goal, and in further consequence of which the journey of self-realization can go on forever, the basic Socratic image remains unchanged.

The doctrine of justification is very directly an attack on this anthropology. There are a variety of ways of getting at the point. The shortest is simply to observe that no substance, no possessor of potentialities to be realized, can justly be so addressed as the gospel addresses us if the gospel is what the doctrine of justification says it is, an unconditional message. For the whole point about a "substance" is that it possesses itself, that whatever is to come to pass within it is always already there as potential: the acorn may well need dunging and watering and pruning, but the good thing that the acorn is to be is in fact in the acorn all along.

The doctrine of justification says that righteousness is not potentially in the acorn, that it has to be given to the acorn from outside it, that the acorn is not what it is to be but must receive what it is to be. It simply is not cricket to come to a *substance* with talk about *gifts* of reality. Over against a substance, such talk would be an imposition; as my old seminary teacher, who I fear was better at Aristotle than at Paul, used always to insist, "God never violates human personality." But if the gospel is true and is true in the way the doctrine of justification suggests, personality violating is all God ever does.

God *crucifies* human personality in order thereby and only thereby to bring it to fruition. What my professor had in mind, you see, was that fundamentally, "potentially," what I am to be is already there in what I am, and that the preaching of the gospel must reckon with that. The preaching cannot, he thought, just say, "Your righteousness is in Christ." It must say, "Your righteousness is in Christ and you may appropriate it if you only will take this little step, this little step that is no more than accepting it, than *really* believing it." The concern is to make an adjustment with the righteousness that is already there — potentially only, to be sure. But that is exactly the Socratic understanding.

More particularly, of course, the Reformation began as an attack on medieval counseling practice, which in those days they called the rite of penance, and precisely insofar as the practice was based on the anthropology just described — that is to say, precisely insofar as medieval counseling practice resembled modern counseling practice. I have two points.

First, the Ninety-five Theses say, "When our Lord Jesus Christ said, 'Repent,' he meant the whole life of the believer to be repentance." That is, there is no progress in human life in the sense of the Socratic journey of the potential self toward fulfillment. I do not repent and then move on; I repent and then repent again. Every day I find myself back exactly where I started.

The standard medieval concept of sanctification, identical with the standard modern concept of sanctification, was and is simply the theological version of the Socratic image of the self-realizing self, of the growth of the self from possibility to actuality, of the pulling together of those attributes by which I am what I am to be. And that standard concept of sanctification was the initial target of the Reformation: "When our Lord Jesus Christ said, 'Repent,' he meant the entire life of the believer to be repentance." "Every day, every hour, what do I do to be a Christian?" asked Luther. And he answered, "I creep back to baptism, I go to the beginning and start again."

That is not a pessimistic doctrine. For what is *in* the baptism that I creep back to is nothing short of the Kingdom of God, the *eschaton,* my perfection. But I do not arrive at that perfection by a journey of self-realization. I arrive at that perfection by never budging from baptism, by never budging from my starting point. And every time I observe that I have moved from it, I go back to it. I reclaim the same promise I did the first time.

Second, the whole business of "satisfaction" in medieval counseling practice was a way of adjusting the notion that fulfillment is the fulfillment of the potentialities that I always already have to the Christian practice of forgiveness. Medieval penance was not nearly as bad as we paint it in order to denounce it. The penitent appeared and confessed his sins. We Protestants automatically assume that the priest then said, "Go away and do such and such; and if you do it, then come back and I will forgive you." But that is not what was done. The penitent confessed his sins and the confessor absolved him on the spot. Then the confessor said, "Now go away and perform such-and-such satisfactions." The satisfactions are not there as conditions for the absolution. Rather than preceding it, they follow it. But what then is their function? Their function is to join the potentiality for righteousness that supposedly is in the penitent with the radicality of the absolution, by giving the penitent something to do out of his own possessed possibilities and powers that can join up with and testify to the righteousness granted in the absolution.

It was exactly this practice of adjustment between the Socratic image of the self as the potential possessor of righteousness and the Christian practice of absolution that the Reformation set out to overcome. The great, magnificent Socratic image of human reality was directly the target of Reformation polemic. And the counseling practice based on that image was the Reformation's immediate occasion.

Let me leap straight from what I have been denouncing to what I propose instead, an alternative anthropology, upon which will follow the proposal of an alternative counseling practice. The alternative anthropology I have to propose is for the most part not original with me, although some of the language is. For the most part it is what has emerged in millennia of Christian confrontation with the Socratic anthropology. More of it is out of Thomas Aquinas than is out of Luther, and some of it is indeed the product of my own further reflection. I present it necessarily in extremely brief outline.

First. We are not any kind of substance, temporal or eternal, supporting ourselves in being by holding on to certain attributes. We are *creatures,* and that is to say, we are radically contingent. There is nothing we are, do, or can do about maintaining ourselves in being. The most radical and precise formulation of this was by Thomas Aquinas, who — within the Aristotelian framework but in drastic violation of it — distinguished between "existence" and "essence." My "essence" is the sum total of all the attributes that I indeed do manifest. My "existence" is the sheer fact that I am. Said Thomas: if we could list everything that is true about me, if we could give a complete description of my essence, on the list we would find no reason that I should be in the first place. None of the characteristics that I manifest are attributes in the genuine Socratic sense; that is to say, none are the support of my contingent reality. Rather I am supported in being and exist at any instant solely because it is willed that I be.

We are intrinsically — now let me use some language that comes out of my own systematics — *objects* of God. He knows us, he wills us, he chooses us. Putting all those together, he *intends* us. His consciousness is aimed at us as mine is now aimed at you. The difference between God and me is that you are there whether I intend you or not, but all there is to our being is being intended by God. God knows and wills us; and in that we are thus his objects, we are.

As Thomas said of the difference between God's knowledge and ours, we know what is already there whereas what God knows is there because he knows it. Switching now to my own system I say: we are in that God talks about us. The converse that between the Father and the Son in the Spirit is the life of God, the eternal, dialogical word that God is, is a word about us. And in that we are thus spoken about in the divine converse, we are and are what we are.

Second. The above is true of all creatures — amoebas, grains of sand, quarks. The specificity of humankind among the creatures, I suggest, is that whereas all creatures are that *about* which God speaks, humans are those creatures *to* whom he speaks. The law and the gospel are the intra-trinitarian converse of God, between the Father and the Son, let out so that we may hear what is said. To be specifically human is to be let in on that converse, to be not merely an object of it but a hearer of it, to be not merely one of those about whom the word of God speaks but also one to whom this same word of God is spoken. To be human, therefore, is to hear the law and the gospel.

Third. If I am not only spoken about but spoken to, I am established not merely as object, not merely as the target of intention, but as subject also. For to be spoken to is to be called upon to reply. Thus humans are those called upon to reply to God; that is, the behavioral reality of specifically human being is *prayer*. The doing of specifically human being, of being addressed by God, is prayer. An Aristotle-style definition of human being would be: humans are the praying animals.

I really should tell you about penguins. On several occasions I have taught seminars on theological anthropology for the students at Gettysburg. When the discussion thus stretches over a whole semester, we of course spend a lot of time on this matter of what it means to be human as over against being other kinds of being. We run through all the suggestions that are made: humans are the talking animals, or humans are the reasoning animals, or whatever. And then we always get long disquisitions on those chimpanzees that can be taught to use language. Of course, one does not need experimental results; all one has to say is, "Well, how do you know termites don't talk?" In one seminar, we settled on penguins. For every suggestion that was made, one student always asked, "But Jenson, how do you know penguins don't . . . ?" (At the end of the semester the class chipped in and bought a wall hanging of penguins, which now hangs on our wall.) The answer is that one does not know. I do not know even that penguins do not pray. But if they pray, then they are human in my sense. In any case, the point that I would want to make is this: the specificity of humankind is not that we talk; the specificity of humankind is to whom we talk.

Fourth. Over against God, that is to say, we are not only objects but also subjects, not only spoken about but spoken to and drawn to reply. That is to say, we are participants in the conversation that is the divine life. And that is to say, the soteriology of the Eastern church is better than we have thought. Since Harnack, it has been assumed that the Eastern church's language about "divinization" was a smuggling of Hellenistic mysticism into the pure gospel. This is an error. The Eastern church's talk about divinization is the message that the final fulfillment of human being is to become not merely spectator but participant in the triune life of God; for it is the *triune* God of which they spoke. And that seems to me to be precisely what the Bible says.

Fifth. We are not merely objects of God but also subjects to God; and that duality replicates itself in our existence, for we are only what we are over against God. I am both subject and object, and the marvel is that I am object to myself as subject. This mysterious phenomenon is the first thing anthropological reflection notices whenever such reflection occurs. Somehow I can be outside myself so as to look at myself; somehow I am beyond myself so as to be my own object.

But now, this object that I am to myself as subject, what sort of being is it? It is a subject, just as you are objectively a subject for me. So there are two subjects here. And that means — and here is, I think, the legitimacy of Augustine's doctrine of trinitarian *vestigia* — that like God, I am a conversation within myself, that my lived active being is an interior dialogue. As subject, I know myself as object; but the weird thing is that this object answers back. This is widely observed; depth psychology posits a whole populace of interior voices.

I am an interior conversation; and it is this that Christian theology and, following Christian theology, much philosophy calls "spirit." That I am not merely what I am but that I am what I am in a conversation within me about what I am, is what is meant by calling me "spirit" or, alternatively, "free." I am not simply what I am; but I am what I am in a conversation about what I ought to be, what I can be. That is freedom.

Sixth and last in this series. That I am not merely subject but that I am subject and object for myself, and everything that follows from this, is *communally* mediated. That I am subject and then object for myself, and that this is very mysterious, need not remain a mere surd to reflection. Something can be said about how all this comes to pass. You have me as your object. Insofar as we address one another, insofar as we *communicate,* insofar, that is to say, as we establish a common world, within that common world that you and I have together I appear as the object that I am to you. And *so,* I suggest, I am object to myself. Human freedom, human reality as spirit, is communally mediated. I would not have it were I isolated. I am object to myself in that I am object to you and in that you and I share a world in which I am object.

Now then, as to counseling practice. The first thing that must be said is that this gospel-vision of humankind drastically demythologizes the business: there will be no more talk about all the marvelous potentialities that are in me only needing to be released, no more talk about an inward ascent to fulfillment. And the immediate outcome of this is that one can look at counseling a little more calmly; one can notice that most counseling is simply what used to be called "giving advice."

We do not really have to get into the depths of the personality every time, even on important issues. When somebody shows up and says, "Pastor, should I leave my spouse?" the pastor ought to be able to answer *automatically,* "No." Then if that answer does not work, we can go deeper. But initially one ought to be able to operate simply at the level of common moral judgments. What has to be done and how it is to be done in a given case depends on the problem; answers to such questions will be pursued in another *locus* of theology altogether, not in anthropology.

On the other hand, sometimes someone's appearance in the pastor's study — confessional booth, it used to be — does indeed become a joint journey that the pastor and the parishioner make together, does in fact come to involve the structures of at least the one person's life. When that happens, the matter is indeed no longer merely one of giving advice; and the kind of anthropological considerations I just went through indeed become relevant. Let me now try to say *how* I think they are relevant.

The goal of therapy or psychagogy conducted under specifically pastoral auspices, under the lead of a specifically Christian image of human being, should be to enable the person to *hear.* The specificity of humankind is that we are those to whom and not merely about whom the word of God is spoken. Personal pathology, therefore, will on this interpretation be understood as a hearing disturbance: that I cannot attend to, that I cannot listen to, that I cannot sit still for the healing word that grants my reality. Therapy will consist in so speaking about whatever brought the person to the pastor that the penitent can bear to hear what is said.

The subject matter of therapeutic discourse will be whatever it was that occasioned the conversation. But the pastor's goal will be so to speak thereof that the person can bear to hear what is said, that is, to speak *gospel* about the matter at hand, to speak in the way that casts out fear. That does not mean that the classical "Do you really think . . . ?" or "Do you really feel . . . ?" — the chief weapon in the counselor's armory — will have no function. But it does mean that the notion of the counselor as fundamentally listener and of the counselee as fundamentally speaker is exactly backwards. What ails the counselee is that he cannot hear, and what the pastor can do is so speak that the counselee can in fact bear to hear.

Hear whom? Human freedom is mediated by the community: the counselee must be enabled to hear the community. From the viewpoint of a decisively Christian anthropology, all personal pathology is isolation, is inability to tolerate what the community says, is, if you like, "antinomianism." The goal of the counselor or at least of the pastoral counselor must be so to speak on behalf of the community that the necessary, the sustaining and sometimes judging word of the community is heard not as threat but — this comes straight out of Karl Barth — as permission.

The difference between the two Lutheran "uses" of the law and the "third use" of the law is that in the third use the will of God appears not as command but as permission. It is not "You must be chaste" but "Because of the Kingdom that is coming and the resurrection of the Lord, chastity is a possibility; you may be chaste, you can be chaste, it is not impossible or unreasonable." It is not that you must not covet your neighbor's wealth; it is that you can get along without it. The pastoral counselor's function is to speak in a very particular way on behalf of the community, to speak the community's word in the proper form in which the community probably does not not speak it, as permission.

It must be emphasized currently, therefore, that the one thing to which there must be no concession in pastoral counseling is narcissism, that is to say, the attempt to behave as if I could carry on my interior conversation without other voices intruding, the attempt to behave as if I were spirit simply in myself, unmediated by the community. That attempt is, by Reformation insight, the key to all psychic pathology. Pathology results from the attempt to detach my interior dialogue from that community dialogue by which it is established in the first place.

Whether what is to be said as permission is explicitly *the* gospel, that is to say, the story about Jesus Christ and the promises contained in that story, is a tactical decision. Also according to the Reformers, the gospel is not always immediately appropriate. But if I do not come explicitly to speak the gospel, I necessarily speak required permissions not in God's name but in my own; my warrant for permitting the person to live as he or she otherwise would not dare is not the resurrection of Christ but my own presence. Then I must remember that I thereby make myself a surrogate for God. I will often have to act so, but it is dangerous. Probably all the Freudian discussion of "transference" could become relevant at this point.

Next, the logic of the position I have espoused dictates that the final goal of pastoral counseling is to enable people to *pray*. I do not mean that every session must end, "Let us pray" — although I think pastors could well say, "Let us pray" a good deal oftener than they now do. But the goal that swings before me must indeed be that the person shall be able to hear the words that the community always speaks to him or her *as* the word of God, as the law and the gospel, and answer freely because it is the natural thing to do.

And finally, if things go deep, if we get into the realm that depth psychology has explored, Christian anthropology suggests that pathology should be understood as misunderstanding in the interior conversation, as mutual deception between the "father" and the "son" in me, between me as subject and me as the subject that answers back. Depth therapy or psychagogy, if it comes to that — and I think it ought rarely to come to that in pastoral practice — should have as its goal the clearing up of misunderstanding between the voices that speak within the person, as Jungian psychotherapy has sought dialogue between a male counselee and his "anima." I can think little further along these lines because I lack the necessary clinical practice.

The Praying Animal

From a Symposium on "Ritual and Humanizing Adaptation"

I

MY ASSIGNED TASK in this essay is multiple. I shall of course attend to the theme of our symposium as a possible task of my discipline, systematic theology of the Christian gospel. I shall also attend to the peculiar situation of my discipline among those represented; my official intellectual responsibility includes the cultivation of an actually occurring system of religious ritual. Indeed, I suppose I was tapped as an essayist partly because of my involvement in devising the rubrics now more or less governing the ritual of American Lutheran congregations. I am, that is, a priest among the analysts of priestcraft. Thus I shall inquire how the scientific study of ritual and the reflection involved in cultivating ritual may be fruitfully related.

We are to consider ritual as "human adaptation." A theologian already must have some problem with this phrase: "adaptation" to what? If our culture's standard association of terms is to be followed, "adaptation" is to the "environment," a term devised on purpose to bracket out the reality of God. Now by no means is all ritual, also among Christians, expressly directed to God, but the association of ritual and prayer is

Published in *Zygon* 18 (1983): 311-325. Copyright Basil Blackwell, Publishers. All rights reserved. Used with permission.

nevertheless pervasive and is founded, as I will later describe, in reality. If our theme is to be taken as a task of *theology,* then ritual's direction to God must not be reductively explained in advance. But would one ever speak of "adapting" to *God?*

It also belongs to normal usage that talk of adaptation is controlled by the metaphor of evolution, and this control is apparent in the phraseology of our theme. But use of evolution as a root metaphor, as it must be used if it is to tell us anything very interesting about religion, is incompatible with use of the Christian gospel's root metaphor, its identification of God by the resurrection of a crucified one, that is, by the most radical possible disruption of continuity and development.

It is decisive for any reality we might call God that he/she is eternal, is reality in which the ever-threatening divorce of past and future is averted, in which what we have been and what we must or will be somehow rhyme to make a coherent whole. More precisely, religion is behavior over against eternity somehow identified; if eternity is so identified as to make it plausible to *address* it, it is in such cases that we use the word "God." Thus it is always appropriate and decisive to ask about a putative God or other putative eternity, Is temporal discontinuity here supposed to be overcome in openness to the future or in the persistence of a past? We live in the present, but the content of the present is memory and anticipation in some mutual interpretation. We must ask, Is a particular putative eternity an interpretation of the past by the future or of the future by the past? It is not at all my original observation that evolution, as a root metaphor, is an eternity of the persistence sort, rhyming the future with the past by interpreting all temporal emergence as the appearance of what was really there all along. The God who raised Jesus from the dead, on the exact other hand, is eternal as "the unsurety of the future."

We can go deeper. Only a God from the future irreducibly belongs to reality, has more than analytic status — only a God from the future needs to be "adapted" to. If an eternity is the persistence of a past, address and response must belong to a reducible level of reality, to the mere manifestation of the eternity; for in address and response it is the future that appears, in and by other persons and their challenge to us.

If eternity is the persistence of a past, the wholeness of eternity must be in itself a unity deeper than the unity of community, of discourse between persons; it must be a unity in which I am you and so cannot address you or respond to your addresses. Thus a God who is eternal by persisting must be a mere accommodation, made by an eternity not itself properly conceivable as God; and ritual directed to such a God must be, and properly understand itself as, the phenomenon of a preliminary level of spiritual activity. Now we can see why it is funny to speak of "adapting" to God: trust in evolution and its devices as a universal context of understanding is but one case of the religion of persistence, and the reduction of God within such trust but one instance of what always happens in such religion.

So I must reformulate the theme to obtain a task for my discipline. The language for my purpose must be "ritual as humanizing *re*volution." I have no doubt that ritual can be explained as evolutionary adaptation. But if there is God as an irreducible partner of ritual, then ritual is in its own meaning rather the intrusion of the uncontrollable future, the appearance of what precisely is not given in the status quo, the location of that very freedom which explanation within an evolutionary metaphor must explain away.

In this reformulation, humanity has reappeared, after a brief bracketing. It is *human* adaptation with which we are concerned. Our theme asks at once about the adaptation that humans make and about the adaptation by which there come to be humans. I thus have two theological questions. First, What part does ritual have in human reckoning with reality? Second, What part if any does ritual have in the step to the specifically human?

Finally in this introductory section, I can begin to absolve my secondary assignment, pointing to an initial way in which modern study of ritual and theology of ritual are positively related. Such argument as that in this section obviously depends on the work of such writers as Mircea Eliade, although he would deplore my use of it. In the present situation of the Christian church in the world, the church's own life and mission depend greatly on clear perception of Christianity's commonality with other religions and, perhaps even more, of its particularity among them. We will unashamedly take all the help we can get.

II

I turn to the first theological question: How does ritual deal with reality? The role of ritual in human life happens to be one of those few points on which the Western church has effective dogma. Saint Augustine looked at the church's ritual and laid down a dictum, cited by all theological parties since, that the church's ritual is the *visibility of the word:* "The word comes to an element and so there is a sacrament, that is, a sort of visible word."[1] This was both an observation of the general role of ritual in human life, specified for the Christian community, and a dogmatic assertion appropriate to the dominant place of the word in Christian life and understanding. Augustine's definition was of sacrament, God's ritual word to us, but it equally well applies to sacrifice, our ritual word to God; and the church has in fact always applied it to both. The life of the church, by Augustinian lights, is an antiphony of our words *for* God, which if true are God's word to us, and our words *to* God. The whole antiphony is both linguistic and "visible." Moreover, if the analysis is correct for the Christian community, it must in its nearly empty formalism be true for all religion, at least up to the descent of mystic silence, since in itself the analysis is independent of the question of religious truth.

In this analysis, "audible" words are propositions of language, that is, they are signs constructed by syntactical and semantic rules to communicate meanings equally well conveyable by other signs. Such communication is not yet ritual, because linguistic signs, in their overt reality as acts, are always replaceable through suitable application of the language's rules. The theological tradition's habit of referring to such words as "audible" over against visible, or simply as words over against visible words, rests on the evolutionary contingency that our ability to generate sounds with great freedom of modulation makes them the initial and permanently most convenient artifacts for use as linguistic signs.

No actual act of human communication occurs sheerly as the transmission and reception of propositions; neither does the Christian gospel or Christians' prayer. The preacher's uttering is not only an emitting of propositions; it is a posturing, an incanting, and so forth. The act of specifically human communication is given only in the ensemble. In our society, if I come close and say, "Good afternoon," but do not extend my hand, my utterance misfires. The forgiveness of sin is promised not by sentences only but by sentences with a bath — that is, by baptism.

1. Augustine, *In Joh. 80, 3.*

It is all our communicative action over and above proposition transmitting that the theological tradition calls visible words, even though much of such action is in fact acoustic — or tactile, olfactory, or gustatory. The use rests on the simple circumstance that sights, by further evolutionary contingency, make the dominant content of our more-than-linguistic communication.

It is this aspect of community, in religious context, that is religious ritual. Repetition, of which some other essayists make so much, is so prominent a feature of ritual just because irreplaceability is, over against linguistic utterance, the distinguishing character of visible words. And it is observable that the visibility of human communion increases precisely as the communion is religious, as it comes to involve eternity. I will consider shortly why this is so.

Not all such ritual bears all the marks of "ritual" as the term is used in some scientific hypotheses. For example, not all ritual in Augustine's sense has any more pronounced rhythmicity than does human intercourse in general; a sacrificial aetiological recital, in its more-than-linguistic aspect, may or may not be notably rhymic utterance. Whether we use "ritual" as I do or narrow its reference to ritual that is also "ritual behavior" is of course a matter of terminological decision. But there is powerful reason to retain the older usage. It is surely strained usage that would not allow the Lord's Supper, celebrated in all haste on a battlefield, or a quick oblation to a household deity, to be a "rite," and an odd explanation of religious ritual that would not cover them.

I may now pose the question of adaption, that is, of why visible discourse is needed in our dealing with reality. There is a standard Western-Christian answer, which I give according to Thomas Aquinas: the human person is "composed of soul and body, to whom the sacramental medicine is proportioned, that through a visible thing touches the body and through a word is believed by the soul."[2] It is by visibility, sacramentality, that God's word to us is no mere transmission between pure spirits, that is, pure memory-and-computation devices, but is a communication between persons. And we may continue, saying nothing but what the tradition has always tacitly assumed, that it is by visibility that also our word to each other and to God is the communion of embodied persons and not an exchange between mere spirits.

2. Aquinas, *Summa Theologica,* III, 60, 6.

In our communion with each other and God, my body is myself insofar as by my address to you I make myself your object and do not only make you my object, insofar as by my address to you I make myself the reciprocal destination of your address, locatable by you, available and even vulnerable to you. But it is by the visibility of my address that this happens. Thus, when community is the horizon of our analysis, we may equate visibility and embodiment; we may even say that my body is the ensemble visibility of my address to you. So the God whose word to us is sacramental is the God who not only claims us but gives himself over to us, who not only speaks but makes himself available to us to be spoken to, who has "body and blood."

Since our topic is human adaptation, we are more concerned with sacrifice than with sacrament, that is, we are chiefly concerned with the ritual reality of our word to God and with one another. What does my ritual accomplish between me and the rest of reality? I suggest that it makes me *available* and therefore *vulnerable* to the world beyond me, to the rest of you, and to the God who encompasses all. It is by the ritual of my communication with the world that I — more nilly than willy — precisely give up control of the world. Rather, it is by addressing me ritually and so demanding my ritual address that reality takes control from me. Insofar as my address to reality is embodied, is sacrifice, it is indeed "sacrificial" in the popular sense.

Is such behavior adaptive? It is in any case revolutionizing. It disrupts the continuity of my developing project of control. From my side, it is the desperate effort to make a new beginning of history within history, to break control by what is. History's sacrificers and revolutionaries are the same persons.

It is possible that revolution is always based on illusion, but if there irreducibly is God, then he and not I in fact controls events, and then new beginning is mere realism. Then the ritualization of my addresses to reality reckons rightly with the metaphysical case, which is that indeed there is interruption and the hope of new life athwart the path of mere development. Of course, if there is not irreducibly God, then the interpretation of ritual just offered leaves the persistence of ritual unexplained, and some explanation by origins and development will have to be extended to be the whole truth. Indeed the *origin* of ritual may well be the attempt to control, since control is what the Bible means by sin and sin is notoriously original.

A first explanation of the association of ritual and religion may now be offered. However we may interpret our prayers and however we may address or misaddress them, if their partner is in fact God, then prayer is the situation of all situations in which we cannot escape being also objects and not sheer subjects, in which our controlling runs into its limit. So long as we keep talking over against God, we will find our talk becoming visible, making us visible, embodying us forth. We can escape only by eschewing God and ritual even as preliminary manifestation and tactics, by turning instead to meditation in the currently usual sense and to its goal of union with an ineffable eternity.

Two great types of religion stand here systematically opposed. It is because Christianity is unambiguously on the one side that it never willingly dispenses with ritual, with sacrament and sacrifice. The sort of union with eternity in which silence permanently falls has always been suspect as an alien phenomenon within Christianity; and meditation in the central Benedictine tradition has not meant emptying consciousness except as a preliminary tactic, but rather the exclusive and concentrated filling of consciousness with one particular text or memory.

Finally in this section, we may note a second way in which the scientific study of ritual and theological reflection of ritual may be positively related; again I report a benefit of the former to the latter. If ritual is visible words, then those who study how ritual works in the context of community, abstracting from the question of ritual's truth, may be regarded as grammarians of ritual, in the same sense in which philosophers in their analytical capacity are grammarians of language. Surely grammarians of ritual are then at least as vital to the work of theology as are grammarians of language.

Of course, anyone engaged in a discourse can, if compelled to it, reflect back upon its grammar; and Christian theology has always made grammatical observations about ritual. But since theology is itself a linguistic enterprise, theology is strongly tempted to suppose that ritual's sense is guaranteed by correct propositions about it, that a visible word says whatever theologians propositionally assure us that it does. If some current theology is ever so slightly less fallen to this temptation, we have the grammarians of ritual in large part to thank for it.

Let me give an example. The history of baptism is mostly a lamentable history of progressive visible incoherence. In the third- and fourth-century church baptism was visibly an initiation, a classic rite of passage clearly structured in three acts, including a time of exorcistic and disciplinary liberation from the old life, the starkly liminal naked immersion itself, and the rite to give the Spirit, that is, to inaugurate new life in the church. The dismantling of this drama was accomplished by a variety of historical contingencies, but at each step the dismantling was legitimated by a theology that abstracted from ritual meaning. Finally theology asked only two questions seriously: first, What really — as *against* visibly! — happens at baptism? And second, What must we ritually do to make this happen? To the first question, the standard Western answer has been "justification," an answer not wrong but notably undramatic. To the second and disastrous question, the official answer has been that application of water, with proclamation of the triune name, suffices. At the end of the historical dismantling, we have our familiar damp-finger pettings of the cute infants.

By the inherent grammar of visible discourse, baptism as now mostly practiced cannot say visibly any of what we keep propositionally insisting that it does. It cannot say end-and-new-beginning, and this is surely much of the reason for the feeble self-identification of Christian congregations. None of us in fact believes that entering the church is death and resurrection or that remaining in it is risky, for we regularly see with our own eyes that we enter by a harmless rite, a rite that speaks, if of anything, of continuity and the sanctification of the given. The modern liturgical movement in all denominations is informed by awareness of this deficit and by understanding of the need to recover a ritual structure analogous to that of ancient baptism. The clear analysis of how initiations work, provided by Victor Turner among others, was decisive in the emergence of the liturgical movement's insight.

III

My second question is, How does ritual humanize? To deal with it, I must recite some Christian theology of whose unsecured situation in this context I can only say I am aware. I have to sketch nothing less than the doctrine of creation if I am to say what sort of adaptive step ritual is in the coming-to-be of humanity, since the coming-to-be of things is the matter of the doctrine of creation.

The primal Christian assertion about all reality other than God is that it exists by God's word, because and only because God said and says it shall. There is, of course, an ancient problem here: since this assertion makes God's word anterior to the creature as God is anterior to the creature, to whom is this word addressed? The doctrine of the Trinity is in part an answer to this question. God rightly identified, the doctrine says, is to and from all eternity both subject and object of an address and its response; indeed, his being is specifiable as *conversation.* Thus the more precise form of the claim that all but God is by God's word is the claim that all but God is by and in its place in the triune conversation. Stated metaphysically, the final Christian insight into reality is that all reality is intended in a consciousness and a freedom and that this personhood is not abstract but constituted in address and answer, as are all persons.

The actual God, according to the Christian gospel, is the one who can be named "Father, Son, and Holy Spirit." There are many ways to get at the suitability of the name; I will develop further some ideas already discussed. Any eternity is a putative triumph of identity over temporal discontinuity. The normal way of positing such identity is by abstracting from time to putative timelessness, by digging in against the future's threatening novelties under the protection of a serenely persisting identity, one that gives no hostages to time, that is impassibly all that it is. But if God is "the one who raised Jesus from the dead," or "the one who rescued Israel from Egypt," then God is not as this move needs him to be. There is only one other move: to appeal not to the cancellation of time but to the success of time, to take a plot in and of time as in itself the transcendence of temporal discontinuity. One plot offers itself.

The infamous trinitarian relations — that the Father begets the Son, and the Son is begotten by the Father, and that the Spirit is breathed by, or by and through both — are initially but a summary of the plot of the biblical history of God's acts, of the temporal and personal structure of what is said to have happened and to be going to happen between Jesus the Christ, the transcendence he dared address as "Father," and the rest of us. The assertion of this summary as relations subsisting in God is the assertion that the plot of saving history is real not only for us and as a context of our lives but for God and as a context of his life, which of course must be himself. Just thereby it also is asserted that what is true of the identity through time of any plot, that it is conversational, is also true of God's identity with himself, of the relations to himself in which his self is constituted. We are back where we began: the self-identity that transcends time is not one in which personhood and discourse are obliterated; it is rather personhood's and discourse's own kind of victory through time, occurring absolutely.

Thus God can rightly be named, Father, Son, and Holy Spirit, because his life is not that of a monad or solitary but is the conversation of Christ and his Father in their Spirit. The Father loves and sends the Son, and this act is not a dumb act but a self-address of the Father to another. Jesus obeys his Father; and this obedience is real audible and visible prayer. The actual divine Spirit is not just any arbitrarily upsetting numinous impetus, but the Spirit of this specifically contentful conversation. Finally back to the doctrine of creation: other reality than the Father, Son, and Spirit comes to pass in that it is mentioned in their conversation that is eternity, in that the word that is God is so spoken as to posit referents other than God. God says, "Let there be . . . ," and just and only so where there was and would be nothing there is now obedience to this *Torah,* this beneficent mandate.

The great problem of theological anthropology has always been to stipulate the difference of human creatures from others. The traditional Western procedure, in and out of theology, has been to stipulate characteristics that are supposed to fit only humans. Thus Aristotle, and following him most Christian theology, defined humans as the rational animals, marked off from most other creatures by interior vivacity and from other animals by rationality. I have modulated the doctrine of creation as I have to set up a quite different sort of proposal.

First let me quickly say why the traditional method will not finally do for Christian theology. The point is straightforward. All delimitations of humanity in the style of Aristotle are compelled to put the concept of potentiality at the center of reality. To stay with our example, humans in fact rarely act rationally, so that the proposition that humans are rational must be qualified to be that humans are potentially rational. The same will be found with any stipulation in this style, where the defining characteristic is simultaneously a value. Thus all such patterns of thought eventually generate the root metaphor of development.

We can avoid this outcome by finding a value-free differentiation, perhaps simply by boiling the moral demand out of the concept of rationality. But it is the utter unacceptability of this move for Christians, which posits no *ontological* difference between humans and other creatures, that led Christianity to make such prompt common cause with the heirs of Socrates. For to abandon the claim that humans fit in time differently than do other creatures, that we are whatever we are in a way that is different from the way in which other creatures are whatever they are, is to give up any ground in reality for treating humans by standards different from those by which we treat creatures of other sorts. And if humans do not demand different standards, then why not, for example, weed out the human population as we weed out the equine population? Adolph Hitler's policy about Jews depended on the spectacularly erroneous empirical assertion that Jews are deleterious to the gene pool. But what if the assertion were correct? It was against the threat of declining antiquity's moral nihilism that Christians once made common cause with Socrates' heirs, once the philosophical question about kinds of being had been raised also for the Christians; and the threat is now yet more severe. Believers insist: humans are a particular ontological sort.

Humanity must therefore begin with an event athwart mere development. What event that is, is supposed already in my claim that there is one. Creatures are what God speaks about other than himself. I now suggest: among creatures some are distinguished in that God speaks not only about but to them. They are taken as not only referents but addressees of the conversation that is God. It is by this role that we are to recognize sisters and brothers among the creatures. No doubt our species — or species (plural) — is created equipped with whatever active and dispositional properties are requisite for this part. But it is not by these that we are human, nor need we suppose any monopoly of them in order to specify our humanity. If we are not ontologically different from other animals, then the search for a line between prehuman and human is unimportant; if we are, then the line does not necessarily coincide with any developmental step at all.

Humanity thus begins with God's revelation (a dubious term but handy here). All branches of Christian theology suppose that believers are sent to speak God's word in the world; our sisters and brothers among creatures are those to whom this sending draws us. All branches of theology suppose also that God speaks to all these sisters and brothers — whoever they may be — also before we arrive with the gospel, in the discourse of their polities and religions. The standard term for this general word of God is "the law," humans' word to each other insofar as it claims absolute authority. Who were Adam and Eve? They were the first community of our biological ancestors to hear in their mutual discourse, "It is in any case good for us to . . . ," that is, to overhear the Trinity.

An odd sort of behavioral specification of humanity is thus after all possible. The unproblematic complement to an address, unless all goes wrong, is a response. If the triune conversation takes us as additional hearers, he thereby solicits us as additional speakers. That is, we are bidden to pray. We are specifically the praying animals. Of course, prayer may display an illusion; and on that supposition, we would need an explanation of the human function of the illusion. There is no reason why such explanations cannot be produced and be illuminating, whether or not they are actually needed.

As we have noted, it is just at the juncture of prayer that discourse is ineluctably embodied. Who were Adam and Eve? They were the first community of our ancestors to have a cult, and it is precisely the ritual of that cult that let it be an ontological beginning. That is, whatever place religious ritual may have in the *evolution* of the species homo sapiens, it has a decisive role in the coming-to-be of *humanity;* one can even say that it simply is that coming-to-be. We are as reluctant and perverse sacrificers as we are reluctant and perverse reasoners; but on the proposed account that which we can and do fail is not a potential in ourselves but an event that involves us, God's word.

Once more I turn to the question of mutuality between scientific study of ritual and its theological consideration. This time I will suggest benefits that run the other way from those I have so far mentioned.

Our symposium was provided with an "Introduction" by Ralph Wendell Burhoe, setting very interesting questions for all essayists. Let me here pick up some of these, and the language in which they are posed. It is suggested that religious ritual emerges as the "coadaptation" of "earlier-established neural levels" of animal behavior with "a phenotypically and behaviorally different set of characteristics" created by a "living sociocultural system." And this seems to me a priori very likely. The informationally somewhat more loaded proposition also seems to me likely, that these two sets of dispositional properties are wired in different, earlier- and later-evolved parts of the nervous system. Now suppose we are able to go on to learn much more about all this than we now know — what precise adaptive steps required these neural arrangements, details about the interaction in ritual performance of specific areas of the brain, and so on. What will we thereby discover?

It really would not have required much research to make me tentatively assent to the opinion that the evolutionary history of the brain is synchronically reflected in its structure and that the structure in turn maps boundary conditions of our ritual performance. Just for that reason, the So what? question inescapably poses itself.

Let me first answer that by such research we will discover a great deal of truth about evolutionary history, neural anatomy, and so on, and that for any worshipper of the Creator such discoveries require no exterior justification. But of course we never leave truth quite so brazenly at that; our technical and cognitive longings are not so clearly separable, even the itch for celestial mechanics was never quite distinct from the itch for improved bombardment. Likewise, Burhoe's questions end with these: "What do [new pictures of ritual in human adaptation] suggest for further developments in religious education, for renewed richness and authenticty of religous faith, hope, and charity?"

We need to ask what such neurophysiological explanations can add up to for our understanding of our own behavior. Surely they can only add up to self-knowledge of the very sort that Socrates attributed to his predecessors and dismissed. Christian theology cannot simply join Socrates' dismissal, and the reason has been gratifyingly reflected in this discussion. In much of the discussion there has been some consensus that ritual is located at the intersection of determination and freedom and that this intersection itself is built into our embodiment — which is just what Christian theology ordered.

However, I have two caveats. First, if this consensus is to be affirmed, we must then say that the body itself cannot be understood one body at a time but only as a communal phenomenon.

Second, we must note the abiding truth in Socrates' position. What indeed may neurophysiological or other quantitative explanations of ritual add up to for our practice of ritual? Those concerned to make ritual work obviously must welcome every piece of knowledge about ritual's workings. It is the case, however, that the knowledge now in question never presents itself in quite that state of cognitive purity that celestial mechanics can achieve if pressed; it always indeed suggests things about what would be "further" and what would be "rich." The evolutionary track projects itself on choice. And it is the experience of those concerned for the church's ritual that such suggestions are regularly bad for it. That may say something sad about Christian ritual, or it may suggest something of the epistemological situation of those sciences that take humanity for their object.

Western science achieved itself by eschewing teleological explanation, including, partly inadvertently, eschatological explanations. It does not follow that science at all levels and at all times can go on that way. Insofar as science becomes history, as evolutionary narrative does or as the most advanced approaches to a unified field theory now do, the same questions must come to afflict it that afflict all historical study. Why should what an event or condition comes *from* explain it more appropriately than does what comes *of* that event or condition? Is historical knowledge possible at all apart from some posit of the whole of history, which in turn depends on some posit of the end of history? Is historical knowledge possible apart from methodical reckoning with freedom?

Science that can tell us about ritual always hovers on the verge of such questions. Antecedent decision to ignore them has decisive consequences for the suggestions such science, as an actual human and social enterprise, makes for the conduct of specifically human life, including ritual. It perhaps has consequences also for the immanent practice of the science. The decision to seek all argumentative warrants in the past rather than in the future is a sheer metaphysical choice. And it must, unless there is great personal incoherence, decide policy generally: it must decide what is to count as "rich" or "further." The decision is against freedom.

Scientific study of humanity that is done sheerly apart from the posit of freedom in which humanity occurs will necessarily generate a replacement eschatology from the decision that governs its own practice. We cannot but do what we do *for* something, if not for the Kingdom of God then for something else. The act of renunciation by which Western science emerged must *by itself* generate ideals of stability, of satisfaction of perceived needs, even of mystic escape from time. The current coalescence of popularized psychology and bowdlerized Eastern religion is most instructive.

To the extent that American religion has opened itself to suggestion from behavioral science, it is such reactionary norms that have in fact mostly been suggested. Moreover, the theological distant observer cannot but note science's extraordinary tendency to schism whenever it touches such questions as those set for this discussion, and the tendency of each scientific sect to establish itself by composing a creed precisely about "genesis." May one suggest that the sectarianism may partly be accounted for by these creeds' common lack of an article on the Spirit to go with the article on creation, that is, of an article on the reality and power of the future.

It is not to be expected or wished that science, even when it touches ritual or other central human matters, will begin referring in its argumentative warrants to the will of God or to the character of the absolute. However, one may suggest that it would be beneficial for scientists to take it as belonging to properly mandated method, for certain matters of investigation, to listen in to modes of discourse that do make such references, to put themselves regularly under reminder that there is such discourse and that it might touch reality. Scientific method is after all a set of moral commitments. One necessary commitment may be that scientists never limit their own reflection to the sphere marked out by the repudiation of teleology, precisely for the sake of what is to be known about that sphere, but rather that they let themselves with methodical purpose participate in speculation about what, for our present instance, ritual is *for*.

One such speculation is that proposed here by Christian theology. Ritual is our discourse athwart our self-development, marking the irreversible intrusion of God and making us vulnerable to reality. That is, we are the praying animals — or, as I would have said had I been able to forgo the pun, we are the sacrificing animals.

Toward a Christian Theory of the Public

❧   ❧

I

IN THE WEST generally and in America preeminently our understanding of political and economic life has for over two centuries been provided by the ideology of the great Western Enlightenment; we are unable to conceive even the church's polity and economy in other norms than those of function and representation. Arguing whether this has been mostly a good thing or a bad would be pointless. But it is arguable that we should not go on so. There are two reasons.

First, even if Enlightened political and economic theory was once a practical success, it seems to have played out its innings. A necessary function of political and economic theory is to aid the identification of good public policy. But, for example, even supposing that you have been able to sort out your adherence to one or another of the public moral policies made available by Enlightenment theory — you are "liberal" or "conservative," or perhaps even "socialist" or "reactionary" — how will that help you vote in this election year? How will it help me personally decide between one set of candidates who are — to me,

Published in *dialog* 23 (Summer 1984): 191-197. Reprinted by permission.

astonishingly — both "antimilitaristic" and "pro-choice" and another set who reverse the prefixes? Or between those who somehow manage to be for "family" and "capitalism" and others who are for "individual rights" and "compassion"? Less anecdotally: by nearly unanimous observation, the conceptual set by which we interpret our public reality to ourselves is in utter confusion. New thoughts would be timely.

Second, once one stops to think about it, it seems plain that Enlightenment politics and economics, even if they for a time produced blessings, must simply be false if the gospel is true. Argument for that assertion will be a chief burden of this essay. That for centuries few Christians did stop to think is understandable, but perhaps the Enlightenment's wind of doctrine has lost sufficient of its apparent balm to let now be the time. The theory of representative and bureaucratic "democracy" and the economic theory that encompasses socialism and capitalism were derived the same way: by stretching the mechanistic metaphor for Newton's physics to make a general interpretation of public humanity. Surely, this was a most unlikely project by Christian judgment.

II

Throughout its whole range of thought, eighteenth-century theory mostly drew lessons from seventeenth-century experience. The seventeenth century's great disaster was the wars of religion, from which the eighteenth learned its deep suspicion of "dogma." The seventeenth century's great triumph was an unprecedented flood of knowledge, at once interesting and practical, produced by its practice of the new science; this achievement was personified for the eighteenth century above all by Isaac Newton. And the seventeenth century's dream was for the extension of Newton's physics to embrace our specifically human lives; perhaps, it was hoped, also the intractable problems of moral existence could be resolved by the same cognitive policies that had been so successful with the mysteries of nature. About the individual, the dream was set before the eighteenth century by the writings of John Locke; about the public world, which is the theme of this essay, by Locke and Thomas Hobbes.

The great attraction of Newton's physics was the vision it opened of universal harmony, the possibility of seeing all nature subjected to the same laws that govern the moving symphony of the Copernican heavens. If the human mind is to enlighten all the obscurities of reality, all reality must be amenable to mind; and that is to say, it must be despite many appearances orderly, for amenability to mind is all we mean by "order."

And here a fateful choice was made. Our civilization harbors two proposals of encompassing order: the biblical word of a coherent total history and Greece's vision of a "cosmos," an itself unmoving inter-relation of moving parts. The normative Enlightenment could tolerate no such theological dogma as the first and chose the second. Newton's world is beautiful, the normative Enlightenment said, because its encompassing system is stable even as it is inwardly dynamic. Moreover, the new technology offered an impressive image for such order, the image of the mechanism. We are all still intimately familiar with the resulting universal metaphor of the cosmos as a great — doubtless Swiss — watch or mill or engine.

When, then, the enterprise was launched of a "scientific" interpretation also of human life, what was in fact cultivated was a mechanistic inter-pretation. It is vital to see that it was not Newton's physics that were extrapolated, but what was already a metaphor for them. When Locke described the dynamics of atom-ideas in the space of consciousness, or when Madison and his fellow Constitution-makers, confident in the "improvements" which the "science of politics" had "lately received,"[1] set out to design a better polity, they did not in fact extend Newton's laws to the workings of the mind and of society, they elaborated a metaphor.

The American polity is the pure model of Enlightenment political theory, for only here did the philosophers have opportunity to start from something close to scratch, to emulate the great Engineer they wor-shiped and construct a polity that by an exact arrangement of forces could — like a great mill — be at once stable in itself yet productive of civil goods. Madison and his fellows worked according to a political technology that treated human persons and groups as inertial vectors, and their interactions as transmissions of energy.[2] Interest is opposed to interest, faction to faction, to the greatest good of the greatest number. Despite all subsequent modifications of the machine's design,

1. *The Federalist*, 1852 ed., p. 39.
2. *The Federalist*, e.g. pp. 39, 43-45, 241, 283.

[134]

our understanding of politics is still entirely swayed by this dream of the "system"; and our anxious question after each challenge is "Did it work?" Just therein we have been a model wherever the Enlightenment reaches and — despite all disillusions — remain so fascinating.

Of special importance and everywhere regarded as the essential of a modern, that is, Enlightenment-approved polity, is the principle of representation. I am thought to be the free citizen of a free country if and only if my government is conducted at controlling points by persons who "represent" me, because they are elected and subject to reelection by a population that includes me or because they are of my color, sex, class, or whatever. But what exactly about me can be represented? It is of the first importance that my moral personhood cannot be represented.

Moral existence is precisely the submission of impulse, of what I antecedently *want* to happen, to *discourse* about what *should* be done, in expectation of new and not fully predictable commitment. Thus my moral person cannot be effective in a deliberation in the course of which I cannot be brought to change my mind and thereafter to speak for new purposes, as repeatedly as may be. And therefore what some other person can represent of me in a forum from which I am absent is always and only pre-moral impulse, what I wanted when he or she last checked, that is, that sort of my agency to which the metaphor of mass and energy is in fact quite apt.

The ideal of political "representation" is but another segment of the machine metaphor, not in this case of cogs and levers but of an impact-transmission chain, like the famous dominoes. What can be represented is — as American's constitution-engineers fully grasped — "interests" only, those directions of agency that inhere in persons and groups independently of moral choice, as it is and remains my personal interest, since I am the salaried employee of an institution with inelastic income, that inflation be restrained at whatever industrial cost. My congressman can represent this interest; he cannot represent my moral struggle with it, since he cannot predict the course thereof.

With the notion of "interest," we may move from the polity to the economy — as, indeed, it was mostly economic interests that such as Madison had in mind. The great communal event of the eighteenth century was the rise of the bourgeoisie, of those brought to dominance by rapid, technologically enabled expansion of the markets and of the division of labor. It was in their interest (!) so to interpret economic life as to make the market the center and efficient production the goal, and theorists obliged.

The mechanistic metaphor was almost demanded, and here fits so well as nearly to be an actual proper theory. "The market" is what a polity never can quite become, however it may try, a system for the pure interplay of interests. Adam Smith laid it down with all possible bluntness: the "meaning" of every event in the market is "Give me that which I want and you shall have this that you want." "It is not from the benevolence of the butcher, the brewer, or the baker, that we expect our dinner but from their regard to their own interest."[3] Smith did not theorize so because he was a moral cynic, or because he understood about original sin; he in fact based all his ethics on the posit of inherent benevolence. He only thought ethics irrelevant to economic theory, since it is a machine that is the object of the theory.

Karl Marx in no way abjured Enlightenment mechanistic economics. For our purposes, we may say he added two things only. First, he recognized the inhumanity of mechanistic interpretation. But he did not dispute its truth, short of the eschaton. Second, he attributed mechanistic interpretation, and the existence of the economic system it indeed nearly fits, to the interest of a class, thereby merely identifying previously unregarded carriers of inertia, classes, as constitutive in the system. The opposition of capitalist and Marxist economics is real enough, but it is the opposition of rival theories of the same kind.

III

Despite its best efforts of self-accommodation, Christian theology has never been able comfortably to inhabit the Enlightenments's machine-cosmos. Christians, after all, worship a God whose reality is invested in discontinuities, in resurrections and forgivings and new creations. Every attempted combination of the Bible's God with the normative Enlightenment's great Engineer falls victim to the village freethinker's question of all these 250 years: "If God designed such a perfect machine, why should he interfere in its workings?" If the gospel is true, the machine-society is a mere illusion — and vice versa.

3. *The Wealth of Nations*, bk. 1, ch. 11.

There have been Christian thinkers who grasped the problem, the best from within the Enlightenment itself. Piety suggests that one of them should lead our reflection. The most penetrating of all — as far as I can see — was himself a noteworthy devotee of Newton and Locke, an eighteenth-century figure of the true style, and an American: Jonathan Edwards. At the age of eighteen or nineteen, he laid down the metaphysical task of Christian thought over against the normative Enlightenment: to show that in fact "there is no such thing as mechanism."[4]

It was neither Newton's physics properly as such nor Locke's psychology properly as such to which Edwards objected — quite the contrary. From his first reading of their works, he apparently never doubted that the new science had the right cognitive policy. But unlike most, he discerned the difference between scientific method and achievement, and the metaphysical metaphor by which his age mostly dealt with these. Whatever "matter" or "motion" meant within Newton's laws, they meant for Edwards; it was the associated metaphysical interpretation of the notions that he attacked. And his critique went to the heart of the machine metaphor, to scientistic ideologists' unthinking bondage — despite all those polemics against "scholasticism"! — to the old Aristotelian notion of "substance."

"Mechanism" Edwards defined as "that whereby bodies act each upon another, purely and properly by themselves. . . ."[5] Mechanistic nature-interpretation's initial error, according to Edwards, is precisely the assumption that bodies *can* act "properly by themselves," that is, the unnoticed extension of the concept of substance, of the *self*-contained *subject* of a real thing's overt attributes and actions, to physics' masses in motion. "Substance," Edwards noticed, is an intrinsically *theological* notion: if "philosophers," he wrote in his youthful notebooks, "must needs apply that word . . . , they must apply it, to the divine being. . . . And here I believe all those philosophers would apply it, if they knew what they meant themselves."[6] What Edwards is up to is a project of demythologizing: there are no little self-sufficient agencies besides God, nor is the universe one middle-sized one. Natural entities are not

4. Jonathan Edwards, *Of Atoms*, in *The Works of Jonathan Edwards*, vol. 6, ed. W. Anderson (New Haven: Yale University Press, 1980), p. 216.

5. Edwards, *Of Atoms*, p. 216.

6. Edwards, *Of Atoms*, pp. 215-216.

godlets, and therefore masses in motion do not act "properly by themselves:" there is no universal mechanism.

Edwards's eye for natural events was severely phenomenalist. Watching a body under acceleration, he saw no need to posit a force "pulling" it, and watching that same body suddenly decelerate or rebound when it reached the boundary set by another body, he saw no need to say that the second body "stopped" the first, nor yet that the first body's acceleration and sudden deceleration were different sorts of phenomena. These are rather resistances appearing in contiguous parts of space/time and in coordination with one another. With its metaphorical wrappings thus stripped away, the Copernican-Newtonian universe appeared to Edwards as itself a mystery of universal harmony through space/time — the same mystery with which contemporary physics, having in its own way banished the substance-concept, presents us.

Edwards believed he knew the identity of the mystery: the Triune God. If we must ask "what substance" resists at points in space/time and communicates resistances among themselves and from point to point, the answer must be: the "immediate power of God."[7]

Thus Edwards cleared the way again for the radical biblical interpretation of God, of the Will more immediate to every grain of sand than the grain is to itself, of Martin Luther's Spirit who "moves and agitates all in all,"[8] in whom good and evil and life and death are equally if differently swept to a goal.[9] Yet Edwards affirmed also the Newtonian vision of encompassing created harmony, as the expression of the harmony this God is in himself as the specifically *triune* God. The world-harmony is founded in the coherence of the inner history God is as Father, Son, and Spirit.[10] The world-harmony is therefore a lively harmony, a harmony through time, and is itself the appropriate "stage" for a history:[11] the world is created precisely to be redeemed,[12] to "provide a spouse" for Christ.[13] And so it may be said that each "atom in the

7. Edwards, *Of Atoms*, pp. 214-216; *The Mind*, in *Works*, vol. 6, pp. 377-380; *Natural Philosophy*, in *Works*, vol. 6, pp. 234-235.
8. Martin Luther, *De Servo Arbitrio*, Weimar ed., vol. 30, p. 709.
9. Luther, pp. 709-10, 585.
10. Edwards, *Miscellanies* (unpublished), 104.
11. Edwards, *A History of the Work of Redemption*, Doc., II, 1.
12. Edwards, *A Dissertation of the End for Which God Created the World*, II, III, IV.
13. Edwards, *Work of Redemption*, Imp., I, 3.

universe is managed by Christ so as to be most to the advantage of the Christian. . . ."[14]

Edwards appears in this essay by way of liberating us from the machine. I will write only two sentences about his more specifically social thought, to record that the liberation occurred also for Edwards himself. He elaborated an understanding of personhood in community that was in radical dissent from the normative Enlightenment's individualism and the theories of representative republicanism it developed: human reality is, according to Edwards, composed of "hearts" united in "affections" in all shadings and intensities, and these unions are in some modes so decisive that what counts as an individual within the communal field depends on for what purpose we distinguish. As for the new capitalist impulses, Edwards, for all his modernism, saw no need to regard them as anything but Pelagianism manifest.

What then are, positively, politics and economics? The politics first.

IV

Let us take it that Luther — with Edwards and Barth and Athanasius and all Christianity's most venturesome spirits — was right in thinking that because the real God is the *living* God, he has a *purpose,* and that the gospel tells us what it is. God "has created us for this, to redeem and sanctify us. . . ."[15] The question of political theory is then, As God moves all things to this goal, what part of his urging is he up to in what we call our politics? When he brings us together to argue about, for example, armaments, he is on his way to his Kingdom. How is the political event on the road to the eschatological event?

It is an ancient problem, and there are at least two recognized boundary-positions. First, we may not, if we are on God's way, simply skip by the political event. "Let every person be subject to the governing authorities" is not quite a general statement of principle, but "For there is no authority except from God . . ." assuredly is. God is the Agent of our politics. Second, politics will not save us; the Kingdom is not, for example, the last stop of a progress of disarmament treaties. If our

14. Edwards, *Miscellanies,* ff.
15. Luther, *The Large Catechism,* Creed, 64.

politics are God's work, he must work with at least two hands, since he saves us with another, the gospel.

How to begin to construct? Let the first thing be to notice that "Kingdom of God" is not a metaphor. The biblical hope is not for "fulfillment" or "salvation" in general, for which politics and other parts of life then provide a variety of "images." Israel's eschatological hope simply was hope for the gift at last of what her national polity was to be and had not become. It was precisely Israel's political sins — her failures of righteousness and peace and mercy — that the prophets judged in the Lord's name. It was thus the destruction of Israel's polity that was the threatened and performed judgment — the people merely as such, after all, with their "private" lives, persisted and sometimes even thrived. When the prophets then promised new life beyond this death, it was precisely new righteousness and mercy and peace, under, according to some, a new King, that was the content of their hope. And it was this prophetic hope that Jesus renewed in immediacy, spoke also to the excluded, died for, and now lives to guarantee. It is quite literally God's Reign, his Kingdom, the polity constituted by his sovereignty, that is the content of the biblical promise.

Now perhaps, of course, what I have just described is how the gospel-promise is merely a religious sublimation of Israel's political failure and disillusion. But Christians *believe* the gospel: they assert that when we hear it we are told the final mystery of God's creating purpose. Therefore we can and must reverse the viewpoint and, looking back, ask again: What then was God up to with Israel's politics themselves? And from this vantage the answer seems obvious: within God's creating will, Israel's politics were established to be the necessary *context of prophecy.* The Lord set his chosen to be a polity among the world's polities in order that they might be the immediate hearers and utterers of the word he in fact chose to say.

Can this statement be generalized to provide the theoretical proposition that *politics are the context of prophecy?* I think it can, if we work carefully. On one side, Israel's politics were, insofar as they were politics, of the same sort as and continuous with the politics of the rest of the ancient world. The political history of humankind was the total matrix of Israelite prophecy. Nor, indeed, did Israel think prophecy was a phenomenon unique to herself — consider only the stories of Balaam or of Jonah. It was the *identity* of the God who spoke and the *content* of his word that were particular to Israel. On another side: we must be careful to observe that Christ's death and resurrection cut across all such plottings of saving history as I am now attempting; failure to observe that "now is the judgment," that God's labor on history does not simply *continue* after Christ's resurrection, is one cause of "liberation" theology's often arbitrary allegorizing of Israelite history. But prophecy itself did not cease with Christ. On the contrary, "all flesh" are now prophets; our prophecy is, "Jesus will reign." And again, it is the identification of the Lord that we specifically bring as we prophesy to the nations; that prophecy is possible among them is antecedently given with their political entity. Politics are the context of prophecy. How does this work?

A community's polity is the arena in which its ethics are done, in which it is decided what sort of community it chooses to be in future. A community's polity is the arena in which the question is posed, with possibility of decision, What should we do about . . . ? This forum may be an assembly of all citizens, the inside of a tyrant's head, or a representative and bureaucratic apparatus, to mention only a few possibilities. But somewhere and somehow a community that still breathes will ask, for example: Under what circumstances if any should abortion be allowed? What is to be taught the children? What sorts of violence shall we offer our enemies, and under what circumstances?

For long stretches of a community's history, its moral reflection may go unprophetically, in that new decisions are reliably guided by established vision. But the sheer reality of time and the plurality of human communities guarantee that sooner or later moral creativity will be demanded of every community, as when a newly "organized" city neighborhood, morally united around authentic but limited ideals of justice and solidarity, is confronted with immigration of an ethnically alien group, or as when gynecological technology continually reduces the age of fetal viability, demanding of liberal America that it face moral questions that could once remain obscured. At such times the community can live only if two marks attach to its moral discourse: if (1) in the community's moral discourse there is spoken not only the community's word to itself, but a word to the community from beyond the community; and (2) in the community's moral discourse not only command is spoken, but also promise.

When moral creativity is demanded, it will do no good for the community to say only, "Come let us reason together," for it is precisely the basis for the authority of that "us" that is then in question. When established vision does not guide, the community drifts in its own moral void. Then somehow it must be said in the polity, "This is the will of heaven." And the morally creative word then needed is never the word that says only, "This is what we should do," but is rather the word that says, "This is what we may await" — in the Declaration of Independence, "life, liberty and the pursuit of happiness" are promised, not commanded.

Putting the two together: the morally creative word is the *eschatological* word, the word of final promise. A polity is, indeed, the institutionalization of an eschatology, and must, to be itself, be from time to time the forum of an explicitly eschatological word of prophecy. In times of challenge, if prophecy fails, the community's discourse will disintegrate into threatenings and sophistry — as is happening to America's discourse about nearly all truly political questions.

The considerations of the previous paragraph yield by themselves a first practical maxim within this theory: right polity holds itself open to prophecy. Right polity will, as the traditional political ethics of the church have always said, open and guard a space for the public speech and reception of the community's speakers of godly promise. In the West, these are still the Jews, the Christians, and the articulators of the civic religion Judaism and Christianity enable. The "separation of church and state," were it possible, would be any Western polity's suicide. If we can find no more creative way to deal with "pluralism" than simply silencing all explicit civilly affirmed faith — in the schools or elsewhere — we must expect the disintegration of our polity to continue apace.

In any polity that lives on, prophecy — words purporting to be the word of heaven — will occur. If we think there is no heaven, we will explain these irruptions reductively, and — the chief point here — posit no necessary coherence among them. Then we will seek the polity's self-identity precisely in the moral or mechanical continuities prophecy interrupts and even threatens. But since there is God, the words from heaven that occur in any polity's life must be coherent among themselves, as the one God's urgings toward his one goal, and it is in the eschatological vision held before a polity that we should seek its self-identity. Therefore we should theorize: what sort of polity a community is depends on what sort of prophecy it hears; and what the right polity is depends on what prophecy is true.

When Christians appear, they prophesy, "We may await Jesus' reign." The vision held up is of the biblical Kingdom of God's Messiah. What sort of polity will the Kingdom be? Some polities, by traditional theory, find their center in a person; others find it in a system. The Kingdom will be of the former sort; its coherence as a community will be constituted by Jesus' self-giving to all his members. This self-giving is a suffering self-giving; it is real as *forgiveness*. Thus also the question of political hierarchy is settled: none will be closer to Messiah than others, whatever other distinctions may obtain; the forum in which the community lives its moral creativity will include all directly. Blessing and prayer will continue for all eternity, to be the true polity.

Since the Christian prophecy is true, right polity for any community at any time is that which would emerge from the meeting of its then historically actual polity with the vision just described. God is in fact urging all polities on the way so stipulated; believers' claim, here as in other reflective realms, is to know about human life what is true also where it is not known. Our question about our own right polity must then be, What mandates would emerge from an interpretation of our present actual polity by the vision of Messiah's Kingdom? I suggest that the chief such mandate must be to create and recreate all possible forums of communal moral discourse, with power of decision, into which all citizens may have entry in their own moral personhood. A second practical maxim within this theory is limited by its materiality to a particular historic realm, the West: right polity will restrict representation and similar hierarchic devices to the minimum. Doubtless there must be forums of decision also for populations too large to assemble democratically, as Madison and company insisted when they devised our polity-machine. But let us accept exile from the political center only for matters about which it is entirely clear that this is necessary.

V

The economy is the public realm in which there are no choices to be made, only calculations. There are indeed choices to be made *about* economic matters: How heavily shall we burden the credit supply in order to build up the armed services? How progressive shall the income tax be? And so on. But these are questions of political economy, and are made in the polity. The economy is the public realm not constituted by argument; in the economy, "information" merely "flows," and an omniscient participant, however wicked, would never have to change his mind. It is this truth about the economy that has throughout the post-Enlightenment period preserved the plausibility of the — intrinsically far-fetched! — machine metaphor for the whole public reality.

When God binds us to the operations of economic necessity, when he binds me to the "butcher, brewer, and baker" for my supper and they to me for theirs, what is he up to? How are economic transactions events in the urging by which he moves us to the Kingdom?

Perhaps the first thing to be said is simply that this question is legitimate. Liberated from the machine metaphor, we can say what is obvious: if there is God, he and not "the market" or any other such entity is the Agent also of the economy, and to understand the economy we must inquire after him and his purposes.

It is a mere reformulation of positions reached in the previous section to say that theory about the economy must be derived from theory about the polity. No new basis is to be laid in this section, for it follows stringently from what we have said about the polity that the economy has no basis separate from it. As the polity is for prophecy, so the economy is for polity.

The suggestion seems to me to follow immediately: what God is up to in the economy is *compelling the polity.* In the economy God rules us in the same way as he rules galaxies and amoebae: without our choice. We must eat, take shelter, and the like; and we are an economy insofar as we cannot manage these singly. God so arranges his creation that we cannot but deal with one another. Just so, communal moral choices become inevitable, and with them politics — and with politics prophecy.

I have room and ability for only a few somewhat scattered maxims about right economy — whereby it should be remembered that presenting and arguing such maxims is an act within the political public, not the economic public. The first is: if necessitating politics is God's goal with the economy, maximum production in itself is not. Of course, since I must eat, I cannot but want to eat well. But not even the possibility of substituting "we" for "I" in the previous sentence can make the promotion of production the automatic right choice for every situation. In a right economy, the GNP would not be a norm.

The second maxim is like unto the first: an economy that produces such inequalities of wealth as to dispense some from and incapacitate others for communal moral deliberation is just so evil, counter to the economy's godly function. "Safety nets" are nothing to the point; it is not poor citizens' mere survival that is the polity's responsibility, but their freedom for the polity. And every self-aware polity has appreciated the necessity of "sumptuary" laws.

Continuing to one last set of considerations, we begin by noting that the butcher, the baker, the brewer, and I will not meet for our exchanges in the first place if we have no roads or market hall, nor yet if there are no butchers, bakers, or brewers. The market never did, does not now, and clearly cannot arrange all that must be arranged. The provision of transport, communication, and education — to name the minimum — has traditionally and unavoidably been regarded as a chief function of government; indeed the need for these things may have been government's historical occasion, as, for example, was the need to maintain water-control works and schedules in Mesopotamia and Egypt. The distinction is not between the "private" sector and the "public" sector, since the modification of "economy" by "private" produces an entirely meaningless phrase. The distinction is between decisions made without freedom by calculation and morally free decisions. Given the purpose of government, the maxim is, right economy delivers as many decisions as possible to the moral deliberation of the community.

Of course, we know all that, but in America our mythology makes us work hard to forget it. When bourgeois development and its Enlightenment ideology came to us, they did not, as elsewhere, transform an existing economy, they created one from near nothing. Therefore capitalist slogans, properly hypotheses to be considered, have tended among us to function as myths of the Beginning, sacrosanct and encompassing. And so we regard, for example, communication as a proper sphere of "private enterprise," even, when the myth is especially upon us, "deregulating" the "industry." It must be emphasized that when we turn decision in such fields over to "private enterprises" we do not thereby depoliticize the decisions; rather we politicize the enterprises, turning them into units of the polity — and then, inevitably, entirely tyrannical units, since decision in them will be unfree, controlled by interests unchallenged in debate.

A right economy would be neither a "free" economy nor a "directed" economy, nor yet some judicious mixture. It would be one for which the polity had taken full moral responsibility, using the economy's necessitarian causal structures as instruments in the service of communal freedom. Would that be "socialism"? One hesitates to say so, flinching from the expected charge that socialist economic goals always seem to being tyrannical polities with them. But the socialist states we know have pursued socialism within the mechanistic interpretation of the public, that is, as communities that have, like the capitalist states, antecedently given up on moral freedom. In such cases, it was only to be expected that the attempt to subjugate the economy to the polity would end up in fact working the other way around.

It is a staple of capitalist apologetics that political freedom depends on "economic freedom," meaning by the latter a situation in which the causal structures of the market are not bent to communal moral choice. The proposition reveals capitalism's profound agreement with Marxism: that the economy, in its apparent mechanism, is fundamental to the apparently unmechanical polity. Within the shared Enlightenment position, capitalist apologetics have a point. Where communal moral choice is anyway given up, capitalist attitudes and procedures do tend to leave more room for a certain kind of freedom, the individual's freedom from the community, his or her space to be self-determined. And that is no small advantage. What *neither* Enlightenment position values is true political freedom: free access to the community in *its* moral self-determination.

VI

The vision of a community that interprets itself quite differently than is suggested by any branch of the Enlightenment will, of course, be denounced as utopian. But since this is the vision enabled by hope for Jesus' Kingdom, it is not. For Jesus in fact lives as Lord.

[1986]

Beauty

I

I WILL NOT ASK, What is beauty? At one level, I do not need to ask, because we all know what beauty is; we are perfectly able to judge, "That is beautiful." At another level, of the phenomenological or logical unpacking of what we all know, I cannot ask, because that task is too vast for this paper. Instead of pressing the analytical question anew, I will rely on the great tradition of Western reflection thereon and simply affirm the mainline answer. Thomas Aquinas will serve nicely as spokesman: "Three things are required for beauty. First, integrity. . . . Then proportion or harmony. And finally clarity. . . ."[1] That is beautiful which is a harmonious whole and is lucid in its harmony.

I will rather ask, What realities are beautiful? Where is beauty found? I announce the answer for which I plead: the specifically triune God is beautiful, and whatever he perceives on the pattern of his own self.

---

1. *Summa Theologica*, i, 39, 8.

Published in *dialog* 25 (Fall 1986): 250-254. Reprinted by permission.

II

There is a notorious answer to the question about beauty's location: beauty is in the eye of the beholder. The answer is surely somehow true. Beauty includes "clarity"; the particular harmony in question is not there unless it is perspicuous as such, unless it is there for a subject. As Kant observed, we call that beautiful which without our effort satisfies our need for the order otherwise achieved only by moral action. Beauty is *perceptible* good. The question is, In *whose* eye? For *which* subject?

There are only two candidates: God and I. Perhaps my eye unifies what it sees and calls the unity beautiful, only without the effort being noticed; or perhaps the fit between some objects and my eye is purely serendipitous. Either way, beauty is there where my eye, following its own dictates, puts it. The alternative is that what I find beautiful is beautiful antecedently to my finding, because it is first beautiful in the eye of God, who somehow shares his perception.

Worship and the experience of beauty can therefore, again notoriously, compete. For beauty is thus a value that we attribute alternatively to our own creation or to God's; in the experience of beauty we can interpret our own consciousness as located where, if there is God, he must be. When Kierkegaard made the "aesthetic" mode of existence the pole to the moral and religious modes, he but codified a chief lesson of modern Western history: since the sixteenth century there have been few who have lived at once for beauty and for God.

But Western history has gone on to teach another lesson as well: the experience of beauty does not survive the cessation of worship. Precisely those who thematically dedicate themselves to beauty, and who within the modern Western tradition regularly just so abandon worship, are in wave after wave driven at last to deny beauty as well. The avant-gardes of nineteenth- and twentieth-century art have one upon the other denounced beauty, proclaiming that to be art which anybody calls such. And if the one artist hangs a toilet seat on the gallery wall, only to have it pointed out that he chose a fine example and placed it artfully, the next ideologist will choose a wretched example and bury it underground.

So long as only the accepted movements are noted, the history of late modern art appears as a sequence of nihilisms, of rebellions against art's constitutive purpose. The appearance is illusion, of course. There have been in every field great artists who have continued successfully to labor at beauty. These are persons who have somehow — perhaps only by more profound alienation! — been preserved from dominant ideology. They are not necessarily religious, only not self-substituted for God. Nor are the nihilisms all trashy; some — one thinks of Beckett or Duchamp — are magnificent and profound. It is only that each is a specific dead end. Where now is Andy Warhol but on the talk shows?

This second lesson is simple, even banal. If things are beautiful only in that I see them so and if there are more than one of us, the judgments "This is beautiful" or "That is not" must be experienced as arbitrary. And if they are arbitrary, the word "beauty" is meaningless. The nihilism of artists who find themselves committed to a meaningless pursuit is fully understandable.

III

My eye or ear cannot found *in* the thing it sees the beauty it sees there, cannot ground judgments of beauty that are not arbitrary, because I am only one. God's eye can found in the thing it sees the beauty it sees there because God is one in three. A merely unitary god could perhaps create a world possessed of being and truth; it would not, however, be beautiful. And perhaps with a sufficient access of power and wisdom to make me a god, I too could create an existent and true world, but not a beautiful one. The reasons for this thesis follow.

The perception of beauty is perception of the sort of harmony otherwise created by moral effort, given without such effort. But consciousness is intrinsically self-consciousness; I will take this also as sufficiently argued in the tradition. And a finite self-consciousness cannot but first value itself; even in the gospel, I am called to love my neighbor as I in any case love myself. Thus when I perceive given good in other objects than myself, it is because I perceive in them some image of myself. It is given in the inevitable dialectics of the case: I find *myself* beautiful, and what is like me.

But what sort of harmony can *I* have? Jonathan Edwards made the decisive observation: "One alone cannot be excellent" (his word for beauty), because in it there is no plurality to be in harmony. Thus, he argued, only a triune being can be beautiful in itself.[2] To be sure, centuries of Western self-knowledge, guided mostly by the faith's trinitarian interpretation of God, have revealed that I too am inwardly complex; Augustine's analogies of, for example, memory, knowledge, and love to Father, Son, and Spirit truly obtain. I can and do confront myself; thus I can and do perceive myself as given good, as beautiful, and so perceive what is like me in the same way. Were it otherwise, the perception of beauty could not at all occur for me.

Nevertheless, the self I perceive as *my*self always remains an evanescent and unreliable other. For my confrontation with myself can always be fudged; apart from the intervention of lover, confessor, friend, or therapist, my self can always be made to reply as I wish or fear. Therefore the harmony I have with this unreliable other, my self, is also unreliable, now of one sort and now of another. Should my judgments of beauty be in fact constant, this will only suggest inflexibility, an increase of arbitrariness.

I have, to be sure, just mentioned the intervention of other consciousness than I, and the reliability they can give my self as an other for me. Fixed by the address of my spouse, my self can indeed sometimes truly confront me. Here there is a clue to part of the truth: the role of community in the objectivity of beauty. But my eye, after all, remains one and my spouse's another; our interaction is in itself but a mutual impingement of arbitrary instances. And therefore the historical observation that communities agree on what they judge beautiful only increases the suspicion of arbitrariness.

According to the doctrine of Trinity, Jesus is the one as whom God confronts himself. The Augustinian point, that in the dialectics of the eternal consciousness the Father is the "I" and Jesus the "myself," fits what we see in the biblical narrative. But the confrontation between this subject and his self is a true confrontation; in the narrative, Jesus petitions and even cries out against the Father. The object as whom *this* subject, the Father, perceives himself is a genuine other, reliably a partner. Therefore, as the plurality of Father and Son in God is reliable, so their harmony is reliable: in all its creative liveliness always *their* harmony. As the triune God values himself, he is drawn to a harmony not produced by moral action and in no way evanescent, a truly given

2. Edwards, *Miscellanies*, unpublished, 117.

and objective beauty. And so finally, when and if God contemplates other things than himself and construes in them likenesses to his own harmony, the construal follows a more-than-arbitrary standard. Which is what was to be argued.

IV

The triune God is beautiful. He perceives himself so, and in so perceiving registers a fact. And if the Father and the Son are the harmonious many, the Spirit is their harmony: the Spirit is God as Beauty.

Beauty is in the eye of the beholder, yet vanishes if it is not just so an assertive character of the thing perceived. Vice versa, beauty is an objective harmony of things, which yet is not given if it is not given for a subject. On this polarity of what is and what is perceived to be, Western reflection has foundered ever and again. Which is to say that Western reflection has foundered ever and again on God, who is God because what he is and what he perceives himself to be are neither confused nor separated.

In Scripture, "spirit" is personal life, subjectivity as it does not merely apprehend objects but in apprehending intrudes upon and determines what it perceives. We all know this reality of life in ourselves, we know what it is to be "lively"; but we also know that life fails in us. In that there is God there is one Life that does not fail. God has a Spirit and so "*is* spirit." He intrudes on himself, to know himself precisely by determining himself. It is not true of us, that we "are our own project" (Jean-Paul Sartre); but it is true of God. Thus in the triune Life, the Spirit spans precisely the polarity of beauty.

Finally in this section, we can now say what sort of beauty God has. Throughout Scripture, the harmonized plurality in God is a *historical* plurality and harmony; it is — as I have been tacitly supposing — indeed a story that can be told, of Jesus and his Father. If we take that with full seriousness — and if we do not, we will not anyway think of God as triune — we will perceive God's harmony as displayed first across time and only therein across space. Therefore God's harmony is first that of discourse rather than of vision; Jesus is first the Father's *word* and only so his image; the divine life is first a conversation and only so a cosmos. God's beauty is that denoted by the original sense of "poetic": it is the beauty comprised in drama, rhetoric, music, and dance. God is a fugued song. I must at this point switch from the platitudinous "eye of the beholder" to the ontologically accurate "ear of the listener."

Such speculations do not establish a ranking of human arts, with music or poetry then at the top; the analogy between God and creatures does not work that way in Christianity. But they do perhaps offer some understanding of the *differences* among the arts, especially of the different ways they intersect with worship. It is surely no accident that Christian liturgy is drama and can hardly survive without music, while the icons are always controversial. I owe much of these last two paragraphs' insight — if insight it is — to Edwards again: "When I would form . . . an idea of a society [including the triune society!] in the highest degree happy, I think of them . . . sweetly singing to each other."[3]

V

Therefore, to perceive beauty otherwise than arbitrarily, and so otherwise than self-defeatingly, we must be given to share God's perception of things. Scripture speaks of God "giving" his Spirit, and theology has often suspected that it is by this gift that the reality of beauty must be understood. But for those who live as little in Scripture as we do, the idea of "giving" can be misleading, as if the Spirit could be detached from God's life and handed over. The Spirit God gives is the harmony of his life; that is, what God can give is *inclusion in* his own life. For the triune God, to create is to open in his lively eternity a space, called "time," for unnecessary but welcomed further participants therein. Whose story is told in Scripture? God's or ours? Plainly the answer is, God's enveloping ours.

God takes us into his conversation by, tautologously, addressing us. He speaks his law and gospel, and we respond by praise and petition. So there is established an expanded eternal community that is beautiful with God's own harmony. What its members speak about and by means of cannot be themselves only; a community needs a world in and through

3. Edwards, *Miscellanies*, 188.

which to come together. So galaxies and amoebae exist also in God and are harmonized in his community's life.

Thus it is that the Spirit appears at both of created beauty's poles. It is by the Spirit that we hear and see things in their beauty, and by the Spirit that things are beautiful for our ears and eyes.

At the one pole, the Spirit appears in Scripture as the Spirit of the prophets' word: as the liveliness with which God's word intrudes on the prophet and as the liveliness with which the prophets' word then intrudes on events, not returning until it has done what it says. Since God creates his community by calling it forth, by speaking, it is in the nature of the case that the New Testament, when God's call has sounded fully, discerns this Spirit of God's word as the Spirit of the community. Every community, quite commonsensically and unmysteriously, has a common spirit; the mystery of God's community is that its shared spirit is none other than the Spirit of God and his Word.

The addresses of others, I noted, give my self solidity, so that when I then love others as myself I do not love at random. But others' addresses to me may be themselves discordant. In a true community, possessed of a common spirit, the community's intrusion on my self-perception is not discordant; by the self established in a true community I can perceive beauty faithfully. But there may be competing and discordant communities, so that even each community's shared perception of beauty must still be arbitrary; only in the *universal* community of a universal spirit, it seems, could the perception and judgment of beauty transcend arbitrariness. God's community has indeed a common spirit, and that spirit, as God's, can be broken by no discord. And God's community is indeed universal.

There is a final point on this line, which is foundational. In the community that by its mutually spirited discourse establishes for me a reliable self, and whose mutual Spirit is the triune God's own, I do not perceive myself except as I perceive God's self, Jesus the Christ. In the community whose discourse is the prophetic word of God, the self by whose lineaments I trace beauty in other objects is the same self by which God antecedently traces beauty in those objects and thus creates it there.

At the other pole of the aesthetic relation, the Spirit appears in Scripture as Creator Spirit, and with special reference to creation's beauty. "By his power he stilled the sea; by his understanding he smote

Rahab. By his spirit the heavens were made fair" (Job 26:12-13). This line of biblical testimony has beckoned throughout theological history, both as opportunity and as temptation. Perhaps I may here simply assert that part of my own reflection that is most immediately relevant.

It is regularly forgotten, even suppressed, that creation is, like all acts of God *"ad extra,"* an act not of one trinitarian identity but of the Trinity, in which act each identity participates according to its inner-triune role. Thus in creating, the Father commands, "Let there be. . . ." The Son, who is this commanding word insofar as the Father hears therein his own self and intention, gives himself to be the meaning of the creature, lets the creature be intended for God himself. And the Spirit, as the intrusive liveliness of this exchange, intrudes also on the creature that is now an item in the exchange, so that the creature is not merely in fact and statically intended for God, but temporally *lives* for God. Facet here of these divine complications: the creature, merely in that it exists in time, is opened in the Spirit to be construed in the pattern of God's self, to be beautiful for God and for whatever other subjects God may admit to his Conversation.

VI

The previous section glosses over a problem that readers will have noted: it speaks as if all God's human creatures were believers, who hear the word and are gifted with the Spirit. This is false — yet surely also unbelievers see creation's beauty? Often more readily than do the faithful? A sequence of insights flows from this objection, to each of which I will here merely refer, to suggest matters of other reflection and to end this essay.

That God's believers and his human creatures are not the same group is the fallenness of the race. That the world and the church shall coincide is the final hope. In the meantime, the community of those who do not yet believe — not necessarily each who belongs to it — does indeed have an historically fragile grasp of beauty; that the grasp is at this juncture of Western history actually palsied was an initiating observation of this paper.

But there is also a positive implication of the universality of beauty's apprehension: somehow, all must be hearing God's word and be enlivened by his Spirit, also those who do not believe. Lutherans will interpret: if some do not now hear God's word as "gospel," they hear it nonetheless as "law." Other confessions propose other ways in which God's word is universally heard; whether there are then specifically Catholic, Lutheran, Reformed, and sectarian aesthetics would be worth investigation.

The division between church and world draws attention, on the other side, to the specific internal life of the church: to the praise and petition by which God's community speaks up in the triune conversation. The liturgy is the church's specific art form. Let me in this connection draw only one conclusion from this essay's positions: the reality of the Spirit in worship, the spiritedness of the church's praise and petition, is not another thing than the beauty of the church's worship. Labor on the liturgy's beauty is not accidental to labor on its authenticity, and what may be called liturgical aesthetics is a vital part of the doctrine of the Spirit.

Finally, I must acknowledge an earlier problem: Was Kierkegaard right? Can one not adore both God and beauty? Plainly one can if the beauty adored is God's own. And at the End worship and art will be one. In the meantime, however, there is indeed a problem, acute in our time. The Lutheran distinction of law from gospel again suggests a particular solution: we can serve both beauty and God when beauty is clearly perceived as that of God *or* that of the creature. Located within the triune life, we suffer no hindrance to hearing that distinction.

The Church and Mass Electronic Media: The Hermeneutic Problem

For a National Council of Churches of Christ in America Study
of "Theology, Education and the Electronic Media"

I

AMONG THE MANY QUESTIONS discussued by the study commission on "Theology, Education and the Electronic Media," this paper addresses one only: Of what characteristics of the modern electronic media should the church be most aware, in using these media for its own purposes? The question is stated in the mode of suspicion because of a history of self-betrayal in the church's use of modern media. Considerations adduced in dealing with this question will, to be sure, bear also on other issues studied by the commission, such as, How should the church judge the existing media, as currently decisive components of society? What reforms should the church advocate? But these questions are not directly addressed in this paper.

Central to all problems in the church's use of any medium of com-

Reprinted from the journal, *Religious Education,* Volume 82, Number 2, by permission from the publisher, The Religious Education Association, 409 Prospect Street, New Haven, CT 06511-2177. Membership information available upon request.

munication is the hermeneutic question: How particularly does this medium *work* within the unitary enterprise of human communication? Thus, for example, the perennial argument about the Bible's exact role in the church's life is in large part concerned with the role that a *written* document can play in the living communication of the gospel. The medium is never the message, but assuredly each medium specifically enables and constricts the message.

We must indeed inquire: Of the things the church is to say within itself and to the world, which can be said by contemporary electronic media? It has been argued that the church cannot faithfully speak by them at all, that the church's message is not one that can make any part of its way through such structures. Experience teaches that this cannot quite be the case, but something so close to it seems to be true as to mandate great discrimination in churchly use of electronic media.

There are two quite different inquiries we must pursue to understand the electronic media. First, we must understand the electronic "media" as existing social institutions. They have not been produced simply by the existence of electronic technology; they exist by political choice. Our one question therefore is, How do the existing institutions work within the total enterprise of society's communicating? And how, if at all, can they fit in the life and mission of the church?

Second, we must understand the electronic media simply as a new — by the church's timescale — technology of mediation. Then our other question is: How does electronic mediation work within the congeries of means by which we meet one another? And how then can this medium appropriately function in the church's life?

II

The *political* structure of the media in question is aptly denoted by the usual label, "mass." The existing television and radio networks — like large-scale print journalism — are all precisely "broadcast" systems. The lines of communication run out from a common center to termini along the radii; and these radii of communication line their hearers or see-ers or readers up alongside each other, facing a common center but with no intrinsic contact with each other. If there is cross-talk, it is extraneous to the grouping established by the medium. Therefore the mass media cannot create or foster a community. What they create and foster is precisely a mass: a collection of persons who have a common focus, who are located at points along the radii of a circle and face toward the center of that circle, but who contact each other, if at all, only by way of that focus.

To the gospel, however, cross-talk is vital. The gospel does not first create individual believers, whom the Holy Spirit then perhaps gathers into a community. In the New Testament, the gospel is precisely the means by which the Holy Spirit gathers a specific community; to hear the gospel and to have sisters and brothers is exactly the same act. Therefore in a situation where I am structurally isolated from my sisters and brothers, I simply cannot hear the gospel at all.

There is empirical confirmation of this. The airways are saturated with Christian religion, which in fact does not greatly resemble the New Testament message. What the existing media do to the gospel, when we try to proclaim it over them, is to transform it instantly into Protestant Christianity's false teachings: moralism and sentimentality. For the mass media intrinsically make a mass, a collection of individuals; and a collection of individuals cannot be auditors of the Christian gospel.

We must repeat that there is nothing inherent in any technology that compels all this. The telephone company and the broadcast networks use the same technology; but the telephone company creates a network in which unlimited cross-talk is in principle possible. We could set up a conference call between every phone in the United States and have a national town meeting, if somebody would control who speaks next. Thus the telephone company creates an entirely different communication structure than does broadcasting. That the technology is in fact used to create broadcast structures is a political choice. We could nationalize the phone company and make conversation among the American people free. It would be expensive; but that therefore we do not do it is a political choice, not a technological choice.

When a congregation broadcasts its services as a way of allowing shut-ins and absent members of the congregation to listen or see, and when this is done in the context of close pastoral and fraternal care, then of course the cross-talk that creates community is there. Then the broadcast does not itself carry the burden of integrating its hearers into the congregation. Then the medium, whatever its technology, is not in fact used as a *mass* medium; the medium is internal to the congregation. There is thus no problem about a denomination or a congregation co-opting available technology for internal use. The problems arise when the technology is used in its presently institutionalized character as the creator of a mass audience.

This must be grasped clearly: the existing institutionalization of electronic mediation is, for the church, the enemy. By their need and power to replace human communities by a human mass, these media contradict the church's message. As the church necessarily deals with and uses them nevertheless, it must above all, therefore, move *warily.* Indeed, insofar as the church derives from the gospel a general vision of possible human community, it must be the church's responsibility to that community to combat the media's disintegrative effects upon it, and with other forces in the community to seek and create communal institutionalizations of electronic communication — but this is to the side of our present thesis.

III

The electronic media have a specific *technological* structure. Their defining character is that they involve a translation from one means of transcending space to another: from sound waves to electromagnetic waves, or from one part of the electromagnetic spectrum to another. The possibility of such translation depends upon the reduction of communication to *information.* This may be seen from the circumstance that very shortly what passes over the lines or through the field will all be "digital," that is, answers to yes-or-no questions. The problem is, is there more to communication than information, so that something must be lost in the current means of translation?

At least one component of communication cannot be reduced to information: whatever is communicated by touch. While touch can of course be used to transfer information, it has a separate communicative function. The reason touch itself cannot be broadcast, or even shared through a network, is that there is involved in touch no *space* for a medium to occupy. Electromagnetic transmission is involved in touch; but this occurs not between us but inside each of us. Technology that overcame this barrier, to enable transmission of touch across space, would literally invade us; it would instantly create a totally unfree world — but we will leave this apocalyptic possibility out of our consideration.

What does touch itself communicate? We suggest: what touch communicates is availability, indeed vulnerability. Touch communicates the sheer *fact* of embodiment. The touching body of course is also seen — and heard and tasted and smelled — and for some theological purposes this is the decisive point. But the test of whether what I see — or hear or taste or smell — is in fact your body, is whether I can touch you. My body is your object in many ways, some of which are indeed electronically transmissable. But that what is mediated is truly my body is communicated only by touch, or by the otherwise perceived possibility of touch in situations where there is no prima facie reason to suspect illusion.

What I have to say to you I can say without touch or the possibility thereof. But communication has an additional aspect. When I address you, I merely thereby make you my object: I reckon with you, try to work my will on you, intend you. If the goal of my address is your subjugation, I will seek to withhold myself from becoming by my address your object in turn. Conversely, insofar as my address does *not* subjugate you, it is because in it I do become your object in my turn — available to you, the target of your intention, the material of your intelligence and will.

The presence of the body of the one who speaks — that she is *seen* or *acoustically* heard or smelled or tasted — is the condition of freedom in communication, in that it is the availability, the vulnerability of the one who speaks. This can happen without touching or even the perceived possibility thereof. But *that* it happens is communicated by touch only. In any free communication I am in fact available and vulnerable to you; but *that* I am available is itself communicated by touch exclusively.

Full human communication, therefore, in or out of church, requires touch; or at least it requires that the embodiment of those who address each other be verifiable by touch, if it is questioned. For it is as bodies that we are available to one another, and when that availability fails on either side or even becomes doubtful, how is the partner to remain free in the discourse? But when we speak the "gospel" to one another, when we claim to speak *God's* word, embodiment and so touch becomes a matter of life and death.

Not only does God, in speaking to us, make himself available and vulnerable to us, but it is an essential part of the gospel itself to say that he does so. Consider for instance, the Supper. Always there have been two questions. How *can* Christ be "bodily" present in our gathering? And what sort of God would let his body be pushed around on the altar, divided between the communicants? It is decisive for the meaning of the Supper that these are the *same* question. Not only does God embody himself in his address to us, but that he does so belongs to the content of what he says about himself in this address. The specific communication of the Supper is precisely this "that."

Not even, therefore, as a democratic network could electronic media constitute the whole community of a Christian group. There is no reason, however, why an electronic democratic network could not make an important *part* of a congregation's communication, so long as touch is otherwise provided for. There is no reason, for our same example, why those who cannot attend the Supper should not, the elements being brought them promptly by the deacons, share more fully in the congregation's celebration by means of such a network.

IV

By virtue, therefore, of both their political and their technological structure, modern mass media cannot mediate that message that the church calls "the gospel," for community and vulnerability are essential to the communication-situation called "speaking the gospel." What then *can* the church do by the media? We have already noted how they can be bent to the uses of the church's interior life. But can they carry some part of the church's address to the world? Only if the church is very clear about what they cannot do, and steadfastly refrains from perverting the gospel in an attempt to make them carry *it.* That self-discipline established, we see the following legitimate churchly mass communication.

One thing that will go over the media, as the gospel will not, is *theology.* Theology is *about* what we must say to be saying the gospel; it is a second-order activity over against the actual speaking of the gospel. Therefore, theology can go where gospel itself will not — as of course vice versa. We may understand it so: the gospel must be proclaimed, whereas theology is *taught,* and teaching is the great possibility of the broadcast media — though also here there are pitfalls.

One thing we can do over the mass media is thus to educate about the faith. And here the possible internal and external uses of the media merge; we can, perhaps without too much distinction, use them to educate both our own scattered flock and the world out there, insofar as the world has any curiosity about the phenomenon called Christianity.

There is a second thing the church can do over the mass media: we can present not the gospel but ourselves as the people of the gospel, for better or worse. We can use the media as permission for the world to spy on us — much as the windows which St. Peter's Church opens onto Lexington Avenue in Manhattan draw a constant group of liturgy observers, some of whom later come in to participate. We can use the media to make the world aware that we exist. What is to come of this peeking is perhaps not to be specified by us; we may leave it to the Spirit to make of it what it will from time to time and person to person.

By mass electronic media, we cannot speak the church's primary message, both because the media are mass and because they are electronic. But we can teach theology and we can invite the world's observation. That is very much, and is surely enough to keep us busy.

On the Renewing of the Mind:
Reflections on the Calling of
Christian Intellectuals

I

DURING THE TIME set aside to compose this essay, I confirmed Allan
Bloom's suspicions about my intellect by following the crowd and
reading his book. Especially in the middle section it is a much better
book than I expected.

The Closing of the American Mind is a meditation on the state of
American intellect, over against two landmark and remarkably paired
diagnoses of Western history. The one is Nietzsche's: that the outcome
of philosophy, of the West's multimillennial effort to be reasonable
at all costs, is the discovery that there is no reason to be reasonable
— and indeed that there is no reason to be anything else that we are
not already. If history is not to halt in bourgeois self-satisfaction, we
will therefore have to tap irrational passion and arbitrary decision
precisely to move us to reason. The other is de Tocqueville's suspicion

Published in *The Cresset* VI, no. 4 (February 1988): 10-16. Reprinted by permission.

that the regime founded on reason, the democratic republic, must prove inhospitable to the actual exercise of the reason on which it is founded.

Professor Bloom judges that de Tocqueville's fears have been fulfilled. The nation built on Enlightenment has not merely become ignorant and unthinking, or even anti-intellectual in Richard Hofstadter's sense, but is becoming incapable of thought. I have to say I agree, and that such diagnoses do not seem to me prejudiced by sentiment for good old days. Bloom argues also that Nietzschean profundity, imported into the Lockean nation, has with appalling irony come to provide the justifying ideology of our superficiality. The derivations he traces in this connection have been much controverted among the symposiasts and reviewers, but I cannot turn aside to that discussion.

Now — if de Tocqueville is as right as Bloom thinks, that would seem to be a historical confirmation of Nietzsche's position. Vice versa, if Nietzsche is right, then de Tocqueville's prediction was not a warning but a prophecy. And both of these are, I think, what Bloom in fact believes — which would seem to leave Nietzsche as the only true guide. Yet what may come of acting on Nietzsche's kerygma has already been tested in Europe, and none of us will favor further experiments on those lines. In this interesting situation, Bloom can suggest only a last-ditch defense of the liberal regime, for however long this proves possible. Huddling around the embers is his image.

The place of defense or huddling is to be, despite everything, the "university," a term that he so uses as to encompass many institutions not officially so denominated; indeed it is first of all the colleges of liberal arts, in or out of "universities," that he has in mind. The university must again become the place where reason can be advocated against the hostility of reason's regime. It must be the haven, for the sake of democracy, of dissatisfaction with democracy, the place where all those questions are asked that democratic folk need to hear but that are natural only to aristocratic and monarchic regimes. It must administer Nietzsche straight, to awake us from the sleep induced by Nietzsche diluted.

It may reasonably (!) be doubted that academia can perform the Münchhausen trick that Bloom proposes for it. How exactly are we to persuade a society as hostile to reason as Bloom says ours is to license a privileged class whose sole function is to be rational? And how are the deep thinkers to be studied seriously when it is known that they are being used as calculated medicines for the health of the regime they abominate?

It is the insight of the whole line from Rousseau to Nietzsche that reason undoes itself because it undoes God, without whom reason — as every other interesting virtue — is groundless. And Bloom hammers this point home. But with respect to it he has no proposal. The university is to be democracy's temple, but it is to house no God. *The Closing of the American Mind* ends very much as did another recently influential book, Alasdair MacIntyre's *After Virtue*. MacIntyre ended by saying that what our civilization must have to survive is something like the Benedictine order. Many who read this wondered how there could be Benedictines without St. Benedict, or a saint without God. MacIntyre appears to have read his own book and wondered the same things, whereupon he reconverted to the faith.

II

In one part of Bloom's book the scholarship is demonstrably slipshod: his account of the university's origin. Most certainly, even the "modern" university was not created from nothing by the decision of Enlighteners to extend Aristotle's educational program to the many, in the unlikely case that there ever was such a decision. Bloom seems to have stopped reading with Aristotle, not to have started again until Machiavelli, and to have hypothesized what happened between from thin air.

The Enlightenment may have conceived the university as the place of "reason." But in its medieval origins and in some strands of its self-understanding to this day, the university is not a *universitas rationis*, a world of *reason*, but a world of *letters*, a *universitas litterarum*, the gathering into one place and one discourse of all those arts whose substance is *books* and *argument*. In the university's founding period, instruction was thus accomplished by the minute examination of texts and by the institution of debates; and anyone who has examined the record of one of those debates or read a medieval commentary on Aristotle will not suppose that this method was in any way inferior to the methods inaugurated in the eighteenth and nineteenth centuries as to openness, dedication to logic, or pedagogical impact. The university may properly and faithfully be conceived, alternatively to liberalism's conception, as the place of discourse, of the *word*.

Reason as the Enlightenment understood it is a sheer capacity and as such an individual endowment. The Enlightenment proposed to establish a regime by harnessing the elemental passions to reason, by turning them into *rights;* also passions and rights are private possessions. Thus if reason and rights are our foundation, we are bound to individualism; then our choice is indeed between clinging to Locke and capitulating to Nietzsche.

And in that case, bowdlerized Nietzsche will surely win in the end, nor is it easy to see how a university founded on reason and rights can do anything but exacerbate the problem. Foundationally, however, the university was not the place of reason but the place of discourse; and the *word* is no one's private endowment. It is the ontological status of community and of the word in which community is constituted that was forgotten by the Enlightenment — and has not been remembered by Professor Bloom.

For some generations, topics such as this have been discussed on the assumption that we know what an "intellectual" is — or "the liberal arts" or "the university" or whatever — and have only to consider how Christians can be called to this field. I have begun with Bloom in order to summon witness for the bankruptcy of this assumption. I doubt that the traditional way of putting the question was ever appropriate; it is anyway now antique. If there ever was a separately definable "intellectual" office or community or fate out there, to which believers might be called, there is none now. If we have a calling, it is not to join a predefined intellectual enterprise but to reinvent one. And there is nothing preposterous about the notion, since we invented the West's intellectual enterprise in the first place. For of course, that the *word* has ontological status — so that the arts of the word might together make a universe — is an insight from the Bible.

III

Mediterranean antiquity's specific ideal of knowledge would never by itself have made the university. The organ of truth, in the classic tradition, is the "mind's eye"; knowledge is *theoria, seeing.* Every self-interpretation of the knowing subject takes one of the senses as its metaphor; Western antiquity's metaphor was sight. And the thing about sight is, it objectifies the other.

It is a point I have found illuminating in many contexts: we have flaps on our eyes and none on our ears, and we can easily aim our eyes and only with great difficulty aim our ears. Which is to say: I control what I see but can always be surprised by what I hear. It is with the eye that I fix the other in space and time, that I nail down what you/it are/is, so as to be able to get back to you/it. It is, oppositely, by the ear that you grab me, also when I am trying to overlook (!) you. An ideal of knowledge that takes sight for its metaphor makes the other the object of knowledge but does not solicit reciprocity, does not offer the knowing subject to be the object of the other.

That is, to knowledge for which sight is the metaphor, the response or solicitation of the other is not *constitutive*. In the final versions of Greek reflection, which became the theology of all late antiquity's cults, this ideal of knowledge is paradigmatically and foundationally instantiated in Aristotle's Unmoved Mover under various aliases. This God is a sheer act of vision, wholly agent and not at all sufferer, receiving and expecting nothing from what is seen — if, indeed, it is acknowledged that anything other than itself comes within its purview. The philosopher king, reentering the cave for the good of its inhabitants, asks them no question.

There was originally a countervailing factor: the actual *practice* of philosophy. Whether Parmenides or Heraclitus indulged in other discourse than description of what they had seen we do not know, but for the sophists and Socrates and Plato, who were not coming *from* vision but trying to be on their *to* it, conversation was the daily work. It was the Socratic conviction that the way to vision is by question and answer, and that real questions have to be actually asked, which rescued Greek *theoria* from the inhumanity that was always its temptation.

Thus it was philosophy as *practice* in which the gospel, when it appeared on the scene of antiquity, found both a rival and an ally. The gospel is a message, and its reflection therefore an argument; the first Christian theologians were simply journeymen philosophers who had found new matter. The difference between Christian theology and pagan antiquity's theology is that the latter, for all that it consists in talk, *leads* to silence, is the handmaiden of cognition as pure seeing, while

Christianity's talk leads precisely to more talk, to the purification and enlivening of a message. And also the gospel's ideal of knowledge is instantiated, in the God who *is* his own word.

Pagan antiquity had many and very talkative circles of seekers. But what they sought was silence. A "university," per contra, is a *universitas litterarum,* an independent world founded on and for discourse, a world in which discourse is its own justification, which some enter never to leave, and which initiates also those who are to leave into precisely the talkative callings. The university was founded by believers, to have a place in which to exegete their Book and argue interpretations of their message. Just so, no book and no argument could be foreign to it. In particular, the practice of ancient philosophy and the books that documented it were simply adopted, now in service of speech rather than of silence.

When the Enlightenment revolted against theology in the name of reason, it thus revolted also against philosophy as anciently practiced, since it was theology by which that practice was now carried on. Thus in the Enlightenment's understanding and practice of "reason," the countervailing factor is gone. Reason becomes what even Aristotle did not make it: sheerly the individual's ability to see truth. And for that, the university is, when push comes to shove, not really needed at all. It is that last point that Professor Bloom's book — to make one last reference to it — finally lays before us, willy-nilly.

IV

Christians' calling to intellect is the calling to nurture the word, to tend books and foster argument. This was always the case, but in our present circumstances we must be unwontedly clear about it. We serve a talkative God, who does not even seem to be able to do without a library. In his service, we will be concerned for talk and libraries. And some of us will have the privilege of spending a lot of time at that concern; if anyone wishes to call these "Christian intellectuals," there is no great reason to interdict the label.

The model and origin of our care of books is the church's care of that library called the Bible. I understand that this is backward to the usual conceptions, but the usual conceptions, if they were ever appropriate, are anyway now mere anachronisms. So I will reverse the usual conception, and inquire first what the church does with the Bible and second what the university might therefore do with its books.

The church, first, reads the Bible *liturgically.* The writings that are canon for the church and that together we call the Bible are recited in the gathered community, to shape its imagination, suggest its argumentative warrants, cast its moral vision. The university, the community of Western intellect, also has a canon of writings. It is not quite so clearly marked as the canon of Scripture — though the contrast must not be overplayed, since also the canon of Scripture is intrinsically open — but it will serve; at least its center is indicable. In a living university, the sheer shared *experience* — never mind *interpretation* or *understanding!* — of such as Plato and Augustine and Newton would be the foundation of everything else. That experience is now indeed embers, but the embers need blowers, not huddlers. Christians are the only ones around who have clear and arguable and imperative reason to blow on them.

Second, the church *researches* the Bible, it labors on its book with the kind of reading that is misleadingly called "historical-critical method" as if with old texts there were some other. We persistently ask, What did the author *say?* What really *happened?* These are life-and-death questions for the believer. The first need not commit the famous "intentional fallacy"; we cannot ask what the author intended to say, but we must ask what she/he in fact got — past tense! — said. Neither is the second question hopeless of answer, nor does it lead us necessarily into historical relativism, though there is no opportunity here to retrace theology's long and in my judgment hopeful struggle with "hermeneutics."

Christianity did not invent such reading, but only for Christianity does salvation ride on it. Thus the techniques that we all assume and that created the nineteenth-century German university, still more or less our model, were all invented to deal with the Bible — if in many cases only to get clear of it. In a living university, a certain historicism would always infuse the various undertakings; not even natural science would regard its own history and great texts as beside its enterprise. A world that forgot historical-critical reading would be one in which the church could not live; our calling here is imperative.

Finally, the church looks to the Bible for *paradigms* of its reflection, of "theology." The church is to preach the gospel and all its thinking is about what to say to be doing that. But "the gospel" is simply a label for what the apostles said. So while the apostles' theology, that is, the thinking they did to form their message, may not have been and for the most part was not very *good* theology, we can at least be sure it *was* theology. The theological authority of Scripture is fundamentally methodological: we look to it to see what the reflective labor was like that we are now to undertake.

When the university has been healthy, it has looked to its books in much the same way. In the high medieval period, reverence for Aristotle did *not* mean unwillingness to disagree with him; it meant that he was the master of analysis, to whom those who sought to analyze should be apprenticed. In the eighteenth century, the authority of Newton and Locke did not mean there was no more to be discovered; it meant precisely that if one did as they did one might discover as much as or more than they did. The fundamental collapse of the university in our time is that it does not know what specifically it is to do, and it does not know what it is to do because the triumph of Enlightenment reason deprives the university of its drillmasters, including the Enlighteners. Here, too, Christians may have a word of quite specific comfort: do not be afraid to look to Western intellect's masters and see what they did.

So much — in this essay — for the Book and books. Discourse does not consist in books, it consists in argument using books. Christians' calling to nurture argument can be very bluntly and so quickly stated. Since the message we have for the world contradicts everything the world could possibly suppose, argument is guaranteed whenever we show up — unless we have forgotten ourselves. It is not Nietzsche who will effectively challenge our current discursive sloth, or rather, it is Nietzsche precisely in that the challenge he made was a version — an unbelieving and despairing, but nonetheless faithful version — of the Christian challenge. Proclamation of the meaninglessness of the world will not now startle anyone — if it really ever did; the claim that a first-century Palestinian is the meaning of things is another matter.

I do not mean that direct proclamation of the gospel is our calling to the intellect — though a bit more of that could hardly hurt. But those involved in the gospel's general argument with the world will necessarily fall afoul also of whatever are the self-evidences of their special "disciplines." I have arrived at my next and last main matter.

V

The title of this essay is "The Renewing of the Mind." The title is intended in a double sense. In the one sense, it refers to our calling to re-establish the intellectual enterprise, as I have just been discussing that calling. The other sense depends more directly on the passage from Paul's letter to Rome from which my title is a citation. "Do not be conformed to this world but be transformed by the renewal of your minds" (Romans 12:2). The passage's location is significant: Romans 12:1-3 is Paul's capsule description of Christian existence, a thesis set at the beginning of the whole parenetic section of his most reflective writing.

The word translated "mind" is that same big word of antique reflection, *"nous."* A survey of its appearances in Paul's writings quickly makes his use apparent. Paul's *"nous"* is not *theoria;* rather, it is much the same as Kant's "judgment" or Jonathan Edwards's "sense of the heart." *"Nous"* is moral choice that is not mere — that is, arbitrary — choice but is precisely as moral choice the discernment of what is really out there. To use Edwards's favorite example, borrowed by him from a long tradition: if I "like" honey, that is my choice, and yet my taste for honey registers reality, for honey does in fact taste good.

It is characteristic of the modern West to suppose that knowledge of facts and choice of goods are two separate acts, so that knowledge is morally irrelevant and choice of the good arbitrary; when I first began to teach philosophy, I regarded this as a dogma beyond challenge. But of course the whole previous tradition supposed that the two must be somehow united, that somewhere in the structure of personhood there must be a grasp on reality that is inseparably knowledge of fact and choice of good, that is precisely taste for what is good. Such was Paul's *"nous."*

But if there is such a thing as judgment, it must guide all intellectual activity, since it is their unity. Vice versa, the dogma that there cannot be any such thing as judgment is the foundation dogma of the intellectual tradition that is dying around us. Christians' calling to renew argument is a guaranteed success if only we are faithful. For we must invariably dissent from the founding dogma of the — barely — existing intellectual world.

Paul's summary of the Christian life is that it consists in the "renewing" *(anakainosis)* of judgment. Paul does not ask how judgment is possible in the first place, not being much of a philosopher. But what he thinks does appear. The transformed judgment has as its object *"to agathon kai euareston kai teleion,"* which are epexegetical upon "the will of God." And indeed and of course the reality of God is the necessary condition of an act of mind that as choice of the good is also knowledge of the fact. That I choose "such-and-such is good" is in itself a fact only about me; that the Creator chooses so is a fact about the facts. Within an intellectual enterprise that either denies God or relegates him to the fringes, judgment is indeed not possible.

Christians' calling to renew judgment — and just so, under the circumstances, to renew argument — will require us to speak of God, right out loud. In our time we are called to renew the "apologetic" enterprise, not so much to enable converts as to tell why judgment is after all possible, since there is God.

Continuing with exegesis of Paul: renewal of mind takes place as a transformation, of which only the *terminus a quo* is explicitly named in our text. We are to wean our judgment, our taste, from conformity to "this world" *(tw aioni toutw).* Paul does not need to name the *terminus ad quem;* it is the Kingdom of God, the "world to come." A "world," an *aion,* is a temporal whole, not so much one big thing as one big history — one narrative, to use the currently fashionable word. Each temporal whole has a *schema,* a pattern of how things go in it, the lines of which our judgment can bend to, or not. Since an *aion* is a *temporal* whole, its schema is determined by what it seeks. In Paul's understanding, what this *aion* seeks is hate, the perfected encapsulation of each thing in what it already is. But there is to be a miracle; what will in fact come of this age is a new one. And what that age will seek is love, the perfected opening of each thing to the future the other is for it.

We do not live in the coming age. But we can already bend our judgment to its temporal contours, since in the resurrection we see what the scheme of that age will be. At least Paul says we can, and that this bending is the whole substance of Christian life. Besides supposing that judgment is possible and that it is the mind's controlling unity, Christians suppose that we rightly judge when we judge each item and sector of reality by how it opens to the love that is to come of it.

Only when — believers will say — we consider how, for example, the polity will finally undergo revolution into mutuality can we claim to know it. Alasdair MacIntyre has pointed out the peculiarity that the social sciences have found no "laws" in the proper sense at all, yet are not discredited thereby. He suggests there can be only one explanation: the predictions made by these disciplines are not of that sort at all, they are not of the sort that can be falsified by one contrary event. Of what sort are they then? Readers of the Bible can hardly refrain from suggesting: perhaps they are prophecies, to be verified or falsified conclusively only by the character of the Kingdom when it comes. A renewal of argument where such opinions turn up would seem assured.

For another and historical example, Jonathan Edwards, a far more careful reader of Newton than all his contemporary vulgar Enlighteners put together, proposed that the physical world is the intersubjectivity of universal personal communion between God and created persons and between the latter, that the physical world is what God thinks in order to think a community that can include others than himself. Edwards argued that such an interpretation sticks closer to the actual features of Newtonian science than does interpretation by the metaphor of the machine, which was dominant around him. Moreover, if that is so, then what it is to be physical is malleable to transformations of relations in the universal community. The saints, Edwards once speculated, "will be able to see from one side of the universe to the other" since they will not see "by such slow rays of light that are several years travelling. . . ."[1]

Perhaps such thoughts may not seem quite so ridiculous as they once did; the boundary between science and its philosophical self-interpretation is not nearly so plainly marked as formerly. Why *should* such speculation be barred from physics classrooms? And how do we know that the movement of science itself must be immune to them?

Or again, whatever *are* the "humanities?" Somehow, they are the disciplines that study humanity, yet are not social sciences. But what can that distinction mean? In practice, the humanities seem to comprise the several activities of interpretation of the arts, plus about half of what historians do. Perhaps this is not so unsensible a grouping, and perhaps those made contrary by the gospel may have something to say to it.

Western reflection has traditionally — prior to romanticism, which opens other questions — traced the fissure in human life as running between the true and the good, what is and what ought to be, and has

1. Edwards, *Miscellanies,* 926.

looked to the beautiful as the possible reconciliation. The arts are thus interpreted as judgment in action — we may think of Kant's interpretation of the beautiful as serendipitous good or of Aquinas' interpretation of it as truth's attraction. If now the good is eschatological, if the good is the *aion* to come, the arts are the presence of the future, the enacted "groaning" and "longing" of creation for what it is not but will be. Christian interpreters might tell of the arts in such terms; and such telling and the telling of history would not go ill together. On such a basis, there might even be reason to practice and teach the humanities.

VI

I could continue with examples — or anyway, someone could. But instead one final point must be made. Christians' calling to the intellect, whether because of its nature or because of our present situation, is not an individual calling. It is *communities* that can be dedicated to discourse and to the renovation of judgment. And a dedicated community is an institutionalized one: it is institutions like universities and colleges that might undertake to reinvent the West's intellectual enterprise.

It is the enterprise as such that needs to be reinvented, the total discourse of the university that we are called to renew. Readers will divine that I conclude with the traditional insistence on what is usually and disastrously named "interdisciplinary" discourse, and with the not quite so traditional insistence on its institutionalization. But perhaps there is one difference between my insistence and that which we have so often heard, which may even make mine a bit more plausible.

The failure of good resolutions to get the disciplines together is easily explained: for the most part, they are given nothing to do together except to be together, or they are given some momentous "topic" artificially invented for the purpose. But Christians are now called to nothing less than the reinstitution of that common discourse within which and only within which our several "disciplines" can exist at all — at least, as human undertakings. We have decidedly urgent "interdisciplinary topics": restoration of the liturgical, scholarly, and paradigmatic experience of the books by which the university lives, and the institution of a university-saving argument between the prejudices of modernity and the truth of the gospel.

The Intellectual and the Church

I

THE CONCEPT of "the intellectual" is specific to the modern West and the West's cultural colonies. To be an intellectual is not just to be intelligent, or even actively and persistently intelligent. A poet or other artist may or may not be an intellectual, without prejudice to the intelligence of his or her art. Nor indeed is even the person consumed like Socrates in the power of the mind thereby "an intellectual"; not Aquinas nor Plato nor Aristotle were "intellectuals." "Intellectuals" are a historical class.

The class of "intellectuals" results from appropriation to created individuals of something always known in Western thought but through most of the West's history considered divine rather than human: what Aristotle called the "agent" intellect. Through the great pre-modern tradition, the created mind was not itself conceived as an *agent,* a *doer* of knowledge; the mind was rather a *mirror* of reality, or at most an eye, constituted in its knowing by what appears to and in it. Mirrors and eyes need light; to be mirrored or seen reality needs light. It was believed that God is the one who sheds that light. Insofar as "agent

A lecture given at Gustavus Adolphus College in 1989. Previously unpublished.

intellect" pointed to an anthropological factor, it pointed to the place in us where God's light shines.

It is, in the tradition, *God* who is finally the intellect who is an *agent* of knowing, who makes things to be known. As the divine knower he grounds — in Christian theology, "creates" — all things in their knowability. God, we may say, is the unmoved knower who just as knower is indeed also the mover of all things. When God is revealed as the Creator, then, insofar as knowing must be considered someone's *work,* it must be *God's* work.

The modern West has been making the titanic experiment of claiming intellectual agency for created subjects. To be sure, not all of the original idea of agent intellect can with much plausibility be appropriated to creatures. The outcome of simply declaring ourselves agent intellects in the full sense would be the claim that we create the world by our knowing of it — though indeed just this claim is the hidden dynamic of some idealist proposals, and of hiddenly idealist proposals such as "deconstructionism." But such titanism always, though sometimes rather later than sooner, proves too much even for Adam's descendants to sustain. If we give it up but still claim intellectual agency, we end in a very specific situation, three characteristics of which I will here mention.

First, whereas God's work as agent intellect is the world, our work as would-be agent intellects can at most be work *on* the world. Knowing as agency, predicated of created agents, can only be the work of explaining, clarifying, predicting, and the like.

Second, we must note a nice irony: titanic knowing thus takes its place among many other sorts of work on the world in which created subjects are necessarily engaged. Putting this point together with the previous, we derive: "an intellectual" is a kind of *worker,* the kind whose work on the world is knowing it in the modern active sense. Such a person may very well be an amateur; only in very decadent modernity is only the paid worker honorable.

Third, a created agent intellect, unlike God, must include him or her*self* in the world on which he or she cognitively labors. Once this object of explanation, or whatever, comes into view, it is utterly fascinating. The physical sciences would probably have emerged in the West without the presence of intellectuals, but without such persons there would not have emerged those sciences and reflective enterprises of which the human person and human society are themselves the object.

II

I have described the origin of "the intellectual" in terms that may be taken as pejorative. And indeed I think it vital to understand the grave problematic of the intellectual's claim and position. I do not, however, think we should repent of our history at this point, or try to escape from our historical situation. We should not, that is, wish that "the intellectual" had not appeared. That some humans, at least during some periods of human history, *labor* on the world to explain it, to understand it, to get hold of it, is surely a good thing.

So to the second term of my title: the church. The relation between the church and intellectuals is personal: the church is a community to which intellectuals may belong. It is such persons, *baptized* intellectuals, who are this essay's remaining matter.

Given created intellectual agency's inevitable infatuation with itself, the intellectual who belongs to the church will promptly make this community, as his or her *own* community, an obsessive object of intellectual labor. It is the experience of centuries that thereby the intellectual regularly and promptly falls into conflict with the church and, if he or she remains faithful to the church, with him or herself. The problem, of course, is the claims the church makes, nearly all of which resist being worked over by created agent intellects.

The church claims to be the body of Christ, though no amount of research discovers the slightest resemblance between the church and Christ or the church and a human body. The church claims to be holy and to make holy, despite a moral record that a created "ethicist" — a notable variety of agent intellectual — cannot regard as wholly incommensurable with that of other collectives. And so on.

For reasons falling outside the scope of this essay, the way in which churched intellectuals have mostly attempted to manage this problem has been by cutting back the claims of the church. To remain with my instances, "body of Christ" will be interpreted as "a metaphor" and "holiness" will be postponed for heaven. The strategy has been unremittingly counterproductive; every diminution of the church's difficult claims has only served to make those remaining yet more offensive.

It may, of course, be that the reason intellectuals have trouble in the church is that they do not belong there, whether because their enterprise is misguided or because the church's claims cannot stand their scrutiny.

Let me, however, make a different suggestion: the reason intellectuals have difficulty in the church is not that the church's claims have been too *great,* but that the church as it has presented itself in Western history has claimed too *little.*

The Western church has by and large vacillated between two opposed but equally pusillanimous self-presentations: as an institution to administer something called "grace" or as a voluntary association of religiously like-minded persons. Predicated of an entity of either sort, the church's claims must indeed be offensive to intellectual agency. Clearly the church administers lots of things, but that these are precisely God's grace will hardly yield to any amount of investigation. Nor is it likely that a voluntary association of religious types can sustain a claim to be the human body of God. For the church to accommodate an internal community of intellectual workers, she will have to understand herself far more grandly than the Western church has customarily done.

To see just how grandly, let us ask once again, *Who* is the agent intellect? Neither the original pagan identification of intellectual agency with the divine nor the modern West's identification of intellectual agency with a certain creaturely labor will do for Christian thinking. The one finally implies an identity between the divine and a certain location in human subjectivity; the other in fact mandates the disappearance of God from the epistemological picture and eventually the degradation of the intellect. But in the church's most vigorous periods of self-assertion, she has in effect claimed that *she* is the agent intellect, the place from which both reality and the mind that seeks reality are illuminated.

If this claim is true, there is indeed a final identity of human and divine knowing at the point of cognitive agency, but this identity is *communally* mediated. No individual created consciousness is or encompasses God's light. The mind that knows the world and just so makes the world knowable is not in us, but we are indeed *in it,* as we live in the community of the church.

For the church is the place where human community is already in this world meshed with the triune community that is God. According to the gospel, it is the destiny of created minds to be included in the life that the Father and the Son live in their Spirit; the claim of the church is to anticipate this divine-human community, to be a "down payment" on the Kingdom of God. To our present concern: thus the church is the place where our destined participation in the cognitive life of God is already in action, so that from this communal context we can see things as they are.

The church is actual as her liturgy. It is in her prayer and sacrifice that the church turns to and moves into her relationships in God. The actuality of the church as the home for intellect is the dramatic and sensual density of her liturgical action, as all modes of created entity are thereby brought into the mutual knowing of the Father and the Son and you and me, in the processions and the icons and the singing and the smoke, and of course above all as the bread and wine and water.

The status of the intellectual is not undone by this insight, but is much transformed. As individuals within the illumining community, intellectuals remain mere workers as before. But from their place within the community of God's active knowing, they may labor with a bright light shining on their work. One or two instances are perhaps called for.

Instance one. From within the life of the church, in which all reality participates in an interpersonal life of the triune God and his churchly community, the created world does not look like a congeries of impersonal things, as it does in the dark. Rather, it is illumined as a community of spirits, and "matter" as the intersubjective distance necessary for their individuality-in-communion. It is lately becoming apparent that such general visions have controlled the history even of "pure" physical research. It is not predictable what truth, also of the "hardest" "scientific" sorts, might await discovery by those able to see the world so brilliantly lit as it is from within the church.

Instance two. From within the life of the church, constituted as it is by communication, by "the word" both audible and visible, human community generally does not look like a mechanism, well constructed a la James Madison or otherwise. In the light of God's shared intellectual agency, the polity appears in its independence as the public sphere of common moral choice and action, and no more as epiphenomenal to the economy, as capitalism and communism teach alike.

III

It must be admitted, of course, that "the church" of whose light I have been speaking is among us so darkened that my encomiums may well appear as fiction. Perhaps here is the calling of "intellectuals" *in* the church.

Hope, the Gospel, and the Liberal Arts

❦   ❦

I

NEARLY ALL American institutions that have in any generous or authentic fashion taught "liberal arts" were founded by the Christian church. Most of these schools are now much secularized. It is a question whether American colleges' cultivation of the liberal arts can survive this development, except as provision of amenities for the most leisured or alienated among student constituencies. The evidence is not encouraging. The sense in which even the most elite schools can now verify their title as colleges "of" liberal arts is with rare exceptions decidedly attenuated. It seems likely that the liberal character of America's colleges stands and falls with their ideologically and liturgically Christian character.

The alliance, of course, long antedates America. The liberal arts are the inheritance of Athens' free polity, of the arts required for public debate of the good and in turn nurtured by the discourse thus constituted; they are, as old classicists like myself never tire of repeating, "the arts proper for a citizen to acquire."[1] The liberal arts, when vital, were

---

1. Aristotle, *Politika* VII:2.

Published in *A Humanist's Legacy: Essays in Honor of John Christian Bale,* ed. Dennis M. Jones (Luther College, 1990). Reprinted by permission.

not ornamental arts; they were the *praxis* of public life as different from private, economic life — they seem impractical to us only because we have made a political choice to restrict serious *praxis* to the private sphere.

So soon as the Christian movement, coming into the hellenized world of later Mediterranean antiquity, encountered the liberal curricular inheritance, it appropriated these arts as its own. Vice versa, since the final collapse of pagan antiquity, the liberal arts have appealed and could appeal to no other protector or promoter than the church.

The question of my essay is: What can be the basis of this mutual attraction? Indeed, of this mutual dependency? "Athens and Jerusalem" are not in general likely allies. Greek religion is polymorphous; the Lord is a jealous God. Greece's deity is eternal by immunity to death; Israel's and the church's God by suffering and conquering it. The free *polis* was indeed an unprecedented public space for those admitted, but excluded most of the population; in Christ there is neither slave nor free, male nor female. The Greeks were incurable elitists; Christ has chosen the lowly of this world. Athens seeks wisdom, whereas Jerusalem seeks righteousness; and the gospel slashes this already drastic polarity with the foolishness and offense of the cross.

Athens and the Christian movement had of course to meet and talk. When the mission of the gospel invades new cultural and religious turf there occurs always a mutual new *interpretation:* interpretation of the gospel claim that Jesus rules in light of the antecedent hopes and fears of the invaded culture, and vice versa, of the culture's antecedent convictions in light of the gospel. So it went also on that branch of the mission that moved from Jerusalem and Antioch into the centers of hellenized antiquity — and eventually to us. At the basis of specifically Western Christianity and of once-evangelized Western culture there are an appropriate baptizing of Hellenism and a reciprocal hellenizing of the gospel. By and large, however, the conversation between *these* partners — unlike, for apparent example, that in black Africa — has been a gloriously productive millennial *agony.* Why then the one area of peace and harmony?

II

The enemy of my enemy is my friend. Let me suggest: the gospel and the life of the free *polis* each perceive an intimate enemy, and it is the same in both cases. When the gospel is heard and not believed, or when freedom is frustrated or merely exploited, the specter of *nihilism* rises. Against this haunt, one can never have too many allies.

It is of course from the writings of Nietzsche that the word "nihilism" resonates among us, but for the purposes of this essay I will follow a usage less convoluted than his. By nihilism I will simply mean lack of hope. Or, what is the exactly same thing, I will mean inability to find reason for valuing human persons by warrants decisively different from those by which we value galaxies or cows or proteins or whatever. Perhaps I may best display the concept by pointing to its most massive historical exemplification: Hitler's variety of fascism. Or by pointing to a trivial and momentarily benign case: the animal-rights movement.

The hellenized world into which the gospel emerged from Judea and Galilee was a world staring into an abyss of anthropological despair and hypnotized by the returning stare. Christianity inherited from Judaism an exploration of the same abyss, wherein "All is vanity, and a striving after wind." Each could thus share with the other the same fear and a dialectical but nevertheless real hope, that hope as such is not in vain.

Greece had drawn the great anthropological line to the contours of the *polity:* she had defined human transcendence as *freedom* in contrast to servility. Accordingly, for all Hellenism the possibility of political freedom was the possibility of specific humanity itself. Thus Greece always had difficulty knowing why the disenfranchised — slaves, the conquered, unwelcomed pre- or early post-partum infants, and in some respects women — should be treated differently than other animals. But what then if the suspicion arises, "Perhaps we are *all,* really, slaves?

The possibility of such suspicion was always there in Greek experience. Since the rebirth of Greek civilization from the Dorian devastations, Greece's energizing terror had been the fear of time's mischances. That old Chronos eats all his children, that what time brings forth, time — and probably rather sooner than later — again devours, was for Greece a founding horrific experience. There had been a glorious, rich, and pious Greece, the Greece of Mycenae and its heroes; and in a moment it had been swept away. Two passages have always defined my understanding of Greece's interpretation of reality. The second decrees that we may "call no one happy, until he has reached the end of his life without suffering misery."[2]

For reawakening Greece, worth and beauty and truth — all together, "being" — could thus lie only in permanence; applied to personal beings, in "immortality." It will be seen that, in Greece, love of freedom must therefore always be on the verge of self-refutation; for it is *time* that is the very horizon of freedom, of making choices that can make a difference, and it was precisely time that Greece feared above all else.

In her search for protection from time, Greece necessarily looked to the one permanence immediately obtrusive on ancient peoples, that of cosmic order. The heavens move, but their very movements exemplify unbending law and guarantee against all surprises. The splendor of the heavens can overwhelm even us, who so rarely attend to them. Ancient humanity could not help but attend to them; and attending so, Greece thought she could see what she longed for, the timeless being in which our hastening times may find standing. We inhabit, she believed, a *"cosmos"*: we, fleeting as we are, may look out from our immediate world, fleeting as it too is, into an encompassing immunity to all time's chances. We are housed within divine immutability.

But cosmic changelessness can be read two ways. Greece initially invoked it as just described, as footing for humanity daring to be free. But it can equally well appear as enveloping indifference precisely to freedom, as the body of a universal determinism. Within reality invoked as *cosmos,* we may be enabled to say, "We can venture to choose our own way, since we need not fear the threats of time." But we may just as well be compelled to say, "There is no point in ventures, since all paths by iron necessity only return whence they came." With the disappearance of actual free polities from the Hellenistic world, the latter reading replaced the former.

When Alexander and the Romans were finished, Mediterranean civilization had become "cosmopolitan"; all were citizens of but one great "city" of the great world as such. But can I be free, if I have the *cosmos* for my only *polis?* In what forum do I speak to *its* future? Where do they count the *ostrakon* I cast against *its* rulers? If the *cosmos* is my "city,"

2. Sophocles, *Oidipous Tyrannos,* 1528-1530.

am I not then the inhabitant of a collective as indifferent to the choices of mortals as were any of the ancient local tyrannies?

It is into *such* Hellenism that Paul and the rest carried the gospel. "Greeks" like Origen who believed, and those like his schoolmate Plotinus who did not, were folk convinced that to be specifically human was to be free, and desperately afraid that freedom was a delusion. Those like Origen saw in the gospel new hope and rejoiced; those like Plotinus derided the new Pollyannas.

The religious and "philosophical" cry of declining Mediterranean antiquity was "Is there any way out of *cosmos?*" "Is freedom possible?" All the religions of the conquerors and the conquered, transmogrified into "mysteries," answered, "You may indeed breach the iron heavens, by sacramental identification with our cult-fugure, who has gone before you." And all the "wisdom" of the "philosophical" ways answered, "Those in the know can find their way through the walls of necessity, to the freedom of pure spirit. We can teach you the secret."

There was only one hitch: all these were indeed ways *out* of the *cosmos,* and those who followed them thus left behind also that human *polis* for which freedom was wanted in the first place. The freedom of the cults and of esoteric wisdom was a private freedom very different from a citizen's freedom; and the cultic and esoteric arts were very different arts from those called "liberal." If the one goal is to die and go to heaven, inwardly now and outwardly later, who needs politics? Or then its arts?

Americans should be familiar with the syndrome, if only in a secularized and therefore pusillanimous version. It is, we say, "a free country," and thousands have dedicated their lives and sacred honor to keeping it so. Yet in that country we have come to interpret freedom as the very opposite of dedication to the community, as a commandeered private sphere of "rights" in which the community is not to meddle. By "a free country" we have come to mean a society with no very peremptory public sphere, a society that demands of us as little as possible. It is no accident at all that mystery-cults and esoteric wisdoms flourish in California or Minneapolis as once in old Corinth or Alexandria. Neither is it an accident that the *liberal* arts languish.

"Can there be freedom?" Also the gospel came with an anwer, but one very different from that of the mysteries and wisdoms: "There is freedom, because the world is *not* in fact a *cosmos,* but instead a *creation.*" Inheriting the doctrine of Judaism, the Christians knew the encompassing world as itself again encompassed, in freedom, in the freedom indeed of a *person,* who can if he will speak to us and attend to our answer. The world, said Jews and Christians, is not a structure of indifferent law but the referent of an encompassing free purpose. The world, they said, is from its deepest reality hospitable to choice that makes a difference, since it *is* itself nothing but the referent of a great such Choice. Prayer is possible, and therein freedom.

Over against despair of freedom in the world to which it came, ancient Christianity thus made precisely freedom a chief slogan of its promises, of the "gospel." The freedom believers proclaimed was, moreover, a freedom that could be, if there were a community to receive it, political freedom, the freedom of that community to choose its courses of action and set out to follow them.

Hellenists who persisted in the memory of free citizenship and — even if merely nostalgically — carried on with its arts, could hear the gospel as a message of hope. They could even see, in the community of the church itself, a restored place for the practice of freedom's arts, for the cultivation of language and public discourse and for the interpretation of texts and of history, as once again communally necessary arts. And that is to say, they could hear the gospel as a promise that specific humanity, just as Athens had evoked it, was not a delusion, and they could see the church as a community in which specific humanity could occur.

Indeed, in the centuries after the final collapse of ancient civilization and the emergence of the new synthesis we have called "Western" civilization, the alliance of the gospel and the liberal arts was to create new free public spaces also outside the church. The great free cities of the medieval empire were democracies far more direct than any we now have in America. Or again, the "holy commonwealths" of Puritan New England provided the very pattern of democratic aspiration throughout the founding periods of this nation's life.

Vice versa, believers could see in faithful Hellenists — which very soon was for most believers to say, in their own past selves — spiritual comrades in all but the identification of the Savior: as Israel had longed explicitly for *Messiah,* the "Greeks" had longed for the freedom he would bring. The "preparation for the gospel," they decided, had been separate but equal in Jerusalem and Athens.

And as the church came to recognize that Christ had not returned so quickly as first expected, that she had to settle down for a longer historical haul, the church needed what all historically continuing communities do, appropriate education. What better curriculum could there be for a community that saw itself as the bearer of God's own freedom than the arts of freedom?

This line of discussion has one more step. After long centuries of Western history carried by the conversation between Athens and the gospel, the eighteenth-century Enlightenment, or rather its more popularized versions, dissolved the conversation, sending, as they superstitiously identified the parties, "reason" one way and "revelation" another — it is this dissolution that has, a bit later than elsewhere, now undone also American colleges of arts.

Thereby antiquity's plight was repristinated: the indifferent cosmos was reinvented. The new prison is duller than the old one; in the meantime, Christian skepticism had made it impossible to see any creature as divine, so that the inexorable cosmos now appears merely as a "machine." But the effect is the same: insofar as we have been taught about "science" by the seventh grade and by Public Television physicists, we again suppose we inhabit an adamant system of predictabilities, alien to freedom, indifferent to our choices and appeals.

III

To compound our need, the alliance of Athens and the gospel has on the way conjured from the deeps a new nihilism, of its very own sort. It has been labelled "historical relativism."

According to Judaism and the gospel, we live not in a *"cosmos"* but in an encompassing *history.* In this metaphysic, being has temporal sequence itself as its horizon, and *consists* in choice of what is not yet but is to be. The coherence of things is not, on this interpretation, lawlike regularity, but dramatic coherence of events across time. The sequence of history has *plot,* so as just thereby to be indeed history and not mere meaningless succession.

Most of Western intellectual and cultural history has consisted in the slow appropriation of this very unhellenic interpretation of reality. We may, for one quick historical instance, think of the Reformation's elevation of "faith" to the key position in human being, as faith is "the assurance of things hoped for. . . ."

In this metaphysic, freedom is not problematic; but the point of freedom may become so. Where the gospel is heard but no longer believed, freedom may become absurdity. My life will be a tale told by a poet, signifying much, only insofar as it does in fact have plot, as it has complication, crisis, and resolution.

The problematic of this "insofar" is that it takes at least two to make drama, so that my life can be *plotted* only in community. And when the reference is made to community, the question of plot is repeated at a new level, for it is again dramatic coherence that makes a group of individuals into a community. But whose story is this *common* story?

As "Enlightenment" had been the spiritual event of the West's eighteenth century, so "historicism" was the spiritual event of the nineteenth. Historicism consisted in the exploration, both theoretical and in political and religious practice, of the question just posed. The Enlightenment, then and still not "overcome," made it seem hard to say boldly as did the Bible, "The common story is the story of God." A series of philosophers unparalleled since Athens therefore attempted approximate assurances: "The common story is the story of absolute Spirit." "The common story is the story of universal humanity." But the slide once underway, someone eventually had to say: "All the common story there is, is the story of *our* community and its spirit. Other communities have other stories." Or even, "How can there by any *common* story? Plot out your own life, even if such an undertaking is absurd." Therewith the demon was out.

"We have our values, you have yours." Or even, "*I* have my values, you have yours." We are accustomed to this historicist sort of nihilism, but it is nihilism none the less. For of course, unshared "values" are no values at all, since "good" and "bad" refer — as we all really know — exactly to what we do with and for one another. A "morality" that I am unwilling to "impose" on anyone else is wholly illusory, and will give no shape to my life either, however privately that life may be conceived and lived. Most who will read this essay entertain in fact "no hope in this world"; or at least so they assure all inquirers, convinced as they claim to be that "values are relative."

Historicist nihilism manifests itself most democratically as sheer inability to reason ethically. I choose an instance that notably infests the academic, reminiscently "liberal" community. A Minnesota Poll recent as of this writing reported that most Minnesotans believe (1) that abortion is the taking of personal human life and (2) that folk should have "the right" to abort as they freely choose. The evil to which I here call attention is not the number of abortions that *Wade vs. Roe* has produced, terrifying as this is. The subtler, more demonic evil appears in our ability simultaneously to entertain the two referenced opinions. The nihilism is the escape of "choice" from community. It is freedom that consists in excuse from responsibility for the other and for the storyline of my life so far, freedom that occurs on a horizon of sheer temporal sequentiality with no plot at all.

In the academy, of course, we expect also explicit ideological appearances of whatever is going; and indeed sundry ways of carrying historical relativism to its spooky end are now the chief menu at conventions of all disciplines but the natural sciences. I mention but one, since it is the currently favored way of displacing the liberal arts. It is, we are told, legalistically repressive — indeed "dualistic," "hierarchical," even "phallocentric" — to insist that any text can have its own sense, which it is a teacher's task to defend against mistaken readings. Therefore it is supposed also to be an arbitrary imposition if we set up any particular set of texts as essential in the curriculum; for since any text can have any meaning, any text can serve wisdom as well as any other.

Where freedom is abstract and arbitrary, and needs no community, neither does it need arts. It is again no accident that where historical relativism rules, the liberal arts die.

IV

There is hope for hope. The gates of nihilism will not prevail against the one holy catholic church — though they may, of course, prevail against particular parts of the church and have sometimes done so — and therefore the gospel will be heard in the world so long as the world lasts, telling of the good for whose coming we may hope. And therefore also there will so long as the world lasts be in the world a community in which hope is practiced.

It is, of course, not guaranteed that Western civilization will last, or that its teaching and practice of liberal arts will last. Even less is it guaranteed that the Western part of the church will endure to the end, or even very long. But just because nothing along such lines is ever guaranteed, neither can we know that these things will *not* last or even suddenly be reinvigorated. In many ways, both surviving custodians of Athens' arts and believers in the gospel find themselves thrown back into the situation in which they first made alliance. A mighty tree came from that inconsiderable seed; why may it not happen again?

The first step is simply the recovery, on both sides of the old alliance, of mere clarity about who we are and what we need. God willing, the Western church might yet remember that it is not an all-purpose volunteer religious society for whatever causes society currently defines as good. We can at any moment take instead to proclaiming the gospel. And if the church did *that*, then *in the Western context* its message would again as in ancient days be a word of hope for freedom, of hope for hope.

All the masters of the liberal arts have ever needed is a bit of such encouragement. And whenever we dare to cultivate our arts as more than decoration, as life-*praxis* of whatever little communities we can find for them, the mere practice itself becomes a spring of hope. Folk who labor on great inherited texts as if they matter liberate all around them to confidence that history does have some plot. Those who practice the arts of public discourse open little polities just by doing so, each time they break their silence. Those who discipline themselves to the outcome of experiment and observation, when they do it for the sake of truth, encourage all to faith that there *is* truth. To pursue beauty is to create it for all to see and hear. When we act as if human deliberation and decision could make a difference, they *do* make a difference. When we act as if community were real, it just thereby *becomes* real.

The gospel gives hope for the freedom that the liberal arts serve. The liberal arts give hope that the free person whom the gospel evokes can actually exist. And this circle is not vicious: we can be swept into its whirl catch-as-catch-can. Hope for hope is, after all, itself hope.

Does God Have Time?

I

THE TITLE of this paper was, so far as I can remember, advanced by Professor Ted Peters. I accepted it immediately, since in fact I have frequently uttered and written the sentence "God has time," intending the same pun as did Peters; an attempt to understand what I have been saying will be the burden of my paper. I have even used the sentence as a statement of what makes God to be God: God has time for himself and for us; we never have enough time for anything; and that is the great difference between us.

It is the common opinion that deity is defined by not having to have time, or in the language of the tradition, by "impassibility," that is, immunity to temporal challenges and opportunities alike. The very concept of eternity is supposed to come about by negating our experience of time. This common opinion is perhaps held by none so firmly as those who think that there is no God, and for whom timelessness defines what a God would be if there were any.

But those more free to ponder the reality of God have never been quite

Reprinted with permission from the Winter 1991 (Vol. 11, No. 1) issue of the *CTNS Bulletin*, W. Mark Richardson, Editor. Copyright 1991, Center for Theology and the Natural Sciences.

so sure of God's timelessness, since the initial experience that draws the devotee is never experience of a reality immune to his or her temporal concerns, whatever may then appear in reflective theory about this experience or at more advanced levels of experience. Of the great theologians of the Christian church, perhaps only Augustine has been willing to make wholly unrestricted and normative use of a rule that nothing can be true of God that might blemish the "simplicity" of his timelessness. As a contrary example, Gregory of Nyssa found the deity of God in the infinity of precisely his liveliness, in creatures' inability to *keep up* with him.[1]

Perhaps the one agreed proposition of religion in general is this: deity, or its functional equivalent, is "eternal" being. But this proposition is so radically multivocal that it is very close to being empty. The word "eternity" by itself is a mere place-marker, denoting *whatever* it is on which a particular spiritual community relies to knit the poles of time.

The substance of every human act is the particular way it joins the poles of time, the particular way it rhymes remembrance and anticipation into lived present meaning. Just so, every human act assumes that the poles of time can indeed be knit together somehow, that the discontinuities of temporal existence are somehow bracketed. Every human act relies on some eternity or other.

But there are as many putative eternities as there are religions, or conversely, as many religions as there are eternities. Putative eternities range from the abstract timelessness of the turning wheel's still center to the contingency-conquering experience of the great ancestors. It is a decisive question about any putative God: *How* exactly is this candidate eternal? Not every possible eternity is the mere negation of time, as is shown by the case of the ancestors.

"Does God have time?" It might seem that the way to deal with this question would be first to settle what time is, then to inquire whether it could possibly be wanted or possessed by a God. But with what would then be my initial question, "What is time?" I would enter a metaphysical and cosmological thicket from which better thinkers than I have failed to emerge. So I will do it the other way around. I will begin by dwelling on the reality of God; then I will inquire what sort of sense, if any, it might make to say of this One, "He has time."

1. For the above, I may perhaps refer to Robert W. Jenson, *The Triune Identity* (Philadelphia: Fortress, 1982), pp. 114-131, 162-166.

Proceeding so, I begin with a specific God. And in fact I begin with the *deus christianorum,* with Gregory's lively God, the triune God. I will make no apology for this, and indeed do not know wherein an apology would consist. I believe the triune God to be the one who in fact is. Moreover, I will leave the questions untouched and open whether incompatible identifications of God can intend the same reality, or whether what I assert might be affirmed by others whose identifications of God are incompatible with that of the church. My question is: Does the *Triune* God have time?

Since not everything can be argued in one lecture, I also assume an orthodox doctrine of Trinity, and will not combat the various relapses into modalist or Arian crudities that continue to occupy popular theology. Indeed, I will assume the current state of discussion. This is characterized by preference for the Cappadocians over Augustine; by dependence on Karl Barth for inspiration though not much for matter; by adherence to Karl Rahner's axiom "the immanent Trinity is the economic Trinity" in an ontological fashion that he himself would probably not have countenanced; and by a remarkable degree of renewed speculative freedom.[2]

II

There are three in God in that (1) the Bible tells a story about God; (2) we cannot transcend the story on the way to find some "real" God, without declaring the story simply to be false;[3] (3) this story about God presents us with three agents of its action; and (4) within the story each of the three agents acts as divine precisely by confessing one of the other two as God and referring away from himself to that other.[4]

The final point above must be made more concrete. Christ refers all homage from himself to the one who "sent" him, his "Father," just so

2. The current state of speculation may be perhaps taken as represented by Wolfhart Pannenberg, *Systematische Theologie,* vol. I (Göttingen: Vandenhoeck & Ruprecht, 1988), pp. 283-483; and by Robert W. Jenson, *Triune Trinity.*

3. These two points were already fully clear to me when I wrote *The Triune Identity.*

4. These last two points only became fully clear to me in discussion with Wolfhart Pannenberg, whose work on the Trinity is now definitively presented in the *Systematische Theologie.*

accomplishing our salvation and appearing as the Son. This God is the Father only as the one so addressed by the Son, and at his central appearance in the story he turns over divine rule to the Son and indeed at the cross "abandons" his role as God, leaving the Son to suffer the consequences of godhead by himself. And the Spirit as God glorifies, and testifies to, only the Father or the Son, just so enabling the proposition "God is Spirit."[5]

It will be apparent that the previous paragraph refers to Father, Son, and Spirit as "persons" not merely in the ancient sense of the words "hypostasis" or "persona," but in the modern sense of a self-reflexive agent. In this, I follow a tendency always latent in the tradition and very deliberate in the current discussion. I think the discourse this initiates can be undertaken independently of whether "person" in this modern sense is the appropriate first designation of each of the three in God. The discourse can also be undertaken independently of affirming or rejecting a so-called social doctrine of Trinity.

Thus it can be said, as the tradition has consistently done, that each of the three *is* his relation to the other two.[6] And further it can be said, as the tradition has not quite so consistently done,[7] that "God" as such denotes what *happens between* Jesus and the one he calls "Father" and the Father's Spirit in whom Jesus turns to him. "God" simply as such denotes the Father's sending and the Son's obedience, the Spirit's coming to the Son and the Son's thanksgiving to the Father, and so on in a dialectic to which only failing insight or imagination sets limits. "God" denotes a life, or as the Eastern tradition has put it, a complex of "energeia."

If, as traditionally has been taught, there is also such a thing as a sheer divine *ousia,* a sheer deity, then it is what Gregory said it is, "infinity" as such.[8] If we ask *what* is infinite, so as thereby to be God, we return to the life among Father, Son, and Spirit.[9] We may even venture to say that the action of that story told by the Bible is the

---

5. Most clearly, Wolfhart Pannenberg, *Systematic Theologie,* pp. 326-364.

6. Thomas Aquinas, *Summa Theologica* 1, q.29, a.4: *"Persona igitur divina significat relationem ut subsistentem."*

7. Inhibited, in my judgment, by remnants of unbaptized theology.

8. To all this, Jenson, *Triune Trinity,* pp. 162ff.

9. I.e., to the *energeia,* as the Eastern tradition from Nyssenus on has tirelessly explored.

referent of "God," in that this story is encompassing, in that it brackets time.

Finally, I must note the connection between the poles[10] of time and the mutual roles played by Father, Son and Spirit in the biblical story of God. That this connection has been the permanent occasion of "modalist" degradations of the doctrine of the Trinity must not prevent us from noting it and reckoning with it. I will abstract and schematize drastically.

The Father appears in biblical narrative of God's life with us as the "whence" of divine events, as the Given from which they come or to which they return. In classical technical formulations, the biblical story about God is summarized in the two "sendings" of the Son and the Spirit; the Father is the Unsent Sender. And when this story is asserted to be true of and in God himself, by the doctrine of "processions" correlated to the "sendings," classical formulations summarize the relational life of God again in only two processions, of the Son and the Spirit from the Father who has himself no procession.

Correspondingly, the Spirit appears as the "whither" of God's life. Throughout the biblical story, the Spirit is God as "the Power of the future," to accept an inevitable cliché. The Spirit is God coming from the future to break the present open to himself. The Spirit is divine self-transcendence, insofar as God does not depend upon what is not God to be the referent or energy of his coming to himself. The "whither" of divine events is not their passive aiming point, but their emergence and activation from the future.

It cannot be said that this biblical character of the Spirit comes very freely to expression in classical technical formulations, at least in the West. Indeed, one aspect of this lack has been a reproach of the East against the West for centuries — I refer, of course, to the Eastern attack on the Western creedal interpolation, "and from the Son."[11]

10. Since I have had opportunity mildly to edit this paper since it was delivered at Berkeley, let me note: the terminological inconsistency that Robert John Russell's response caught in my use of "arrows" at this and similar points was indeed present in the draft available to him; I noticed the problem before reading the paper at Berkeley, and edited to read as in the present text.

11. See especially the writings of the exiled Russian who has most influenced modern Orthodoxy on the point, Vladimir Lossky, especially *A l'Image et a la ressemblance de Dieu* (Paris: Aubres-Montaigne, 1967).

The more general repair of the deficiency is a project of the current revival of trinitarian speculation. In my judgment, the goal of such construction is to learn how to say something along these lines: as there are two sendings/processions of/in God, so there are two — to propose language — "liberations," of the Father and the Son by the Spirit. And these liberations are as constitutive of the identity and reality of God as are the processions.

Finally, we may perhaps say that the Son is God as his own "specious present." It is Jesus the Christ in whom the Father finds himself; and it is Jesus the Christ in whose resurrection the Spirit's liberating activity is actually accomplished.

If the Father and the Spirit are the poles of the divine eternity, it is then the life of the Son, as God's specious present, in which these rhyme, in which the unity of the divine life is accomplished. Death is time's ultimate act; that God transcends time must finally mean that God transcends death. Normal gods transcend death by immunity to it or by being identical with it. The way in which the triune God transcends death is by within himself triumphing over it: by the Son's dying and the Father's raising him again. The whence and the whither of the divine life are one, and so the triune God is eternal, in the event of Jesus' resurrection.

In his treatise on God's eternity, Karl Barth defined the particular "eternity of the triune God" as *"reine Dauer,"* as indeed a duration but a "pure" duration. That this duration is "pure" means that it is not a struggle. And it may be that Barth has said all there is to say on the topic: "That being is eternal, in whose duration beginning, succession and end . . . do not fall apart. . . ." "That between source, movement and goal there is no conflict but only peace . . . , distinguishes eternity from time. They are not, however, distinguished because in eternity there are no such differences. . . ."[12]

III

The life of God is thus constituted in a structure of relations, whose own referents are narrative. This narrative structure is constrained by a

12. Karl Barth, *Kirchliche Dogmatik,* vol. II/1 (Zurich: Zollikon, 1940), pp. 685-686, 690.

difference between whence and whither that one cannot finally refrain from calling "past" and "future,"[13] in some strained use of the words, and that is identical with the distinction between the Father and the Spirit. This difference is not relative and therefore not measurable; nothing in God recedes into the past or approaches from the future. Thus Karl Barth said of evil that in the eternal life of God, as he freely lives it, evil is *defined* as that which is left behind. But the difference is also absolute; there is no perspective from which to see evil as future or the Kingdom as past.

On the supposition that what I have been saying does not strain language utterly beyond utility, Barthian characterizations of God by such words as "history" and "event" have been justified. But is it therefore appropriate to speak specifically of "time" in God? We must indeed say that there are whence and whither in God that are not like right and left or up and down on a map, but are like before and after in a narrative, that are dyadic relations and not triadic. But even so, does it make sense to call this "time"?

Let me propose a pseudo-Thomistic criterion. Perhaps I have established that there is a *likeness* between an aspect of the specific eternity of the triune God and that aspect of created process called "time." This likeness is in my judgment a necessary but insufficient justification for speaking of God's "time." A second necessary justification, which together with the first will constitute a sufficient justification, is that this aspect of God's eternity be the *Bedingung der Möglichkeit* of created time.

IV

In the theological chapter of *A Brief History of Time* — of whose standing among cognoscenti I have no idea, but which has the virtue that nearly everyone claims to have read it — Stephen Hawking distinguishes be-

---

13. Let me again exploit the postpartum editing. I was at Berkeley distressed by Robert Russell's contention that I used a prerelativistic conception of time in speaking of God's "time," having taken, precisely as an outsider to physics, such care to do no such thing. I am, however, convinced by him that if not so much in this paper then in my other writing I have indeed to rework much of my language for these matters, to make plain that I do not suppose an *acausal* past-present-future to be absolute.

tween "real" time and "imaginary" time. "Real time" is the sort of time with which one reckons in construing the course of the universe by classic relativity theory. "Imaginary time" is the sort of time with which one reckons when quantum mechanics are brought into the enterprise.

According to the present data and calculations of Hawking and others, when we construe the history of the universe in classically relativistic fashion we are led back to a beginning of the laws of nature themselves, to the posit of an initial singularity for which no laws can be formulated. But plainly Hawking does not wish to acquiesce in such scientific ascesis, and thinks it might be avoided if a "quantum theory of gravity" could be developed. If we could "discuss the very early stages of the universe" in terms of *such* a theory, there would be nothing about nature to be accounted for which could not be accounted for by nature's own laws — or so Hawking hopes.

Real time is "real" because it can (though it need not, of course) have an arrow, because relations on its horizon can be construed as true diadic relations. Thus in real time it is possible for the universe to have boundaries that can be called its beginning and its ending. On the other hand, the time of quantum mechanics is strictly a "fourth dimension" indeed; two points on its horizon are triadically related, so that which way the "arrow" points depends on the side from which one views the two points. The arrow of imaginary time can only be interpreted as reversible. When we construe the history of the universe in imaginary time, the question of a beginning therefore cannot arise. The universe will just "BE," as Hawking ingenuously puts it.

I wish to use this distinction as the object of a theological experiment, in full awareness that new cosmological observation or theory might render the experiment moot at any time.

One is obviously drawn to ask, Which time, "real time" or "imaginary time," is the *really* real time? It will not do to say, as Hawking does, that it is simply a matter of which calculations we wish to make. For the two are metaphysically different. Only "real time" can be experienced, since only in "real time" can there be experience. Thus if there were to be a big crunch and if the conditions that support life nevertheless somehow still existed, sentient beings contemporary with the event would in fact experience an *end*, that is, become omnipresent and eternal. Or, in the terms of Hawking's favorite fable, that the singularity inside the black hole that "an intrepid astronaut" had trespassed does not exist in imaginary time would not prevent its weird effects on him.

At this juncture, an ancient dichotomy of metaphysical tempers presents itself: that real time is the time of the world as experienced will suggest to some that it is the really real time, and the very same consideration will suggest to others that it is it not. Hawking is no more immune to such suggestions than the rest of us; quite transparently he regards imaginary time as the McCoy, precisely *because* it obviates the need to think of an absolute beginning or ending.

Equally anciently, it has been on the experience of time that advocates of each metaphysical temper have come to grief. When Kant defines time as the horizon of specifically personal experience, we are immediately convinced. Time, more inwardly than space, is what we experience in experiencing anything at all. Something that was in principle alien to personhood and its capacity for experience could not be what we ineluctably mean by "time." But when popular explications of relativity theory describe time as a warp of the world's very geometry, we are just as immediately convinced. Something that subsisted only for us, or even that could be fully assimilated into our inwardness, could not be what we mean by "time." It is an intuition from which we will not easily be driven that time must possess the metaphysical characters of *both* Hawking's "real time" and "imaginary time," if there is to be *time* at all. Time is precisely the *horizon* of *experience,* with both nouns demanding full weight.

V

I am not in the midst of a proof of God; I am not arguing that there cannot be time unless there is the triune God, and that there is time. I am engaged only in considering whether, *given* the triune God, the timelike structure of relations we know in him can be considered the *Bedingung der Möglicheit* for what we otherwise know as time, so that by my pseudo-Thomistic standard we may legitimately call it "God's time." My argument runs: if there is the triune God, then his *"Dauer"* is the condition precisely of the oneness of real time and imaginary time. That is, God's *Dauer* is the condition of the subsistence of any reality that intuition will let us call time.

The Jewish and Christian word for the relation of God to everything else is that God "creates." And it is standard teaching that created reality includes not only all things in time, but time itself. It is commonly supposed also that this must mean created time has a beginning and an end. I think this common supposition is unexceptional in itself, but it is not the whole story.

What must created time be in relation to God, if what I have said about God's life, with its timelike structure, is true? I suggest that if God is triune, then created time must be the *accommodation* God makes in his own life for persons other than the three he himself is. For in the biblical story of the divine life, the whence of the divine life is the whence also of creation, and the whither of the divine life is the outcome and end also of creation. We creatures appear *within* that narrative whose agents — Father, Son, and Spirit — between them enact God's life. We inhabit the story that is the story of God. God is indeed the one "in whom we live and move and have our being."[14]

Now — how is it in there? Or rather, in here? Time is something we experience in experiencing anything at all. Therefore, the experience of time is experience of a total horizon of all things and events, that is, of the creation itself in one of its dimensions. But then, if the foregoing paragraph is in any way true, the experience of time as such is an experience of God's own whence and whither, and of the dynamism constituted therein. It is an experience shared with the Son of the difference between the Father and the Spirit.

Our experience of time, therefore, is our sharing in a personal experience that is within itself communal. Our experience of time is our sharing in a personal life that has *room* for others, and that if it in fact gives room to others *encompasses* them, to be for them a given horizon of all experience, a given externality. Therefore, that real time is the inner horizon of personal experience does not make real time "subjective," does not preclude real time from being "external" to subjects.

The feeling that the "transcendental" factors of personal experience are just so "subjective" factors arose simultaneously with individualistic interpretations of personal being. For all premodernity, the person's transcendental constitution is established in part by his or her relation

14. If someone wishes to say that I am thus a "panentheist," I have no objection whatever to the label.

to others than him or herself, so that such a thing as an "inner horizon" of experience did not on account of its inwardness have to be thought of as private. So, for example, *tradition* was not a heteronomous factor either in cognition or in moral choice until it was declared such by Enlightenment fiat. It may be that pre-Enlightenment understandings of personhood apply to our fallen personhood only brokenly, so that when we have interpreted ourselves by them we have cultivated a "theology of glory." Be that as it may, however, Enlightenment doctrines of personhood clearly do not at all apply to *God*. At least in their use about him, "personal" and "communal" define each other.

To be in time is to share God's life in its temporality. Since precisely as personal he is a community of persons, our time is simultaneously the inner horizon of all our experience, and a given dimension of reality around us, and is each only in that it is the other. God's "time" is thus the possibility that both our demands on time — that it be inner and that it be outer — are fulfilled by the same time.

I have argued that if God's "time" both possesses decisive characteristics of what we call time and is the *Bedingung der Möglichkeit* of there being such a thing as, by our ineluctable intuition, time must be, then we may reasonably drop the quotation marks. It seems to me possible that both of these conditions are fulfilled.

VI

Perhaps we should go yet another step. I have argued that "real" time in fact possesses that externality represented in the beginning of my experiment by "imaginary" time. Is there then no truth about our time, as it is founded in God's time, that is represented by imaginary time in its own character?

It is tempting to correlate imaginary time to that *Abgrund* of God, beneath or beyond God's *life,* of which so many Dominican mystics dreamed. But I am committed to the position that there is no such thing, and will give up this commitment only under extreme pressure.

Or one might correlate imaginary time to that sheer *infinity*-as-such that in Cappadocian trinitarianism gives the life that is God its character as the life that is *God*. Someone who did that would take Wolfhart Pannenberg's side of an argument he and I have been conducting. For it is precisely the infinity of imaginary time that it lacks the arrow that for experience qualifies time as time. I have claimed that also God's infinity must be understood as a "temporal" infinity, using "temporal" in its "real" sense; and that Pannenberg's understanding of God's infinity as God's bottom-line timelessness is a lapse.

I will therefore say no more than that the need to posit imaginary time represents the sheer otherness of God even over against creatures who live and move and have their being in his own life. Jonathan Edwards said there is no limit to blessed creatures' eternal assimilation to God, but also no achievement of identity. Just these paired truths, he said, constitute the eternity of heaven.[15] Accommodated within God's life, we live by that life; but we do not catch him up.

VII

I offer the foregoing merely as a cognitive experiment. I will close by observing that in a certain way it does not matter whether or not we call God's directed liveliness "time." But it does matter that this liveliness and its directedness are brought to words; that the positive character of the relation to time of the triune God's eternity be grasped; and that this relation be pondered anew.

15. Jonathan Edwards, *Dissertation Concerning the End for Which God Created the World*, I,III.

The Political Arts
and Churchly Colleges

🏵   🏵

I

CLEARLY TO UNDERSTAND the present situation of the liberal arts in America, and the specific advantages that a churchly college of such arts might have, it is vital to have clearly in mind that the word "liberal" in "liberal arts" is a near-synonym for "political." We can with little loss of meaning translate "liberal arts" as "political arts."

The notion of the liberal arts comes, of course, from Western antiquity. Aristotle laid down the usage: the liberal arts are those that it is "proper for a free man to acquire. . . ."[1] The liberal arts are those, in the abidingly influential formulation of Seneca, that are *"homine libero digna."*[2] Both the force and the vicissitudes of the conception spring from the antique notion of *freedom* at its heart. As antiquity conceived freedom, it is a strictly political fact: the free person is the

1. Aristotle, *Politika* VII:2.1337b.
2. Seneca, *Ep. morales* LXXXVIII:2.

A lecture given at Concordia College in Moorehead, Minnesota, in 1992. Previously unpublished.

one who participates in the polity, in the governance of his community.

A polity is the forum in which the future of a community is debated, where we argue and decide what sort of community we will try to be. A polity is constituted by discussion of such questions as "What shall we teach our children?" "What force may we allow ourselves against enemies?" "Who *are* our enemies?" The polity is precisely the common *moral* life of the community. It is constituted in communal deliberation of one sort of questions from among the many sorts a community faces: those questions that *can* only be deliberated, that is, the moral questions.

The free person, in the sense of the ancients, is one with access to the forum of such questions, whether this is a representative assembly, a prince's bedroom — in which the case the community includes very few free persons — a club of magnates, or a universal suffrage. And the liberal arts are simply those learned capacities that are requisite for practice in the polity, that are needed to persuade and to understand and to overcome self-interest and perceive the common good.

When the liberal arts have flourished, they have not been thought of as the impractical or the useless arts. Very few, after all, have ever desired an *im*practical education. It only depends on what you want to practice; the liberal arts are the learned capacities of *political* practice, of participation in the common moral life.

Also in antiquity it was of course understood — indeed all too well understood — that the free actions of communal self-governance cannot be the whole of life. We must eat, drink, and find shelter. Besides the political, there is another sphere of life, the sphere of the economy. Therefore there are also the arts of material production, the economic arts.

Antiquity thought — and surely rightly — that the economy cannot itself be a sphere of freedom. For by the acts of material production we become subject to the determined laws of material nature. The economy is the sphere in which right action is that determined as much by calculation and as little by choice as is possible. The economy is the sphere in which competence rather than wisdom must be the chief virtue. The unfree pair to the political forum is the famous "market."

Under the conditions of ancient society, it was believed that practitioners of the political arts and practitioners of the economic arts must be two different sets of persons. These will then be the free and the unfree. The unfree are those who must assume the societally necessary function of making things, whether this be in small or grandiose circumstances, whether they be poor or rich. We will for Christian and good reason protest this distinction. But we should always remember *why* Christians protest it: because we think that no one should be only an economic person and because we believe that in the End no one will be. The pagan ancients had not yet such hope.

Thus Christianity has greatly changed antiquity's notion of freedom. Under the impact of the gospel, we have come to believe that both the political and the economic arts must be suitable for anyone to acquire, because free persons and working persons cannot and should not be simply two discrete sets.

The gospel redefines the notion of freedom. But it does *not* depoliticize it. On the contrary, the apolitical freedom of which Americans now mostly speak, the license *not* to join the community's moral deliberation, is a good deal of what Christianity means by "sin." The gospel insists that freedom consists in service. By its lights, therefore, antiquity's distinction between those who govern and those who serve is perverse. But both governing and serving remain public acts.

Moreover, the sphere of necessity, of material nature and its determined and determining laws, is not by Christian lights an inferior or evil sphere, just a different one. By the lights of the gospel, determining and being determined, doing and suffering, choosing and abiding, are equally human. The gospel's salvation is not escape from the body but the body's resurrection; thus our temporal good cannot be avoidance of the economy for the sake of the polity, but some far more complicated relation. We therefore should not be embarrassed that few churchly colleges are now "pure" colleges of the liberal arts, that they now are also colleges of economic arts.

In the ancient world, the political arts relegated the economic arts to a ghetto of mere materiality, in a world thought fundamentally constituted by mind. The gospel — doubtless among other agents — overcame this prejudice, and that has been an abiding blessing to our civilization. *This* prejudice, however, is not the evil from which we now need to be rescued. The continuing curricular and ideological agony of colleges of liberal arts is determined by the opposite relegation: of the liberal arts to a ghetto of mere intellectuality, in a world thought fundamentally constituted by material and so deterministic relations. We may ask: Does Christianity offer any rescue from *this* ghetto?

II

Let me at this point adduce Martin Luther, from among the many Christian thinkers who could as well appear. The schools Luther promoted — lower schools, gymnasia, and new university departments — were all unequivocally to be schools of liberal arts. They were to teach languages, the more the better; history, which Luther called "the narratives"; literature, which he called "the poets"; mathematics; the fine arts, to use our term; and theoretical physical science. He promoted such schools both to the authorities who had to pay for them and to parents who had to send their children.

The first thing that strikes us about the arguments Luther used with these constituencies is that they were blatantly vocational. We need, he said, the study of liberal arts because we need well-qualified "preachers" and "jurists." (As an admissions counselor, he had, indeed, no shame: persuading parents to prepare their sons for the ministry, he could say, "You can count for yourselves how many pastorates . . . daily become vacant. What are these but so many kitchens and wine-cellars prepared by God for your children . . . ?") We should not by now be surprised by this: the ministry and the law were precisely the *political* offices of the time, the offices that were both public and other than economic. Luther no more than the tradition thought of the liberal arts as impractical; again, it simply depends on what you want to practice.

And the second striking thing about Luther's arguments for the liberal arts is the tremendous horizon in which he sets the ministry and the law. All created reality, said Luther, is but the scene of a universal battle between God and Satan: God battles for the perfecting of his creatures in fellowship with himself and Satan battles to defeat this aim. In the struggle, God has two sorts of created lieutenants: the jurists and the preachers. In God's "worldly rule" he struggles to make and keep us human, as Satan wants to make us "beasts." And by the gospel's ministry God struggles to make us saints, as Satan seeks to make us sinners. God's purpose is *holy humans,* with particular emphasis for each word; and God's means are the political order and the gospel message.

Therefore it is Satan's single greatest stroke, according to Luther, to deprive us of the liberal arts. For both worldly rule and the preaching of the gospel depend on them, so that when the liberal arts fail, both the larger community and the church within it must become "a wild band . . . , a stall of swine, a rout of wild beasts."

The preaching of the gospel and the work of the polity depend on "the languages." Theologian and jurist each has a "book," a deposited tradition running back across cultures and languages, and each must bring that book to speech in a community that is intrinsically international.

Just so, both preaching and politics depend on the kind of linguistic sensitivity and inventiveness that is — apart from extraordinary native genius — attained only by converse with "the poets" and "the musicians." A passage in Luther's *Letter to the Town Councils,* advocating these disciplines, is so characteristic it must be cited: "Let us be warned by the horrid recent example of the high schools and monastery schools, in which not only was the gospel neglected but bad Latin and Greek styles [!] were taught, so that the poor people . . . were nearly deprived even of natural reason."[3]

Finally, so far from automatic is the translation from book to living wisdom that only the widest and deepest human experience makes it possible, for the attaining of which "twenty lifetimes" would be too little were it not for "the narratives." And so little are the spiritually relevant narratives merely spiritual in any Socratic sense that to be comprehensible they demand the widest possible knowledge of the whole created world, and particularly the disciplined pursuit of every kind of predictability in that world, that is, of what we now call science.

The enemy of both preaching and politics is the same: "the belly." "The belly" is what economic concern becomes when it rules alone, when the public spheres of the church and the polity are relegated to a ghetto or to epiphenomenal status. Here the insight of the Greeks comes into its own. For indeed economic life independent of political life, whether by circumstance as among them or by perverse choice as among us, is "the belly," the life of mere animals. And education in the economic arts that is not simultaneously and with vigor and inner connection education also in the political arts is training for pigs, and just so in the service of Satan.

"The belly" is represented for Luther by parents who are interested only in their children learning how to make a good living, by students

3. WA 15:38.

with the same blinders, and by town councils and ecclesial leaderships
that take no thought for their own replacements. Behind "the belly"
stands Satan, angling for his great coup. The power of Satan thus resides
in what we would call "the private sphere," as this is supported by the
economic sphere yet separated from the political. Satan's great weapon
against community and specific humanity is the attraction of *my* needs,
my rights, *my* development and fulfillment.

In the economy I appear as a bearer of needs and interests, and the
processes of the economy are to fulfill these in optimum balance with
fulfilling yours. But in the polity we meet to *transform* our interests,
by deliberation, into common policies for the common good. Thus in
the economy I remain — and should remain — a mere individual; just
so, if that is *all* I am, I remain a sinner spiritually and a dolt morally.
The great disaster feared by Luther was the absorption of the polity
into the economy, the withering of the spheres of communal deliberation
and their replacement in the direction of the common life by pre- or
post-human mechanisms, by the rule of superstition and the belly.

III

Now — what advantages might a college of liberal arts have, that was
itself an arm of the church? I can see two.

The first. The church knows what is at stake in the struggle to
maintain the liberal arts. The struggle is not a matter of maintaining
certain amenities. On the contrary, it is a struggle to maintain the polity
in its distinction from the economy, and so is part of the struggle
between God and Satan over the possibility of specific humanity. In
neither church nor civil community, with respect neither to civil righteousness nor to the righteousness of faith, is humanity possible without
polity, without a forum in which we may together seek righteousness
and perhaps even be given it.

The great enemy of the political arts in our society is simple ignorance
of their purpose. The ideologies of capitalism and communism alike
teach that the political is a mere epiphenomenon of the economic, that
freedom is a function of economic relations. The doctrine is preposterous
on its face, but absurdity has never yet prevented a doctrine from being
believed and acted upon. The church at least knows that moral com-

munity is not an epiphenomenon and why it is not. For the church worships a God who as Father, Son, and Spirit is himself moral community. Therefore the church knows why the existence of a forum in which we may be jointly moral is as necessary to our being as air or water.

The second. A churchly college of liberal arts has one foot in *each* of the political communities for which Luther promoted his schools, whereas what is now a normal college stands within the civil community only. The former situation offers a great advantage just at our present point. For since the church is the community of a message, of "the gospel," not even in deep perversion can the church escape the political. The church's sheer common interest is invested in a piece of discourse. Thus the church's common interest cannot be managed, but can only be deliberated. And therefore, however feebly the church may at any time exist, until she expires altogether there will always be flickers of political life in her body, and the liberal arts will always have a use in her life.

Once upon a time the liberal curriculum at "church colleges" had one great support above all, the entrance requirements of theological seminaries. Those days are of course gone forever. But what if a churchly college were nevertheless to take the necessary daily practice of life in the church, in its ineluctably political reality, as an organizing principle of much of its curriculum? What if a churchly college again set out to train "leaders for the church," and asked seriously what would be involved in that? Such a college would just so have a secure structure for the liberal arts.

God, the Liberal Arts, and the Integrity of Texts

❧   ❧

I

IT SHOULD NOT be necessary to argue the point or even make it explicit, but it now is: the existence of the liberal arts and so their teaching depends on texts. The liberal arts depend on the *use* of texts, on the use of *certain* texts, and on the *subsistence* of texts, that is, on the possibility of distinguishing them from their interpretations. The liberal arts depend on texts because they are the arts of political community, and because community depends on texts.

A community is a historical entity. Like an individual person — in fact the analogy runs the other way — a community subsists in that as a group created by a certain past it jointly chooses a future. The *common* of community is both diachronic and synchronic, but it is fundamentally diachronic and only derivatively synchronic. An individual can perfectly well belong to a community that at present has no other members, while a million momentarily synchronized individuals make a community only when their unanimity ceases to

A lecture given at Concordia College in Moorhead, Minnesota, in 1992. Previously unpublished.

be a mere fact about them and becomes their choice about a future that is to be theirs.

History, however, occurs only where texts accumulate. History occurs as discourse occurs with those no longer there; it is written or memorized texts that enable this. The history of times before texts are produced comes to pass in the texts *we* afterward make telling the narrative we construe for them.

The liberal arts are the arts of political community. They are therefore in each case dependent on the texts by which the political community in question subsists. A liberal art is always in some way the art of exegeting those texts, and its existence depends on knowing them.

Thus the notion of a "canon" of texts for liberal instruction is merely tautologous. The canon of texts for the arts of any community is simply the set of texts by which the diachronic actuality of that community in fact obtains. Nobody has to make up the list or even, except in a crisis of the community, discover it. And the notion of "adding" to the canon, as a deliberately undertaken act, is merely uncomprehending. If, for example, as is surely the case, certain writings of Martin Luther King are now among those by which the American political community subsists, then they are part of that community's canon quite independently of any of us, and that American schools teach them is mandatory. But if acknowledged masterpieces of Taoist wisdom must be admitted hardly to play such a role, then these may be ever so worthy of study, but the notion of "adding" them to the canon of liberal texts, in the name, let us say, of "multiculturalism" would be at best a witless distraction.

II

Such opinions are now of course those of a suspect minority. The integrity of texts and of a community's canon of texts is not only much doubted in academic circles, in the more respectable it is a mark of dark reaction even to doubt the doubt. Let me try to state the problem simply, avoiding the Heidegger-by-way-of-the-French jargon in which it is usually couched.

There is a great difference between agreeing or disagreeing with someone who speaks and agreeing or disagreeing with a text someone has made. If you assert something and I say, "I disagree with your contention that . . . ," you may respond, "But that is not what I assert." Then I can listen further for a clearer understanding of your intention, and again try to agree or disagree. If, on the other hand, I am reading a text, *it* is the object of agreement or disagreement, and not the author. With a text, the question cannot be "What do you want to say?" It can only be "What did someone in fact say? Even if he or she did not intend to?"

A reader is therefore much freer with a text than is a listener with a speaker — indeed a text-user is apparently godlike. A speaker is there to defend his or her autonomy against my interpretations; once discourse has become text it lacks this defender. A text is a bundle of signs left behind by their erstwhile user, and merely as such cannot defend its independence against its readers. If a text is to adjudicate between interpretations, it must have some living defender. Nor can its interpreters individually or collectively be this advocate, since they are the problem. It is the apparent catch-22 in this situation that has driven much current critical theory to decide that texts cannot be independent over against their interpretations, indeed that there is no such thing as the text itself as an other thing than the play of its interpretations.

If a text is to be independent of its interpretations, it needs, it seems, someone on its side who is neither any of its interpreters nor the association of its interpreters. It is now assumed by most critical theory that no such someone is conceivable. But there are in fact two candidates for the role.

The first is discoverable by continued attention to the nature of community. The integrity of a text depends on the existence of a community for which the text in turn is constitutive. Texts are a necessary but *insufficient* condition of community; and where the other conditions are missing, texts lose their integrity.

Let me here call attention to the distinction I have been using — Max Weber's famous distinction between "community" and "association": between collectives in which members find their own selves, and collectives created by the interests and needs of otherwise established selves. In a collective that is a mere association, texts indeed can have no interpreter other than individual interpreters, singly or collectively. The most that can be hoped for is an average interpretation by the association, an accidental group consensus. If the question is asked, "But why *should* we all read the text this way?" no answer is possible. The independence of texts requires an interpreter who is no one or group of individual interpreters nor yet all interpreters averaged or added together. Such an interpreter *is* in fact there, if the text is being read by a vital "community" for which the text is a matter of vital concern.

The currently fashionable doctrine that texts have no "body," no sheer givenness except the play of whatever momentary "language" they have happened into, undoubtedly states texts' lamentable case in mere associations of autonomous individuals. In all cases where the text is not being read by a living community the text can indeed be nothing but the collection of alternative interpretations. Also in a living community, varying interpretations of course pose a problem, but in such a community this problem is precisely the interpretive blessing, for it is problem *for* a communal unity that transcends its own subsidiary entity as an association of individual interpreters.

There is a model of such community and of interpretation within such community. The model is not my arbitrary offering; it is offered by the factual history within our civilization of the problematic we have been tracing. The model is the church. The church is the historical and conceptual archetype of Weber's "community." The church is a unity that transcends its own associational collectivity, in that it is the "body" — that word again! — of someone who is not one of its members. And there is a voice that speaks for that unity, the voice of dogma and proclamation.

Thus a first and utterly scandalous practical suggestion. If scholars of the liberal arts wish to pursue and maintain their calling, they must emulate the church's use of Scripture. If they will not, it is likely that the process now so far along will grind to its completion and the liberal arts will disappear altogether.

But the church is more than a model for liberal scholars to imitate. The church has throughout the history of our culture been in its communal entity the very *possibility* of the liberal arts. There are two ways in which this happens.

The first obtains where a college is itself within the church, as all institutions of liberal arts have been until recently. Such a college can offer itself as a community within which texts *are* and therefore can be read with integrity, and also by scholars who do not necessarily share the church's faith. Moreover, the texts that are in fact canonical for the

West's political community were long ago internalized by the Western branch of the church, and have been read within the church's theological scholarship with an honesty and absence of obscurantism unknown elsewhere.

The second obtains where the church proclaims God. God is himself the unity of truth. And the academic community must know and embrace truth's unity if it is to be able to treat the liberal arts' canonical texts with integrity. For to treat these texts with integrity, the academic community must itself be a diachronic unity, a self-identical conversation carried on across time. That is, if an academic institution is to teach the liberal arts, it must embrace within its cognitive grasp Aristotle and Isaiah and Machiavelli and Luther and the future genius who will yet unify field theory, as partners of a single continuing conversation that is identical with its own single communal reality. That it can do only by faith in the unity of truth, which is to say, in God.

A school of liberal arts will even need to have what in the church is called the *teaching office*. No more than in the church will the location and authority of the teaching office be uncontroversial. But a vital community in the unity of truth will nevertheless somehow and somewhere have heroes and grand old parties and whippersnappers to whom folk listen; it will somewhere and somehow contain *authorities*. A collective in which every opinion is respectable merely because someone holds it cannot be a community in truth. Indeed, it cannot even jointly *seek* truth.

III

Talking of God, we have arrived at the second candidate earlier mentioned to be defender of texts' independence. Fashionable academia's presumption that texts are defenseless is merely a parochial part of a larger phenomenon. The loss of sense for texts' independence is epiphenomenal to our loss of trust in that diachronic unity of our community on which texts' independence does indeed depend. That is, our loss of sense for texts' independence is epiphenomenal to our loss of trust in the narrativity of history.

Is there a *story* to tell about the Western political community? A story that is *true* and the chief thing needed for us to understand our communal life? We are currently much inclined to doubt it. We are even actually able to speak of "narrative history" as if there were some other kind. When I first taught in a liberal arts college, people in the history department were desperately inventing work for themselves that did not involve storytelling. That having proved difficult, without open capitulation to the sovereignty of other departments, "narrative history" is lately in renewed vogue among academic historians, but only as a kind of necessary fiction.

It is clear what has destroyed our confidence in the possibility of telling the true story of our political community. It is the more general loss of confidence that there is a total narrative, an encompassing universal history, a tale to be told about the first beginning and about the last end and about the way from the one to the other. This loss is theological: unless there is someone to compose the universal tale, it is mere facing of the truth not to think there is one.

General Western culture was able to sustain a sense of humanity's narrative reality and so of its own particular narrative reality only so long as it presupposed the reality of God. Whether the loss of theology and the consequent loss of history is permanent for our culture, I will not predict. In any case, there are presently few if any ways for a collective — such as a college — to hold on to its own narrativity except by worshiping the church's God.

Not every God can or would want to be the Narrator of universal history. America's grasp of community in its history has been undone not so much by disbelief in the God of the church as by belief in his great modern Western rival, the great Engineer of a postulated machine-world. History is constituted in contingencies, in new starts and unpredictable emergences. These are the last things a perfect Engineer would want in his machine-creation.

Indeed, only a very particular sort of God could be the Narrator of a world-tale. For to whom would God tell this tale? It is that very atypical God, the *triune* God, who can be the universal Teller of a universal tale. For in this God there is indeed one to tell and one to hear and one to be the telling.

It is a long train of consequences. Because there is the triune God, there can be a universal narrative. Because there is a universal narrative, there can be narratives of particular communities. Because there can be narratives of particular communities, a community can be a diachronic unity, and so then can an academic community. Because an academic community can be a diachronic unity, it can defend texts' independence.

IV

And so the last consequence, asserted of course all along. Because texts' independence can be defended, there can be teaching and study of the liberal arts. And texts' independence can be defended in the church and by believers in God. Whether others will in the long run be able or want to do so may be doubted.

Autobiographical Reflections on the Relation of Theology, Science, and Philosophy; or, You Wonder Where the Body Went

I

LET ME START with a case. The notion of "heaven," of God's place in his creation, has usually been deemed an essential item of Christian theological conceptuality. God, to be sure, is his own proper place; for himself God needs no other place than himself. But if there are to be creatures, God — it has usually been thought — needs a created place at and from which to be among them. Had God no place of his own within his creation, he would either be sheerly absent from creatures or leave no room for them. Heaven is God's pad within his creation.

The ptolemaic mapping of the universe seemed to accomodate heaven quite nicely. The crystalline nested spheres on which the heavenly lights are according to this mapping mounted, and whose rotations account for the observed motions of those lights, divide space into discrete

Published in *Agora* 6 (1994): 11-15. Reprinted by permission.

shell-shaped volumes, at increasing distances from earth. It is not only possible to apprehend these shells as of different ontological dignity, it is inevitable that we will: the further from earth, the lighter and more glorious. And then, if we are trying to place God's heaven, we can take the outermost shell, which will have the highest ontological dignity, as this place. Heaven is thus at once a place ontologically different from the rest of the universe, and so suited for God, and spatially related to the universe's other places. It is vital to understand that there is nothing unsophisticated or implausible about this notion of heaven, given the mapping of the universe that science until recently provided.

Now — if Jesus is risen bodily, it would appear that his body must be *someplace,* if we suppose, as most have, that "this is the eternal truth of any body, that it is contained in its place."[1] Between the Resurrection appearances, Jesus evidently was not walking the streets or holed up in the Jerusalem caravanserai; nor is he, according to Luke, so located since the appearances ceased. Yet if he is risen bodily his body must on the common supposition always be *some*place. And metaphysical interpretation of the ptolemaically mapped universe seemed to provide the place. Again it must be emphasized: the conception that the risen Jesus bodily ascended *up* there, to a region of the universe called "heaven," there to have his place until the final transformation of all creation, is a sophisticated and successful notion, given the ptolemaic mapping of the universe.

Thus the real problem with Copernicus was not the blow he is thought to deliver to geocentric prejudice; and indeed Christian use of the ptolemaic mapping did *not* make the earth the center of the universe in an evaluative sense — quite the contrary. The real problem was that the universe as mapped by Copernicus does not seem to accommodate key portions of the Christian story: *In the universe as mapped by Copernicus, where can the risen Christ's body be, between his "comings" to us?*

But now we should note: it was apparent long before Copernicus, and on strictly inner-theological grounds, that there was a problem with the traditional construction, despite its general attractiveness. For it is a central conviction of the faith that the body of Christ is present on the altar of Eucharist. If the embodied Christ is located beyond the

1. John Calvin, *Institutes of the Christian Religion* (1536), iv.122.

outer ptolemaic sphere, how does he come to be bodily present in First Lutheran Church of a Sunday morning? If heaven is the place just described, it would seem he would have to *travel* from the one place to the other. But at this point another character of the Christian faith kicked in, its aversion to what we would now call myth, central in which are just such divine journeyings. I may cite Thomas Aquinas: "Plainly, the body of Christ does not come to be in the sacrament by spatial motion."[2]

Thus throughout theological history, at least in the West, there was a constant pressure, exerted by the way in which heaven was conceived, to attenuate the understanding of Christ's bodily presence in Eucharist. Surely Christ is only "spiritually" present on the eucharistic altar, or something like that. Where the temptation was resisted, this was done by two linked moves.

The first move was to characterize the reality of the embodied Christ on the eucharistic altar as "supernatural." The embodied Christ does not, according to this teaching, "get from" one place to another at all. By the promise of God, he simply *is* both in heaven and on the altar, contrary to normality though this is. So Thomas Aquinas again, and following him the whole subsequent Catholic tradition. But this move of course meant that in order to account for eucharistic bodily presence, the whole conceptual framework by which the risen Christ's bodily reality was otherwise accounted for was short-circuited.

The second move dealt with the circumstance that the miracle had to be, as it were, a reliable miracle, since we could not at each celebration be left wondering if this time it was happening. The ministry of the church was credited with authorization to petition the presence with absolute assurance that it would occur.

The Reformers rejected the second of these moves, for reasons not our present concern. This broke the issue open again, and in aggravated form. A variety of moves were possible and tried. Two were radical opposites. Some reformers denied the eucharistic bodily presence. Luther and some of his younger followers instead denied the traditional understanding of heaven.

Luther and others were led by their concern for Christ's sacramental bodily presence to deny that heaven is any *other* place than the places

2. Thomas Aquinas, *Summa Theologiae* iii.75.2.

of Jesus' sacramental presence to us, that is, that it is a "place" strictly speaking at all. Thus there is no spatial separation needing to be overcome, between heaven and the eucharistic altar. Against fellow Reformers who clung to the traditional opinion, they could sound like religious skeptics: Johannes Brenz mockingly inquired if in this "spatial and material heaven" of traditional theology, Jesus took "little walks" with the angels?

All the created universe, said Brenz and then Luther, is simply *one* place before God, in rather the sense in which the field of a consciousness is one place for it; and so it is also for the risen Jesus at God's right hand.[3] Therefore the question of Christ's bodily presence on the eucharistic altars is not one of containment in one set of places instead of another but one of availability to experience in one set of places instead of another.

Thus the Lutherans saw no theological problem in the Copernican challenge to Ptolemy. Luther himself thought that Copernicus was, as a scientist, mad, but did not suppose that his madness posed any theological difficulty. Other Lutherans were themselves Copernicans in science. And the writings of Copernicus finally achieved publication when Melanchthon arranged it in a territory politically controlled by the Lutheran movement.

II

When I first learned about all this, now many years ago, I was sheerly delighted. The entire complex interplay between (1) critique of established theological opinion by inner necessities of the faith, (2) change in a scientific paradigm, and (3) metaphysical speculation seemed to me a very model of the way in which truth comes to light. And I was myself launched on two related lines of inquiry that guide me still.

For in untangling one problem the old Lutherans posed at least two new ones — and that they did so is part of what commends them to me. Are now *these* questions posed by inner theological necessity or by science or by philosophy? The alternative seems to me utterly meaningless.

3. Johannes Brenz, *De personalis unione duarum naturarum in Christo* (Tübingen, 1561).

The first such problem: if the risen Christ's body is not now located in its own proper space among other spaces, is it indeed a *body?* If we insist that it is, what can we in that case mean by "body"?

Readers attuned to theological history will know that this question was already hurled by Calvinists at Lutherans in their sixteenth-century broils. The attempt to answer it and similar posers once created an entire school of Lutheran revisionist metaphysicians, lamentably wiped out by the Thirty Years' War. When I took it up, I thought about the reason theology talks in these connections of "body" in the first place, which is that the New Testament talks that way. So I asked, How does the New Testament use "body"? A large body of scholarly exegesis was to hand: in the usage at least of Paul, a person's body is simply that person him/herself, insofar as he/she is *available* to others and so to her/himself.

To say that Christ's body is present as the bread and cup is on these terms to say that these available things are *his* availability, that here he not only intends us but allows us to intend him, not only touches us but allows us to touch him, not only sees us but lets us see him. It is to say that by these objects the risen Christ gives himself to be our object.

But that last sentence is not stated exclusively in churchly language; its last part introduces the subject/object language of German idealism. Let me then continue with *that* language, as Hegel uses it in the great *"Knechtschaft und Herrschaft"* section of the *Phänomenologie des Geistes.* According to Hegel, were someone to be present to me as subject only and not also as my object in turn, I would just so be that someone's object only and not a subject over against him/her. Thus such a personal presence, even were the person the risen Christ, would enslave me.

Why do we need the eucharistic bread and cup? Why must Christ be present to us "bodily"? Now we have an answer: because a disembodied presence of Christ would be enslaving rather than liberating. You see where we can get, moving reflectively with and among Copernicus and Luther and modern exegesis of Paul and German philosophy and not worrying about boundaries between supposedly different sorts of truth.

It is not even clear that our understanding of the physical universe should not be affected by such a revised notion of "body." Science's proper discourse about the world is always accompanied by a different discourse, that attempts to state the "results" of science but in language that does not have mathematics as its only grammar. This discourse is often called "popular presentation" or something of the sort, yet scientists themselves do not in fact get along without it. Indeed it is becoming increasingly evident that the course of research itself is heavily determined by problems and opportunities that arise in "popular" translation. Transitions from one "scientific paradigm" to another often do not occur in the language whose sole grammar is mathematics, but in this parascientific discourse.

It happens that the attempt to transcribe the results of relativistic and quantum-mechanical reflections in parascientific discourse have rendered the very concept of body, once the most obvious of concepts, mysterious. The interplay of Christian doctrine, philosophy, and scientific paradigm just traced offers the following lightening of the mystery: what bodies really are, is *availabilities* that enable *freedom*. It seems to me that both nouns might be suggestive also to more strictly physical research.

The second problem: can theology do altogether without heaven? If all things are as immediate to God's presence as Brenz seems to say, must not God indeed simply engross all, leaving no room for creatures that are other than he? Catholic theology has accused Lutheran theology of pantheism, and so long as no answer is attempted to the question about heaven, there is justice in the accusation. If heaven is not the outermost shell-space of the universe, if there is no place up there for little walks, what *is* it? If anyplace or anything?

If one is convinced that Luther and Brenz were on the right line, but is also concerned to find a place to be heaven, and is prepared to be speculatively brazen, it is tempting to say that the space occupied by the bread and cup, and by the space-occupying aspects of the church's sacraments and sacramental life generally, is God's pad in his creation. I will not here argue that one should say this. But let me at least suggest some of what might follow from saying it.

Saying this would redefine heaven christologically: heaven would exist only in that the Incarnation occurs, only in that God *incarnationally* occupies space in his creation. It would become *conceptually* impossible to describe the Creator's presence to his creatures without reference to Jesus Christ. Someone who made this move would be committed to one side of an old theological divide: *Utrum Christus venisset, si homo non*

peccaverit? "Would Christ have come if humanity had not sinned?"
Someone who made the suggested move would be committed to say
Yes. He/she would be committed to assigning foundational status
within metaphysics to the existence of the God-*man* — as has been done
by Athanasius, the Franciscans, Luther, the supralapsarian Calvinists,
and Karl Barth.

It would also follow that *the church* was constitutive for the reality
of creation: if no church then no big bang. Someone who made this
move would indeed find him/herself looking at the universe very differently than modernist ideology has made us do. But for Protestants,
the more wrenching alteration would doubtless be in their perception
of the church itself. When we come together and the liturgy begins,
where are we? If the space occupied by the sacramental elements is
heaven, then the space the elements define around themselves is the
gate of heaven — just as Orthodox theology, of course, has always said.
And *now* see where Luther, Copernicus, and Hegel have gotten us
between them!

III

I have often wondered why the two theological heros for whom I have
developed the greatest affection — Jonathan Edwards and Karl Barth
— should both be from a different theological tradition than my own.
It is, I think, because both are ruthless in refusing to be confined within
or protected by a special epistemological "compartment" called "theology."

So — to take a second interesting case — Edwards pondered a central
notion of the physics of his time, the notion of an atom, of a geometrically divisible yet physically indivisible unit of matter. What can account for the fact that the smaller units into which it geometrically
could be divided cannot in fact appear? The explanation, he supposed,
must be the operation of a binding force that cannot be overcome, that
is, an "infinite" force. Whereupon Edwards was off and running about
God and his relation to creatures. For what could an infinite force be
but God himself? Are not then atoms simply particular manifestations
of God's infinite will? From a multitude of such starting points, Edwards eventually created a fully developed alternative to the mechanistic

interpretation of Newton, of which everyone *else's* atomism was an integral part.

The case of Edwards is not merely an illustration. Edwards lived though the great moment of the Enlightenment, and was himself one of its most imaginative and determined practitioners. And it is the fact that modernity did not take the path Edwards opened to it, which has compartmentalized our reflective lives.

The "mechanistic" interpretation of Newtonian physics does not necessarily follow from any of its methods or theories, but from the dominance of a particular root metaphor in their "popular" transcription. It is the "popular" transcription that is culturally decisive, also for scientists themselves. When in the culture it came to seem self-evident that what "science tells us" is "how the universe-machine works," and when the practical success of the new science had given it overwhelming epistemological clout, Christian discourse about God and humans found itself the inhabitant of an epistemological ghetto, as it had never before been. For the Christian God is wholly unfit to found or rule a machine-creation, addicted as he is to fooling around with monkey wrenches, to what the machine metaphor can only construe as "intervention," as fixing what ain't broke. And the Christian human is equally unfitted to inhabit such a universe, expecting as he/she does to be ever and again reborn from new scratch.

For two centuries, we have in consequence supposed that Christian talk of God and human destiny must be epistemologically disconnected from scientific talk, and that since what science does is describe reality, Christian talk of God and human destiny cannot describe reality, whatever else it may then be permitted to do. Entire generations and schools of theologians and philosophers have thereupon devoted their careers to inventing some epistemological function for theology. But whether Christian discourse is then taken to be a "higher" discourse than science or a "lower" one, whether it is taken as "expressive" or "evocative" or just as a self-justifying "language game," the disaster is the same. In my judgment, there is nothing at the basis of the entire agony but uncritical acceptance of a — to boot, intrinsically implausible — metaphysical root metaphor.

Do I then say that "$E=mc^2$" and "The Son proceeds from the Father" work *just* the same way? I do not think I do. But I do say that insofar as either "$E=mc^2$" or "The Son proceeds from the Father" is *true*, insofar as either has any purchase on something other than itself, they depend for this purchase on their situation in one total human cognitive discourse, which has no clear internal epistemological boundaries. To put it from the side that will make the point most offensively plain: if science does not belong to the same discourse as does theology, then science is a play of fictions.

I do say that no subregion of human discourse can be a normative paradigm of any other, not because they are so discrete but because their mutual boundaries are so blessedly ill-defined. And I do say — and this is to me the most interesting and liberating point — that where one, on any occasion, gets into the enterprise is strictly and rightly a matter of catch-as-catch-can.

My first grown-up job was teaching introduction to philosophy on Monday, Wednesday, and Friday and introduction to theology on Tuesday, Thursday, and Saturday. I recall spending much time trying to discover the gear I was supposed to shift each evening but Saturday. I have given up. My recommendation is that we all should.